BROOKLANDS BOOKS

CITROEN SM 1970-1975

Compiled by
R.M. Clarke

ISBN 1 85520 0546

AL5? 6E

Distributed by
Brooklands Book Distribution Ltd.
'Holmerise', Seven Hills Road,
Cobham, Surrey, England

Printed in Hong Kong

BROOKLANDS BOOKS

CONTENTS

BROOKLANDS BOOKS

ACKNOWLEDGEMENTS

The first Brooklands book made its appearance over 30 years ago. It was duplicated and contained works from two British magazines.

With the passage of time our aspirations have become known to a wider circle and today we are privileged to be able to include road tests and other articles from over 30 journals. Our objective is, that when the stories are read in sequence, they will create an international picture of the model in question.

This book on the SM joins three other Citroen titles. They cover the pre and post war Traction Avants. The advanced DS and ID models produced from the mid '50's to the mid '70's. And the third volume reports on the ubiquitous 2CVs which are just being phased out after some 42 years in production.

As always we are indebted to the publishers of the worlds leading motoring journals for their help in compiling these anthologies and for their generosity in allowing us to reissue their road tests and other articles in this series. Our special thanks in this instance go to the management of Autocar, Autosport, Car and Driver, Classic & Sportscar, Classic Cars, Motor, Motor Sport, Motor Trend, Road & Track, Road Test, Restoring Classic Cars, Track & Traffic, and Wheels. Our thanks also go to Citroen Uk Ltd for providing the attractive cover photograph.

R.M. Clarke

AT LAST! THE CITROEN MASERATI

V6 Maserati-engined Citroen SM makes its debut in Geneva today

SPECIFICATION

Engine

Block material	Light alloy
Head material	Light alloy
Cylinders	V6
Cooling system	Water; two thermostatically controlled electric rad. fans
Bore and stroke	87mm 75mm
Cubic capacity	2670 cc
Main bearings	4
Valves	two overhead camshafts, chain driven
Compression ratio	9 : 1
Carburetters	three twin-choke Weber 42 DCNF
Fuel pump	Bendix electric
Oil filter	Full flow, with light alloy cooler
Max. power (net)	170 bhp at 5500 rpm
Max. power (gross)	180 bhp at 6250 rpm
Max. torque (net)	172 lb.ft. at 4000 rpm
Max. torque (gross)	170 lb.ft. at 4000 rpm

Transmission

Layout	Front-wheel drive
Clutch	Diaphragm spring
Internal gearbox ratios	
5th gear	0.76
4th gear	0.97
3rd gear	1.32
2nd gear	1.94
1st gear	2.92
Reverse	3.15
Synchromesh	All forward speeds
Final drive	4.375 : 1
Mph at 1000 rpm in:	
5th gear	22.6
4th gear	17.6
3rd gear	12.9
2nd gear	8.8
1st gear	5.8

Chassis and body

Construction	Base-frame monocoque with detachable body panels

Brakes

Type	Power-assisted disc
Dimensions	11.8 in front, 10.08 in rear
Handbrake	Acting on separate front calipers

Suspension and steering

Hydropneumatic self-levelling suspension with built-in dampers and an anti roll bar at each end

Steering type	Rack and pinion with variable weight powered assistance
Steering ratio	9.4 : 1
Tyres	195/70VR 15 Michelin X
Wheels	5-stud disc wheels
Rim size	6 in

Dimensions (to nearest in.)

Wheelbase	9 ft 8in
Front track	5 ft
Rear track	4 ft 4 in
Overall length	16 ft
Overall width	6 ft
Ground clearance	6 in (constant)

Weights

Kerb weight (DIN)	28.5 cwt
Distribution (unladen)	62/38
Max. laden weight	36.2 cwt
Distribution (laden)	57/43

Claimed performance

Max. in gears	mph
1st	38
2nd	57
3rd	84
4th	115
5th	137
Acceleration	
0-100 kph (62 mph)	8.9 sec
Standing quarter	16.2 sec

Few cars have been an open-secret for so long, few have been the subject of so much rumour and speculation. Now, at last, details of the long-waited Citroen-Maserati—the Citroen SM to use its proper name—are out. It is not the most beautiful of cars to our eyes (we've yet to see it in the metal) but its styling does reflect its Franco-Italian parentage. As the pictures show (left and above) you don't have to look very hard to see the influence of the Citroen DS, and there's more than a hint of Maserati Ghibli about the hind quarters.

The SM would appear to be exactly what we all hoped for: a cross-pollination of Citroen ideals on comfort, luxury and safety, and everything that Maserati stands for on performance and sporting appeal—plus more besides. To us, on paper at least, it seems to be the ultimate in Grand Touring cars.

Like the DS the two-door monocoque frame is clothed in easily detachable body panels—the bonnet is made of aluminium. Forward visibility is good because of large windows supported by slim pillars, a low waistline and a flat, sloping bonnet. Despite the almost horizontal fastback, rearward vision appears to be good too as the enormous rear window virtually fills the tailgate over the large boot. Beneath that is a 20-gallon plastic fuel tank to give a grand touring range of at least 400 miles between fills.

The Maserati part of the car is its 2670 cc light-alloy engine—a 90 degree V6 with four chain-drive overhead camshafts and three twin-choke Weber carburetters. Real pedigree Modena material. Claimed outputs are 170 bhp (net) at 5500 rpm, and 170 lb. ft. torque at 4000 rpm. The drive, predictably, is to the front wheels through a five-speed, all-synchromesh manual gearbox with a floor-mounted gearlever protruding, Maserati fashion, from an impressive central console. Fifth gear, giving 22.6 mph /1000 engine rpm, is clearly for long-legged cruising at well over 100 mph.

Citroen claim a top speed of 137 mph (115 in fourth) for which highly efficient streamlining must be largely responsible. The acceleration, though pretty fierce (0–60 in under 9 sec.), is perhaps less impressive due no doubt to the car's weight of $28\frac{1}{2}$ cwt.

Complicated cars invariably are heavy—and the SM is certainly complicated. A hydraulic "mains", supplied by a seven-piston pressure pump driven by a shaft from the engine, supplies the all-independent, self-levelling hydro-pneumatic suspension (as in the DS, this height can be adjusted by a lever inside the car); a twin-circuit system for the all-disc brakes; and the power steering. A separate hydraulic circuit operates the fantastic battery of self-levelling quartz halogen lights; the inner ones of each trio swivel with the steering, as on the DS.

The steering is unique: not just power-assisted but powered to self-centre, even when the car is standing still. A centrifugal regulator, driven from the end of the gearbox, exerts pressure on a hydraulic slide valve, which regulates the amount of assistance to the steering circuit. The effort required to turn the steering wheel therefore varies with the car's speed; very light when parking for large, insensitive deflections, heavier when travelling fast to avoid twitchiness which would inevitably be the corollary of light steering geared like that of the SM. Two turns from lock-to-lock put it almost in the kart category for responsiveness. (The ratio of the quick-steering DS is 14.7:1; that of the SM is 9.4:1.) Citroen also emphasize the safety aspect of their powered centring. Nothing, they say, will affect the car's lock angle when it is cornering—not even a front-tyre blow out.

The equipment and furnishing inside, as the picture on the left shows, is very lavish. Refinements include a steering column adjustable for height and reach (the same goes for the seats); very comprehensive heating and ventilation; headrests adjustable for height and rake; armrests covering door pockets; a battery of warning lights; a heated back window; fingertip switchgear—including that for the washers and wipers; and so on. The exact price has yet to be announced but it is clearly going to be high probably as much as £5000 in Britain, F40,000 in France. Production will not start until September.

Apart from the pictures you see here all this information has been gleaned from a general specification table—the only material we've so far received. We'll no doubt have more to say about the car in our Geneva Show report next week.

Citroen's new performance GT

Technical description of the Maserati-engined Citroen SM

By Geoffrey Howard BSc(Eng) ACGI

CITROEN have never been afraid of complicated design, and there can be no doubt that their first DS when it was introduced 10 years ago was a bold piece of engineering. Since then, relatively, they have stood still, this being their traditional practice, to leapfrog in huge jumps and wait for time to catch up. The trouble with this kind of progress is that it calls for a lot of foresight, if not psychic inspiration, as without small steps there is no opportunity to change paths or redirect development as design influences change.

Thus in some ways the DS design is now out on a limb in relation to the generally accepted thoughts outside Citroen on some fundamentals. Apart from the shape, which has not been copied or even imitated anywhere, the least impressive part of the DS has been the engine. Not for any mechanical reasons of strength, because it is a tough and very reliable unit, but for reasons of refinement and performance, the current Citroen four-cylinder is very long in the tooth. The roots of the design go back to before the war and for several years now there have been predictions of a new unit.

At the Geneva Show last week a new model was announced. It was not what the world had been expecting, a new 2-litre family saloon to take us up to 1980, but a prestige touring car to be built in only limited numbers for a few very rich Frenchmen. It is my guess though that this car is merely a mobile and carefully controlled proving ground for parts to be used

in a new model for mass production at a lower price in the next year or two.

Relating the new SM to the other controlled experiment Citroen are undertaking with single rotor Wankel engines in a coupé version of the Ami 8 (see *Autocar* 27 November 1969), I would expect "next year's car" to have a twin-rotor Wankel and many of the suspension and steering features of the SM.

In many ways the SM is an inefficient design. It is built on a wheelbase 5in. shorter than that of the DS, yet is 2in. longer overall and has less room inside. It is claimed to be a four-seater coupé, although the rear seat legroom is insufficient when a tall driver is at the wheel. This is largely the result of lowering the roofline a full 6in. which has meant that the occupants must be stretched out more front and rear.

For a 2 + 2 an overall length of 16ft is a lot, being 8in. more than a 2 + 2 E-type Jaguar and 6in. more than the Austin 3-litre even. Most of the five-seater four-door saloons built in Europe have an overall length of about 15ft 6in. except for the 280 SE Mercedes, which is 16ft like the Citroen.

Maserati Vee-6 Engine

Far from an admission of defeat, the choice of a Maserati engine for the new Citroen is a rational piece of cost accounting. To give the new model the kind of performance which would be good for the image (and a useful stressing of the running gear in service) a unit developing over 150 bhp was essential. Even in

its most developed form with fuel injection, the old Citroen four was at its limit at 125 bhp. A technical agreement was already in existence with Maserati and they had the design experience and the necessary machine tools to build the right kind of engine.

To fit it into the space available it needed to be of vee configuration and, for French taxation categorization, to be under 2.8 litres. By taking virtually the same bore as the existing Maserati 4.2-litre vee-8 and reducing the crankshaft throw by 5mm, a compact vee-6 of 2,670 c.c. resulted. The only shortcoming was that the firing impulses would be uneven and only the primary forces and couples would be in balance.

One glance at the cutaway or section of the engine shows that it has been built almost regardless of cost. Light alloys are used for all the structural casings, with a crankcase split on the crank centre line and a separate finned aluminium sump. Chains are used in two stages for the camshaft drive, each head having twin cams and opposed valves. It weighs only 308 lb without accessories and clutch.

The crankshaft runs in four main bearings, con-rods being in pairs on the three big ends. In the centre of the vee between the banks of cylinders is a hollow jackshaft running in two journal bearings machined directly in the aluminium. This is driven at half-engine speed by a duplex roller chain off the crankshaft nose. In line with the spaces between the cylinders there are two more sprockets for the secondary duplex chains. On the left-hand side of the engine therefore (remember that for the Citroen installation the clutch is at the front) the secondary chain passes over the top between the front two cylinders, while on the right-hand side another secondary chain passes over the top between the back two cylinders. There is no speed change for the secondary drive, which is tensioned by an adjustable jockey between the camshafts and three nylon rubbing strips on the straight runs.

On top of the jackshaft are three twin-choke Weber 42 DC NF downdraught carburettors; these feed the inner faces of the heads, which are interchangeable. Three-branch exhaust manifolds bolt to the lower faces, feeding into a single pipe each side at sump level.

Opposed valves with an included angle of about 76deg are worked by inverted bucket tappets adjusted by shims on the valve stem. The pistons have slightly raised crowns which protrude into the hemispherical combustion

Above, right: This longitudinal section clearly shows the robust four-bearing crankshaft. Note the unusual main bearing cap arrangement, all four being cast integrally with the lower half of the crankcase. The oil pan is a separate casting
Below, right: Each bank has a pair of overhead camshafts chain driven from a halfspeed jack-shaft. The latter also drives the ignition distributor, the water pump (at the rear) and, via a flexibly jointed quill shaft, the pump for the car's central hydraulic system
Below: Three twin-choke Weber 42 DCNF carburettors are mounted on a one-piece manifold. Cylinder heads are interchangeable. Note the detachable sleeves in the open-deck light-alloy cylinder block

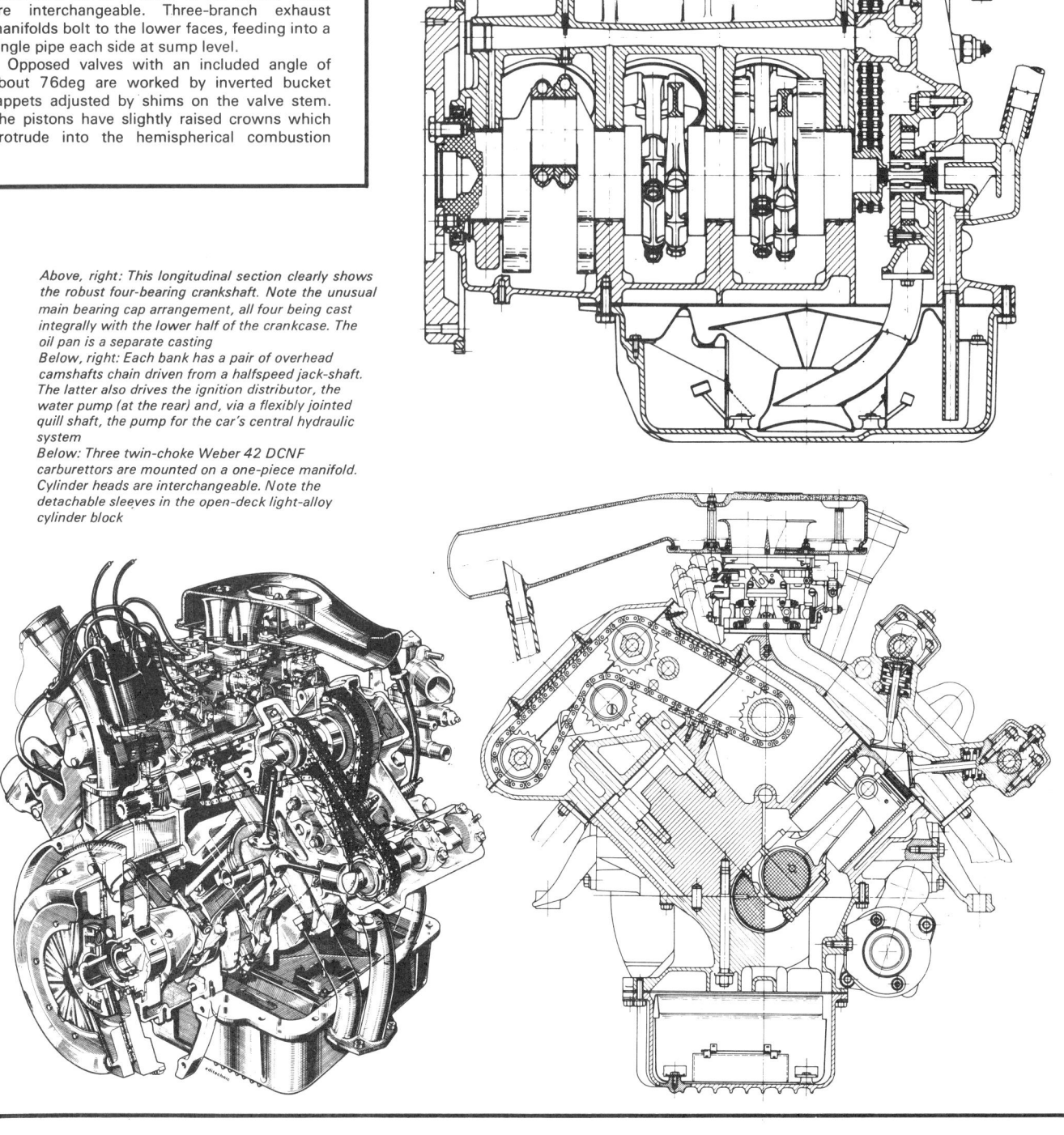

chambers at top-dead-centre; the chamber diameter and the raised part of the piston crown are smaller than the bore size to promote squish. Compression ratio is 9 to 1 and maximum bmep is 157 psi.

A diaphragm spring clutch transmits the drive to an all-synchromesh five-speed gearbox and transaxle unit. It is a two-shaft unit with all ratios indirect, the drive passing to the left of the crownwheel through the gearbox and back to the pinion. Drive shafts have constant velocity joints at both ends and the disc brakes are inboard as is usual on Citroens.

Suspension appears to follow normal DS

pattern, with self-levelling built into the hydropneumatic units and the usual integral damping. The front wishbone pivots now trail instead of lead—a lesson learnt in rallies.

Novel Steering Assistance

Driven by a quill shaft across the top of the transmission, and connected to the valve-gear jackshaft by a flange coupling, is a seven-plunger hydraulic pump for the accessories which include the suspension units and the power steering. Hydraulic pressure to the power steering is monitored by a valve mounted on the front of the gearbox and driven at road speed.

The front wheels have centre-point geometry (i.e. the axis of the king-pin passes through the centre of the tyre contact patch, giving zero offset) and there is a steering box ratio of only 9.4 to 1 (compared with 14.7 to 1 on the DS). Only two turns are needed from lock to lock.

By controlling the assistance of the steering according to two parameters, Citroen are claiming that the SM is easier to handle at high

speed. Steering wheel effort needed increases with the speed of the car, according to the hydraulic monitor driven by the gearbox. The effort needed also increases with steering lock, giving the car a kind of servo castor. In the extreme, with the engine running, the front wheels will turn back to the straight ahead position of their own accord when the car is parked. The degree of effort needed by the driver under any condition is very low and the precision is claimed to be exact.

One of the problems in making steering light to operate and shock-free in use is that a lot of the feel and most of the castor must be removed in the process. It would seem that by using this simple form of hydraulic computer Citroen have provided the best of both worlds. They were fortunate in having a supply of pressurized oil for the other services and an accessible gearbox output shaft available.

Body Construction

The stressed part of the body is built up from sheet metal with a pair of forks at the front to

Left: This view shows the low build and clean lines. Wide doors make getting in and out an easy matter. The steering wheel is adjustable for rake and reach

Right: Unlike the DS and its derivatives, the outer panels form part of the body structure. Only the front wings and associated sheet metal are unstressed

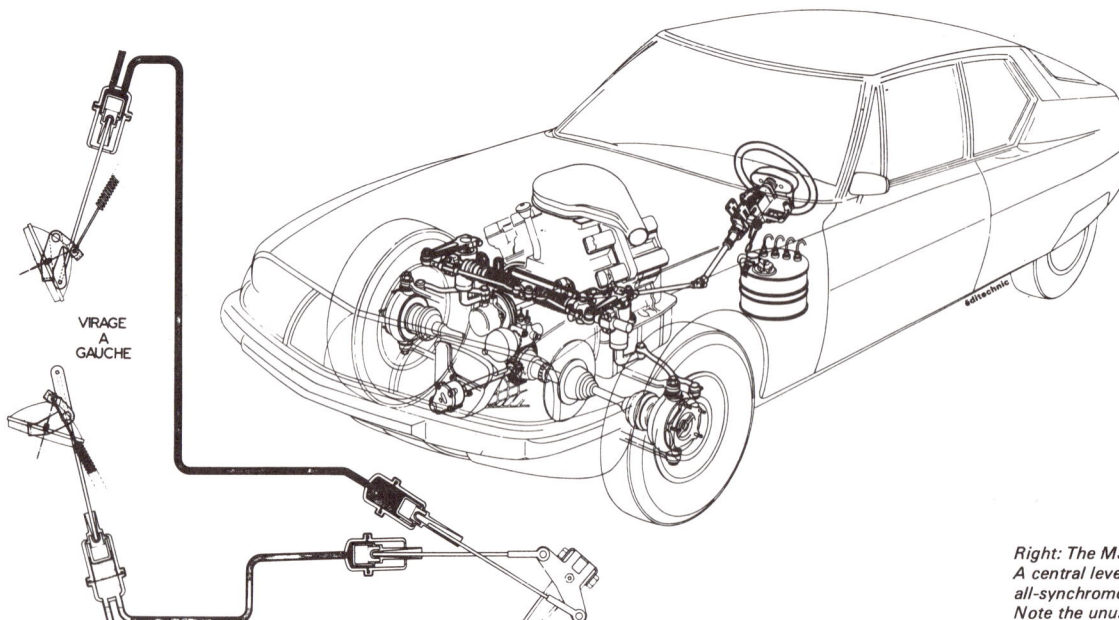

VIRAGE A GAUCHE

Left: Pressure in the hydraulic servo-steering system is monitored by a transmission-driven speed-sensitive valve. This enables parking efforts to be low without the attendant disadvantages of ultra-light steering at higher speeds. Inset is the hydraulic headlamp-guidance system

Right: The MS is luxuriously appointed. A central lever controls the all-synchromesh five-speed gearbox. Note the unusual seat design, with its high backrest fulcrum

carry the engine unit and welded rear wings and roof. The front body cross-member, wings and door sills are bolted on. This is a slight departure from previous Citroen practice where the entire body is bolted on to a self-supporting frame, as on a Rover 2000.

The body shape has been developed in a wind tunnel and is obviously very aerodynamic. The body tapers in plan by 8 in. from front to back.

A further development of the DS lighting system is employed, with plastic moulded carriers for three lamps each side. These boxes are connected to both the front and rear suspension by hydraulic pipes so that all beams stay level regardless of the car's attitude. The inner pair of lamps, which are long-range pencil beams, also steer with the front wheels by hydraulic connections. (The DS lamps, which also self-level and steer, have mechanical connections.) The outer pair of lamps are rectangular and provide a wide spread cornering beam, while the middle one in each group is a dipped beam. All six use tungsten-halogen bulbs.

Interior comfort has not been overlooked and there is extensive use of padding and leather (an extra cost option). Front seats have a single contour backrest which hinges at the base of the occupant's spine for rake adjustment. There is a screw-type micrometer adjustment under the front edge and a quick release lever for access to the rear compartment.

The characteristic single-spoke steering wheel is retained, but with a new padded appearance. Circular instruments are mounted under a hooded facia top and the gearlever is mounted between the seats, true GT fashion.

Production of the new car will run at 20 cars per day, with a maximum capacity of 30. The price has not been fixed, but it should be about 42,000 French francs (just over £3,000). Deliveries will begin in September; there are no plans for importing it to the UK for some time to come.

Performance figures giving by Citroen are:— top speed 136 mph, with 0 to 60 mph in 8.8sec and a standing quarter-mile in 16.2sec. □

SPECIFICATION

FRONT ENGINE, FRONT-WHEEL DRIVE

ENGINE
Cylinders	6 in 90 deg vee
Main bearings	4
Cooling system	Water; pump, fan and thermostat
Bore	87.0 mm (3.42 in.)
Stroke	75.0 mm (2.95 in.)
Displacement	2,670 cc (163 cu. in.)
Valve gear	Four overhead camshafts, two per bank
Compression ratio	9.0-to-1 Min. octane rating: 98RM
Carburettors	3 twin-choke Weber 42 DCNF
Fuel pump	Bendix electric
Oil filter	Full-flow
Max. power	170 bhp (DIN) at 5,500 rpm
Max. torque	170 lb.ft (DIN) at 4,000 rpm
Max. bmep	157 psi at 4,000 rpm

TRANSMISSION
Clutch	Diaphragm spring
Gearbox	5-speed all-synchromesh
Gear ratios	Top 0.81
	Fourth 0.97
	Third 1.32
	Second 1.94
	First 2.93
	Reverse 3.16
Final drive	4.375 to 1

CHASSIS and BODY
Construction	Integral steel hull with bolt-on front wings: aluminium bonnet

SUSPENSION
Front	Independent double wishbones hydropneumatic units interconnected and self-levelling
Rear	Independent trailing arms hydropneumatic units interconnected and self-levelling

STEERING
Type	Rack and pinion, power assisted

BRAKES
Type	Disc, front and rear
Servo	Hydraulic pressure
Dimensions	F 11.8 in. dia. R 10.08 in. dia.

WHEELS
Type	Pressed steel, 5-stud fixing, 6 in. wide rim.
Tyres—make	Michelin
—type	X 70-series radial ply tubed
—size	195/70 VR 15 in.

MAINTENANCE
Fuel tank	19.7 Imp gallons (no reserve) (90 litres)
Engine sump	12.5 pints (7 litres)
Gearbox	3.9 pints
Max. payload	800 lb (363 kg)

DIMENSIONS
Wheelbase	9 ft. 8.1 in. (295 cm)
Track: front	5 ft. 0.1 in. (152 cm)
Track: rear	4 ft. 4.2 in. (132 cm)
Overall length	16 ft. 0.64 in. (489 cm)
Overall width	6 ft. 0.28 in. (183 cm)
Overall height	4 ft. 4 in. (132 cm)
Ground clearance	6.1 in. (12 cm)
Turning circle	34 ft. 6 in. (10.5 m)
Kerb weight	3,197 lb (1,449 kg)

PERFORMANCE DATA
5th gear mph per 1,000 rpm	22.85
4th gear mph per 1,000 rpm	17.64
Mean piston speed at max power	2,710
Bhp per ton laden	95.3

Technical Analysis
CITROEN SM

Citroen enters the luxury GT field, applying its usual unorthodox and imaginative engineering to the requirements of a fast, comfortable motorcar

BY RON WAKEFIELD

THE CITROEN SM is unequivocally *the* revolutionary car of 1970. That status isn't new to Citroen; they've made revolutionary cars a habit for decades now. And their obsession with achieving a particular goal with less than the customary attention to cost and simplicity (not to mention styling) has over the years put them in a more and more embarrassing sales position. The SM, at approximately $10,000 in the U.S. market, is not going to help much in that respect. But perhaps it will give what the admen call "image ruboff" to other Citroen models; certainly it is the first real French prestige car in years, not to mention that it's also the only 6-cyl now available from France. More than that, it comes at a time when many of us were getting the depressing notion that the development of road cars was reaching a boring plateau. Progress of a revolutionary nature may still be possible.

Citroen's current connections with other car builders are intriguing. In January 1968 Citroen acquired a majority interest in Maserati and soon thereafter put Maserati to work

on the V-6 engine for the SM, Maserati's first all-new engine in a long time. Several months later, however, the Italians got their revenge when Fiat bought 15% of Citroen stock. All the more interesting because Fiat also controls Ferrari now. The SM, be it known clearly, is a Citroen through and through with Maserati only in the engine. Viewed with respect to the other premium GT cars of the world, it is not in the top rank as far as performance is concerned but it equals or surpasses the most exotic ones in finish and appointments and may approach the best of them in handling. Certainly, at least on paper, it far surpasses any of them in sophistication and refinement.

Chassis & Body

LIKE THE DS and ID Citroens, the new SM is built on a conventional steel unit frame-body structure; all external panels are steel except for the aluminum hood and the front fenders and sheet-metal assembly are bolt-on. Also as with the

CITROEN SM

DS, the SM's shape is primarily aerodynamic. Esthetically, our styling experts say that as long as it had to look like a Citroen—and it's reasonable that it should—they couldn't have done better on the overall shape. On details, particularly the fussy chrome and lightwork at the rear, the stylists could have done better. Things like skirted rear wheels and a tapering rear end (8 in. narrower than the front), though we don't like the way they look, we accept on Citroens in the name of aerodynamics. The front end, remarkably smooth with its full-width glass cover for all lights including the advanced swivel-with-front-wheels units, will have to be altered to conform to our antiquated lighting laws before the SM is sold here this will be done by a sheet metal panel into which four round headlights are fitted as smoothly as possible.

Speaking of aerodynamics, we're told that the SM has a 30% lower (better) drag coefficient than the DS's. I doubt it; the DS is very good already and that's why it has such a high top speed and good fuel economy for its power output. But in any case aerodynamics are a Citroen strong point and I would not doubt that the SM is somewhat better than the DS—the claim of 137 mph from 180 bhp is not so wild as it sounds. By contrast a typical squared-off sedan of similar size and weight will do about 115 mph with the same power.

U.S. safety standards were taken into account from the start of design work on the SM. Its structure follows the rigid passenger compartment and controlled-crush design practice established several years ago by Mercedes, and a plastic fuel tank mounted between the rear wheels for maxi-

mum impact shielding is a welcome feature. But true safety design, according to Citroen (and us, and thankfully, the new U.S. Safety Bureau director), must be "preventive or passive" —meaning handling, braking and the like. A starter, say the designers, is the driving position:

The padded-rim steering wheel tilts and telescopes for position adjustment. Pivot point for the adjustable seat backrests is about 8 in. up from the base of the occupant's spine and there is considerable bucket effect in the backrest. Also the front and rear of the driver's seat can be raised or lowered independently. This is all manual, not power-operated. Interestingly the SM doesn't have the extreme softness of the DS interior; rather, it's on the firm-padding side. The handbrake lever is in our preferred position between the seats and the shift lever is nicely located in the central console and "booted" by an interesting metal cylinder that rocks and slides from side to side with the lever. The radio—which looks like a piece of expensive equipment from Fisher—is well back in the console, a location of questionable wisdom. Full use is made of control stalks on the steering "column" so that various important things can be operated without the driver fumbling for buttons or knobs.

A large complement of gauges and warning lights, with one master warning light (reading STOP and mounted in the center of the warning light cluster) to accompany any critical light such as that for engine oil pressure, water temperature or central hydraulic system. There are many other highly thoughtful details in the interior—this may be the greatest interior of any car on the road but passing a judgment like that depends upon a chance to live with the car for a while.

The entire rear body section, including the heated rear window and package tray, lifts up to reveal a trunk which is deep but intruded upon by the spare tire, and now there is a height control lever in the trunk so that the tire-changing owner can do his jacking-up (see *Suspension*) without having to go back and open the driver's door!

Suspension & Steering

THE SM's suspension system is basically the same hydro-pneumatic system as on the DS, in which a set of liquid-gas spheres are the springing units. There is one sphere for each wheel; hydraulic fluid is carried in the lower portion of it and nitrogen gas in the upper, a flexible diaphragm separating the two. The high-pressure pump supplies the hydraulic fluid to the system, a circuit of sensors and valves raising or lowering the pressure in the lower portion of the spheres to correct the height of the car for loading. If, for instance, three passengers climb into the car the pressure to the spheres is raised, which in turn compresses the N_2 and increases its pressure; thus the car is brought back to normal height. A 4-position control is provided—located by the driver's seat instead of at the toe-board—so that the driver can raise the ground clearance for rough going, and this is also used for jacking. Jacking procedure consists of raising the car to its highest position, inserting fixed-length props and then "lowering" it, which picks a pair of wheels up off the ground.

Since the SM is a sporting car the suspension settings for it are firmer than they are in the sedans. This is accomplished by starting with a lower static N_2 pressure and hence less N_2 volume in the sphere: the effect is less compression space and hence less suspension travel. With the system in operation—fluid supplied under pressure—the N_2 pressure is thus higher than in the DS, the equivalent of firmer springs.

Geometrically the suspension is similar to the DS's but there is an important difference. The front unequal-length arms, which turn rearward to their pivots in the DS, turn forward on the SM and hence are trailing instead of leading. For one thing, this puts the whole business out front where it is more readily accessible for attention; but more importantly it reverses the suspension's reaction to braking—the front end now tends to squat instead of rise on braking. Since the pure trailing arms at the rear—same as on DS—also tend toward squat on braking the SM has less of an attitude change on braking than the DS. Still, the SM is not entirely free of those odd motions peculiar to Citroens when being maneuvered for parking as the rear end seems more prone to squat than the front under these circumstances. As on the DS there is a torsional steel anti-roll bar at both front and rear. The excellent

Michelin XVR tires—Michelin's best—are the only ones supplied on the SM, size 195/70-15 on 15 x 6 wheels.

The hydropneumatic suspension was revolutionary in 1956 and it is the SM's steering that is revolutionary in 1970. Like the brakes and suspension it is fully powered from the central hydraulic system, but this was true of the DS too. To start with, it's much quicker than before: gear ratio of 9.4:1 vs 14.7:1 on the DS. That's race-car quick, in case there's any doubt—two turns lock-to-lock. Now with steering this fast, a car as rapid as the SM could be a real handful at speed—one false breath on the steering wheel and one would be off in the trees. The solution, according to Citroen: variable assist and powered centering.

Power supplied to the rack-and-pinion steering gear, then, is governed by two things: position of the steering wheel and road speed. As the wheel is turned away from center the power "assist" increases, meaning that parking maneuvers will get maximum assist. But as road speed goes up the level of power assist (onto which the position modulation is superimposed) goes *down*, via a signal from a hydraulic governor unit at the front end of the transaxle unit. Furthermore, the steering return action is powered and this is supposed to have a salutory effect on straight-line stability. Citroen has put hydraulic pressure into the "running on rails" idea, and proof of this is easy to see: with the car at a standstill and the engine running, if one cranks the steering wheel over and lets it go, it returns to center!

Engine & Transmission

THE ENTIRE power package is "turned around," with the engine back at the firewall and the transaxle unit ahead of it. Dare we call the SM a mid-engine car? Maserati has built a new plant near Modena to produce the V-6 engine in quantities that must be quite new to them—Citroen tells us around 7000 per year.

Like Buick's V-6 engine, which was built on tooling for a 90° V-8, the new engine is a 90° unit. Both block and heads are cast of aluminum alloy for a low overall weight of 308 lb and there is a lower block casting of the same material that forms a spacer between main block and sump as well as the four main bearing caps. The mains, by the way, are very beefy at 3.00 in. diameter. Interestingly the sump does not go full-length, its deep pan lifting (probably to clear framework) just ahead of journal no. 2 to a level that's very close to the crankshaft counterweights.

SM's hydraulic steering system is revolutionary, varying assist with car speed and wheel position.

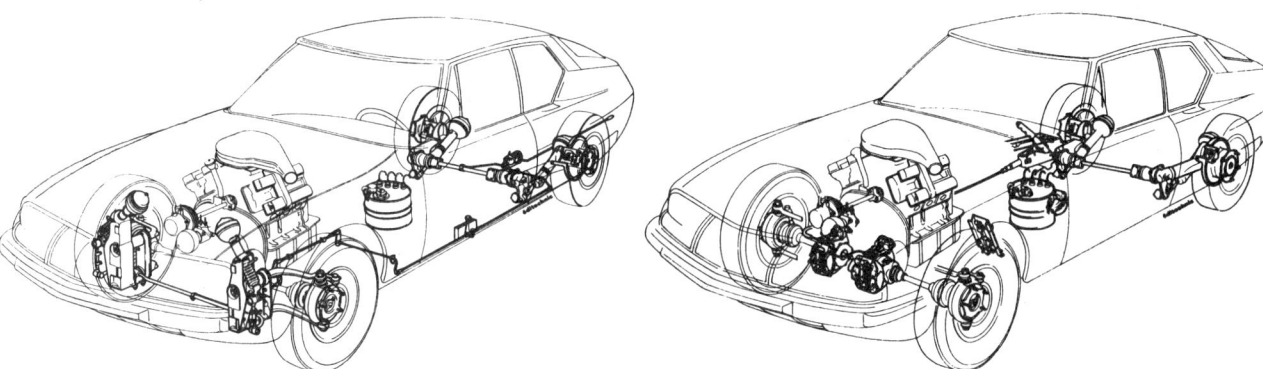

Hydropneumatic springing is basically same as on DS but front lateral suspension arms now trail instead of lead.

Four-wheel disc brakes, like steering and suspension, are fully powered from engine-driven central hydraulic system.

CITROEN SM

Nearly flat-topped pistons form the bottom of hemispherical combustion chambers and operate in unusual wet-dry cylinder liners that are in contact with coolant for about the top inch of their length only. Bore and stroke dimensions are well oversquare at 87 x 75 mm.

The valve gear is the most interesting part of the engine. Four cams, it seems to me, are a mighty expensive way of extracting that last bit of horsepower from an engine and I wonder if they justify their cost in a car costing less than $8000 on home ground—but then tradition is tradition at Maserati. Anyhow, the camshaft drive arrangement is the wild part: a conventional duplex chain on a sprocket at the rear of the engine runs up to an auxiliary shaft whose centerline is an inch or so above the intake valve head and in the center of the V. That shaft, large in diameter but hollow, runs forward to emerge at the front of the engine from where it drives all auxiliaries—alternator, air conditioning pump, main hydraulic pump, air injection pump. On the same shaft are two double sprockets, the left one between the front and second cylinders and the right one between the back and second cylinders, which drive via duplex chains the two camshafts on that side of the engine. An idler sprocket, manually tensioned, keeps chain tension on each cam-drive duplex and there are three rubbing blocks on each side as well. The camshafts in turn operate the valves (approx. 78° included angle between intake

and exhaust) through bucket tappets. Intake-exhaust gas flow is of the crossflow variety, as the engine cross section shows, and three Weber carburetors complete this complex breathing arrangement.

Maximum speed of the engine is 6500 rpm and its output is 180 bhp @ 6250 rpm; the maximum torque of 172-lb-ft occurs at 4000 rpm. Citroen claims a top speed of 137 mph, 0-60 mph time of 8.2 sec and quarter-mile time of 16.2 sec, which figures would put its performance in the Porsche 911T class. In 5th gear the engine is geared for about 22.5 mph per 1000 rpm.

A conventional diaphragm-spring clutch transfers power from the front of the Maserati engine to the Citroen-built 5-speed gearbox ahead of it. The main gearbox shaft (input) passes over the right side of the differential unit and transmits through the various gears to the layshaft below, which drives rearward to the differential. From there constant-velocity universal joints (tri-axis at the differential end, Spicer at the wheels) and halfshafts drive the front wheels. There is no semi-automatic transmission as on the DS: the 5-speed box is strictly conventional and manual, and an automatic (most likely a Borg-Warner 3-speed) is to be available later.

Brakes

THIS IS Citroen's first model with discs at all four wheels but otherwise the SM follows the braking system of the DS—which is to say highly unconventional. The discs are of the solid, not internally vented, variety with 11.8-in. diameter at the front (inboard) and 10.1 at the rear (outboard); a small

CITROEN SM SPECIFICATIONS

Engine:

Type....................90° V-6, dohc
Bore x stroke, mm......87.0 x 75.0
   Equivalent in.............3.42 x 2.95
Displacement, cc/cu in.........2670/163
Compression ratio................9.0:1
Bhp @ rpm...............180 @ 6250
Torque @ rpm, lb-ft........172 @ 4000
Carburetion...three Weber 42DCNF (2V)
Emission control...........air injection
Block & heads material....aluminum alloy
Crankshaft main bearings..............4
Sump capacity, qt..................4.8
Weight, lb........................308

Drive Train:

Transmission......5-speed manual in unit
  with final drive; automatic to be available later.

Gear ratios: 5th (0.757)...........3.31:1
   4th (0.971)................4.24:1
   3rd (1.30)................5.68:1
   2nd (1.94)................8.48:1
   1st (2.92)...............12.8:1
Final drive ratio.................4.38:1

Chassis & Body

Body/frame..................unit steel
Brake type: 11.8-in. disc front, 10.1-in. disc
  rear; actuated by central hydraulic system
  with front/rear proportioning determined
  by vehicle loading.
Wheels................steel disc, 15 x 6
Tires............Michelin XVR (radial)
  195/70VR-15
Steering type..rack & pinion with variable
  power assist from central hydraulic system
   Gear ratio....................9.4:1

Turning circle, ft..................34.5
Front suspension: unequal-length lateral
  arms, hydropneumatic springing with
  automatic leveling, anti-roll bar.
Rear suspension: trailing arms, hydropneumatic springing with automatic leveling,
  anti-roll bar.

General:

Curb weight, lb...................3200
Distribution, front/rear, %........62/38
Wheelbase, in.....................116.1
Track, front/rear..............60.1/52.2
Overall length..................192.6
  Width........................72.3
  Height.......................52.1
Ground clearance..................6.1
  (adjustable by level control)
Fuel tank capacity, U.S. gal.........19.7

This shot from front of car shows location of suspension spheres and engine-driven ancillaries at front of engine.

drum handbrake is built into the front discs. The Citroen system can truly be called "power brakes" and is not to be confused with the vacuum-assisted braking systems used on most cars. Here the brakes are fully powered, there being none of the usual application of them by a master cylinder, hydraulic fluid in lines and wheel cylinders. The high-pressure pump supplies high-pressure fluid via the main accumulator to two smaller accumulators, one for the front and one for the rear brakes—Citroen had this dual-circuit braking long before it was required by U.S. law. Application is controlled by the famous *champignon* pedal and proportioning of front-to-rear brake effort is modulated according to vehicle loading by the same system that levels the car. It was an eyebrow-raiser 14 years ago when the DS was introduced to see a brake system with absolutely no mechanical or conventionally hydraulic takeover in case of failure of the central hydraulic system, but over the years I haven't heard any reports of trouble with this on Citroens. The accumulators store enough pressurized fluid for about 50 brake applications after the engine stops, should it stall.

A FASCINATING car, the Citroen SM. I have not driven it yet, but I did get a brief ride in it over a very bad stretch of road—which seemed to confirm what its sophisticated features promise. A full road test will be forthcoming the first minute a car is available to us.

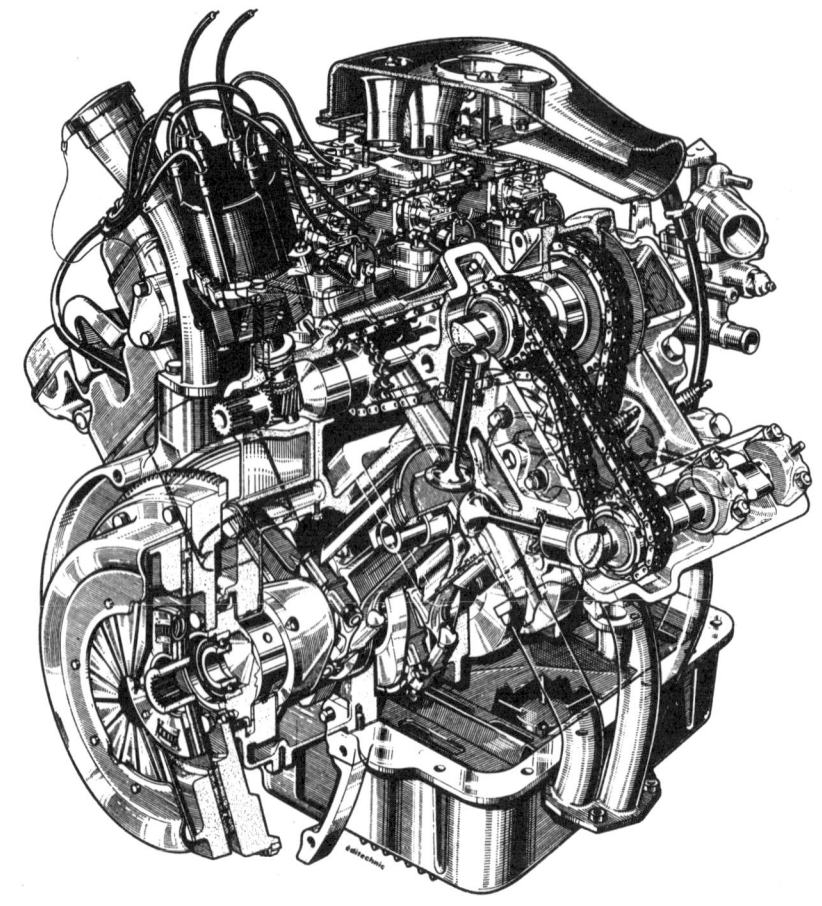

Formidable

Grand Touring Citroen with 2.7-litre Maserati V6; high top speed but weight hampers acceleration; novel power steering requires familiarity; roadholding superb, ride very good; many striking features

.MOTOR TESTED

In some ways the House of Citroen is typical of Parisian haute couture; it sets fashions so daring and way out that few dare to follow. But unlike the fickle world of fashion, the men from Quai Andre Citroen produce new models at infrequent intervals and then largely leave them alone. The fashion that the DS range set 15 years ago is still as highly regarded as it was then. Rumours of a six-cylinder DS were rife five years ago; now a "six" has arrived in a complete change of clothing, not as a replacement for the DS but as the company's new prestige car, the ultimate sporting Citroen cast in the renowned mould of comfort and luxury.

The engine comes not from Citroen but from Maserati with whom Citroen signed a technical agreement in 1968. French fiscal laws draw a line at 2.8 litres, beyond which annual taxes rise very steeply. To get real power from an engine below this capacity

needed the skills of engineers used to thinking in terms of high specific outputs, and with the strong, light 90° V6 Maserati have achieved 170 bhp from 2.7 litres using classic twin overhead camshafts per bank and three twin-choke Webers. Although this might be thought of as a racing specification, refinement inherent in the Citroen reputation has not been sacrificed; it gives real usable power and can accelerate $28\frac{1}{4}$ cwt. of metal masterpiece to 100 mph in 26 sec. That the car can reach 135 mph on half the power that a Jensen needs for the same speed is adequate commendation that Citroen aerodynamicists know more than most how to get the best blend of shape and styling, for the car is as striking to see as its specification is to read.

To describe the rest of the car as pure progressive Citroen would be accurate but insufficient. The familiar hydropneumatic suspension has been developed to be compatible with a responsive sports car—it's firmer than that of the DS to keep the roll angles down and inevitably a little harsher round town. But the ride is still first class at speed. The biggest change is to the steering; the

PRICE: Approximately £5000 when available in UK

DS power steering has always allied accurate response to high gearing but the SM goes several stages further with even higher gearing and variable assistance according to speed and lock. High speed corners are taken with virtually no assistance and it feels very nice indeed. Around town, though, assistance is strong, response is instant and the unfamiliar have to be very careful not to take the usual armful of wheel to get round the corners or the car responds too soon and the rear wheels, some $9\frac{1}{2}$ft. behind the front ones, take a short cut across the pavement. Overall we liked the steering although it takes some getting used to and demands concentration, but we can't help feeling that it might put some people off since it needs more than a 50-mile demonstration for a true appreciation. If your second car is a 2CV the switch from one to t'other could almost be dangerous for the first mile.

Once behind the wheel of the SM you know you are in a rather special car and treat it accordingly. An impressive battery of readily identifiable instruments and switches are fairly easily found and the dials are shape matched to the slightly oval steering wheel. The seats are carefully profiled hammocks (with inadequate side support), and the rear seats allow fairly comfortable room for two in the back—less headroom and knee space than in a DS but enough for two adults on a Paris-Nice run. The boot, too, is adequate rather than spacious.

At the wheel of an SM you are conscious that it is a product of some of the world's top motoring technologists; it looks and is fast, and it's comfortable and quiet. You can spend half the SM's £5000 (an approximate price at the time of writing) on cars with less comfort, but higher performance and more conventional handling. But the SM is a very real contender in the top league and for £5000 it's a triumph of design complexity over production engineering—a remarkable car from a remarkable company.

Performance and economy

Underneath the SM's fallaway bonnet the engine looks almost dwarfed sitting right back against the bulkhead; classic in conception with the twin camshafts per bank chain driven, it is a beautiful piece of alloy casting with the sign of the Trident on the cam boxes. Starting requires just a brief spell of the choke. At fast tickover you can hear a smooth whine with little hint of the lengths of chain inside, and you catch the occasional clatter of the hydraulic pump which is still audible, though less so than on the DS. Winding it up after a customary warm-up spell produces that thoroughbred growl, just like a flat-six Porsche, although the exhaust note is very much quieter. You don't really hear it until about 70 mph, but over about 3000 rpm in the gears it makes just the right sort of noise for a sporting ear without being obtrusive.

With a nice five speed box to play with you aren't really going

PERFORMANCE

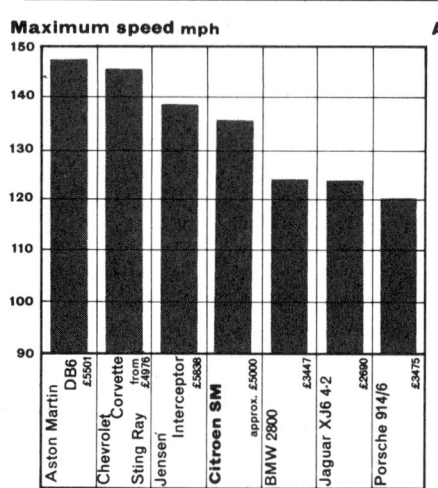

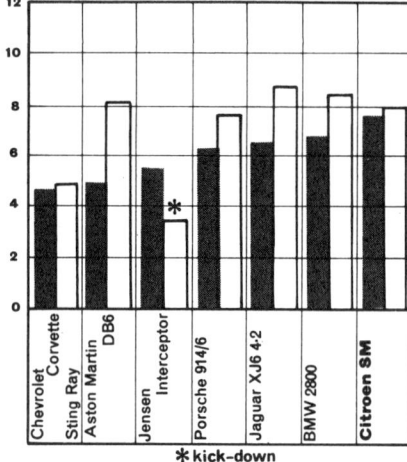

* kick-down

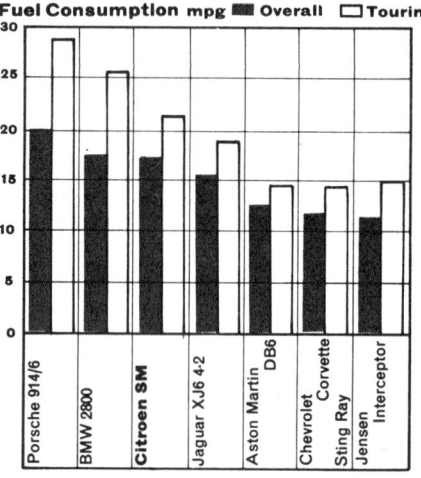

Test Data: World copyright reserved; no unauthorised reproduction in whole or in part.

Conditions
Weather: No wind, occasional light rain
Temperature: 55°F
Barometer 29.4 in. Hg.
Surface: Damp tarmacadam
Fuel: Premium, 98-octane (RM) 4-Star rating

Maximum Speeds

	mph	kph
Mean of opposite runs	135.2	218
4th gear	115	185
3rd gear	84	135
2nd gear	57	92
1st gear	38	61

Acceleration Times

m.p.h.		sec.
0-30	. . . .	3.9
0-40	. . . .	5.7
0-50	. . . .	7.6
0-60	. . . .	9.9
0-70	. . . .	13.1
0-80	. . . .	16.0
0-90	. . . .	20.7
0-100	. . . .	26.1
Standing quarter mile	. . . .	17.4

m.p.h.	Top sec.	4th sec.	3rd sec.
10-30.	—	—	6.4
20-40.	11.8	8.4	5.7
30-50.	11.7	8.0	5.6
40-60.	12.5	7.9	5.5
50-70.	12.2	8.2	5.5
60-80.	12.3	7.8	5.8
70-90.	13.0	7.9	—
80-100	14.5	10.0	—

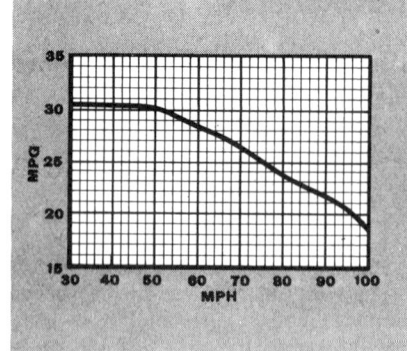

Fuel Consumption
Touring (consumption midway between 30 mph and maximum less 5% allowance for acceleration) 21.5 mpg
Overall 17.2 mpg
(= 16.4 litres/100km)
Total test distance 510 miles

Brakes
Pedal pressure, deceleration and equivalent stopping distance from 30 m.p.h.

lb.	g.	ft.
25	0.43	70
50	0.77	39
75	0.94	32
Handbrake	0.17	177

Steering
Turning circle between kerbs:		ft.
Left		33
Right		33
Turns of steering wheel from lock to lock		2
Steering wheel deflection for 50 ft. diameter circle		0.65 turns

Clutch
Free pedal movement	= $\frac{1}{4}$ in.
Additional movement to disengage clutch completely	= 5 in.
Maximum pedal load	= 45 lb.

Speedometer (corrected to mph)
Indicated	10	20	30	40	50	60
True	10	19	28	37	47	57
Indicated	70	80	90	100	110	120
True	67	77	87	$97\frac{1}{2}$	108	119

Distance recorder 3% fast

Weight
Kerb weight (unladen with fuel for approximately 50 miles) 28.5 cwt
Front/rear distribution 62/38
Weight laden as tested 32.2 cwt

Parkability
Gap needed to clear 6 ft. wide obstruction in front

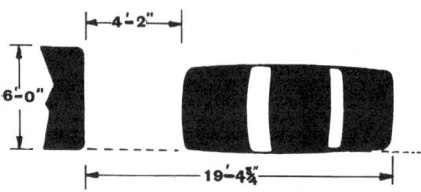

16

to notice that performance is a bit slow in fifth gear until you can floor the pedal at around 25 mph; beyond that mere 1200 rpm it pulls well, its quickest 20 mph band being as low as 30-50 mph, though its not much slower from 70-90 mph where the aerodynamics are beginning to play their part and the engine is reaching the highest part of its flat torque curve. Curiously in both fifth and fourth there's a slight hiccup in the acceleration curve—40-60 mph in fifth and 50-70 mph in fourth are both slower than the figures above and below those speeds. Third gear really displays the flat torque curve well with a steady flow from 20-80 mph, each 10 mph step taking 2.7-3.0sec.

Peak power is developed at 6250 rpm and the red sector on the rev counter starts at 6500 rpm; in search of the best 0-60 mph figure we held second gear just beyond this but valve bounce sets in sharply at 6800 rpm (exactly 60 mph). Although 170 bhp sounds a lot, it had to accelerate over 32 cwt. when the car was laden with our test gear, giving 105 bhp/ton; so it is not surprising that the 0-60 mph figure is only just under 10sec. which equates to a Cortina Lotus in power/weight and figures—aerodynamics being insignificant at this speed. The factory claim 0-60 in 8.2sec. which would have been impossible in the car we drove with two-up with test kit. The SM is rather like the DS on take-off. Too much initial jerk and there is some tramp from the driven front wheels accompanied by a tremendous crash underneath as if engine torque has twisted the

unit into contact with something solid; so unless you are completely unsympathetic (or there is a little more clearance) and the engine allows a few more vital revs, faster times would be difficult. The slight dampness of the road improved rather than detracted from getaway in that it allowed some wheelspin, which was otherwise difficult to achieve. However, we equalled the factory time to 100 mph with an impressive 26sec.

These figures aren't particularly world beating, but the ease with which the car maintains 100 mph cruising and beyond is very impressive. Give a Lotus Elan Plus 2 170 bhp and it would only be about 3 mph faster than the SM given ideal gearing, so the much larger SM (6ft. wide x 4ft. 4in. high) must have a very good drag factor to achieve 135 mph on 170 bhp. Our figures are a product of rev counter readings in opposite directions, and the rev counter proved to be accurate.

The shape of the fuel curve is always a good indication of drag; at 30, 40 and 50 mph the SM returns 30 mpg, the power required for the various ancillaries taking a much higher proportion of the output at such speeds. The curve drops very gradually from this level, only falling below 20 mpg at 95 mph; our touring figure, worked out for 80-85 mph cruising, is 21.5 mpg, and even our overall consumption, which was affected by a higher proportion of performance test mileage than usual, was a respectable 17.2 mpg with 100 mph plus cruising on the autoroutes—legal in France where we did the testing. The

Six quartz iodine lamps hide behind the transparent cover; the outer two swivel with the steering. Heater motor is on left

The spare wheel takes up a lot of space on the boot floor—no room under the bonnet. Parcel shelf lifts up with boot lid

We didn't use our standard Revelation set of cases to go to France, but this collection of one case and assorted test kit fitted in without any juggling

octane rating is for best French petrol corresponding to our 4-Star fuel; the $19\frac{1}{2}$ gallon fuel tank allows well over 300 miles range—we achieved 310 miles before our first fill-up.

Transmission

The DS has also benefited from the SM's Citroen-made five-speed gearbox. With a floor-mounted lever it gives a delightful gearchange and the ratios are very well chosen with a nice widening of the gaps for a useful pull at any speed. The long gearlever sits in a neat slotted cylinder which rocks with the lever into the various ratios as a permanent and effective seal against noise; selection movements almost follow a W-pattern with the lower four ratios in the conventional positions; fifth requires a noticeable dog-leg movement. You get the occasional click as the lever catches the edge of the gate surround but it is a delightful and easy change which a well cushioned clutch keeps permanently smooth; in fact the clutch is pretty heavy with a long travel but you don't really notice this with a good seating position.

We didn't find a 1-in-3 test hill but the SM should be able to start on such an incline. There was no transmission noise.

Handling and brakes

As Citroen's sports car the SM had to be rather special to be able to out corner the DS without sacrificing too much ride comfort. So engineers retained as much as possible of the ideas developed to their utmost in the latest DS21s, like the interconnected hydropneumatic suspension with built-in self-levelling, headlights which stay level, spotlights which see round corners and power-assisted rack and pinion steering. The rear suspension pivots on the familiar trailing arms but at the front are a pair of transverse arms, just single links not wishbones, bent through a right angle to give a longitudinal axis. With slightly different lengths upper and lower, the wheel no longer inclines with the body, keeping flatter on the road to give a bit more grip even than a DS. Colossal 195/70 HR 15 Michelin XVR tyres put more rubber on the road too; these low profile tyres are used on Ferrari's road cars and we were very impressed with them on wet and dry surfaces.

Citroen's other departure is to produce even more direct steering with variable assistance. With $\frac{1}{2}$ ton on each front wheel when fully laden, assistance is necessary so Citroen provide maximum assistance at zero speed building up as lock increases—this is coupled to a self-centring system so that the wheel returns to the straight ahead position with the car stationary.

Round the streets of Paris we thought it was too highly geared and ultra responsive at first; you have to keep your elbows down, control normal fluid movements and just caress the wheel. It pays not to feed it through your hands in the IAM shuffle since this makes things jerky. But with practice and great respect for the response you feel you can swerve it round anything. At medium speeds you hardly notice the assistance although you still have to keep the movements tight. On motorways it really does feel like manual steering with no assistance, but it's very, very direct and we felt that it required a lot of concentration to drive at over 100 mph, particularly on shallow motorway curves, or in the very minor corrections for a side wind twitch. Familiarity over a longer spell might have bred a more relaxed hold on the wheel.

Where we enjoyed the car particularly was in hilly areas with bends in the 50-80 mph region. Grip, even on wet roads, was quite remarkable and at these speeds the steering again feels like a manual system. The SM could be cornered fast and flat with very little roll; what there is builds up with the first movement of the steering. Using full bore out of a slowish corner you can get the car to understeer, betrayed by the noise of rising revs under wheelspin. Citroen claim that the system is so irreversible that you wouldn't even feel the wrench if a tyre blew out which means that "feel" as we know it is non-existent. But it doesn't seem to affect one's confidence at all—the roadholding really is superb. We aren't 100 per cent convinced that the steering is the ultimate system, though.

Power braking through separate circuits is another Citroen hallmark and it seemed much easier to brake the SM smoothly

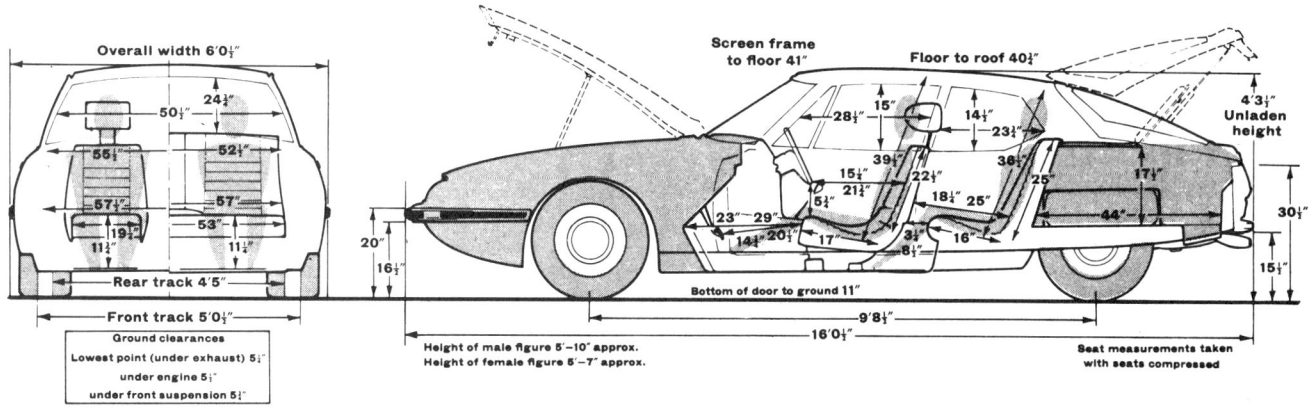

Overall width 6'0½"
50½"
24½"
55½"
52½"
57½"
57"
53"
19½"
11½"
11½"
Rear track 4'5"
Front track 5'0½"

Ground clearances
Lowest point (under exhaust) 5½"
under engine 5½"
under front suspension 5½"

Screen frame to floor 41"
Floor to roof 40½"
28½"
15"
14½"
23½"
39½"
22½"
36½"
25"
17½"
15½"
21½"
18½"
25"
51"
23"   29"
14½"   20½"
17
3½"
44"
16"
6½"
Bottom of door to ground 11"
20"
16½"
4'3½" Unladen height
30½"
15½"
9'8½"
16'0½"

Height of male figure 5'–10" approx.
Height of female figure 5'–7" approx.

Seat measurements taken with seats compressed

Alloy V6 engine with front wheel drive; independent self-levelling hydro-pneumatic suspension

Engine

Block material	Light alloy
Head material	Light alloy
Cylinders	90° V6
Cooling system	Water with pump, thermostat and two electric fans
Bore and stroke	87 mm (3.42in.) 75 mm (2.95in.)
Cubic capacity	2670 cc (163 cu. in.)
Main bearings	4
Valves	Twin ohc per bank
Compression ratio	9.0:1
Octane rating	99
Carburetters	3 Twin-choke 42 DC NF Webers
Fuel pump	Bendix electric
Oil filter	Full flow
Max. power (net)	170 bhp at 5500 rpm
Max. power (gross)	180 bhp at 6250 rpm
Max. torque (net)	170 lb. ft. at 4000 rpm
Max. torque (gross)	172 lb. ft. at 4000 rpm

Transmission

Clutch	Diaphragm spring 8¾in. s.d.p.

Internal gearbox ratios

Top gear	0.81
4th gear	0.97
3rd gear	1.32
2nd gear	1.94
1st gear	2.92
Reverse	3.16
Synchromesh	On all forward ratios
Final drive	4.375:1

Mph at 1000 rpm in:

Top gear	22.5
4th gear	17.6
3rd gear	12.9
2nd gear	8.8
1st gear	5.8

Chassis and body

Construction	Steel monocoque with detachable steel front wings and front panel and aluminium bonnet.

Brakes

Type	Power operated disc brakes all round
Dimensions	11.8in. dia. front, 10.1in. dia. rear
Total friction area	47.4 sq. in.

Suspension and steering

Front	Independent with transverse arms and anti roll bar with hydro-pneumatic springing and self levelling
Rear	Independent with trailing arms and anti roll bar with hydropneumatic springing and self levelling
Shock absorbers: Front Rear	Integral with suspension units
Steering type	Rack and pinion with variable assistance
Tyres	Michelin 195/70 VR 15 XVR
Wheels	Steel with 5 studs
Rim size	6J x 15

Coachwork and equipment

Starting handle	None
Tool kit contents	Wheel changing equipment
Jack	Adjustable stand
Jacking points	In door sills
Battery	12 volt negative earth 70 amp.hrs. capacity
Number of electrical fuses	12
Headlamps	Six quartz iodine for main, dipped and long distance beams
Indicators	Non self cancelling flashers
Reversing lamp	Yes
Screen wipers	Two speed electric
Screen washers	Electric
Sun visors	Two padded
Locks: With ignition key	Ignition/steering lock
With other keys	Doors, boot, glove locker plus fuel cap
Interior heater	Fresh air
Upholstery	Jersey nylon
Floor covering	Carpet
Alternative body styles	None
Maximum load	860 lb.
Maximum roof rack load	Unknown
Major extras available	Air conditioning, leather upholstery

Maintenance

Fuel tank capacity	19.7 galls
Sump	12.5 pints SAE 20/50
Gearbox/transaxle	3.9 pints SAE
Steering gear	Hydraulic fluid
Coolant	23 pints
Chassis lubrication	Every 3000 miles to 6 points
Minimum service interval	3000 miles

Ignition timing	6° btdc
Contact breaker gap	0.015in.
Sparking plug gap	0.024-0.027in.
Sparking plug type	Bosch W200 T30
Tappet clearance (cold)	inlet 0.013in. exhaust 0.020in.
Valve timing	Not disclosed
Front wheel toe-in	0.08 to 0.16in.
Camber angle	0 to ½° negative
Castor angle	1° 42'
Tyre pressures: Front	32 psi
Rear	29 psi

Full address

Maker	SA André Citroen, quai André Citroen 133, Paris XV, France.
Concessionaires	Citroen Cars Ltd, Trading Estate, Slough, Bucks.

Safety check list

Steering Assembly

Steering box position	Above and behind front wheels
Steering column collapsible	Yes
Steering wheel boss padded	Yes
Steering wheel dished	No

Instrument Panel

Projecting switches	None
Sharp cowls	None
Padding	Full width above facia

Windscreen and Visibility

Screen type	Laminated
Pillars padded	Yes
Standard driving mirrors	Interior and driver's door
Interior mirror framed	Yes
Interior mirror collapsible	Yes
Sun visors	Two padded

Seats and Harness

Attachment to floor	Bolted runners
Do they tip forward?	Retained
Head rest attachment points	Head rests standard
Back of front seats	Firm but padded
Safety harness	Lap and diagonal
Harness anchors at back	Yes

Doors

Projecting handles	No
Anti-burst latches	Yes
Child-proof locks	No

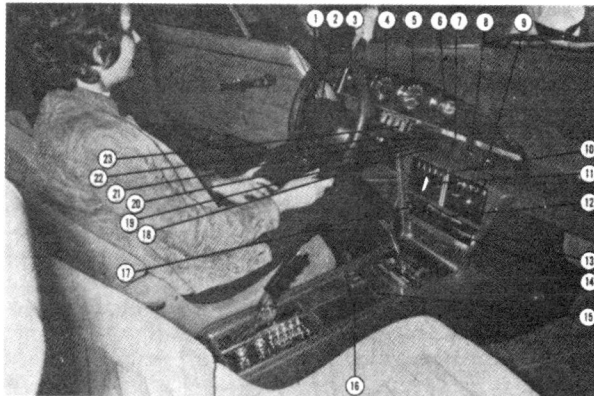

1 horn/flasher stalk. 2 washer/wiper stalk. 3 air vent. 4 speedometer. 5 rev counter. 6 warning lights and tell-tales for hazard warning, fuel tank, main beam, left and right hand indicators, brake level, water temperature, hydraulic fluid level, oil pressure, alternator charge, sidelights, handbrake, rear window heater plus check button for emergency lights. 7 water temperature gauge. 8 fuel gauge. 9 oil temperature. 10 central air grille volume control. 11 direction controls. 12 heater temperature. 13 heater direction. 14 heater volume with fan. 15 ashtray. 16 window lifts. 17 choke. 18 interior light switch. 19 rear window heater switch. 20 parking lights. 21 fog lights (option). 22 lighting stalk. 23 steering column supports

than the DS; the usual rubber button pedal was nice and firm and provided a good pivot for heel and toe operation. With 50lb. producing 0.77g the brakes aren't over-servoed; maximum braking gets the front wheels juddering on damp roads as if the suspension links could do with triangulation, but the car pulls up all square. The handbrake, however, was quite useless for emergency stops although this should never be necessary with twin circuit braking; it was capable of holding the car on quite steep hills.

Comfort and controls

With the sportier outlook of the SM came rather firmer suspension than on the DS; progressive bump stops come in quite early in the suspension travel. The result is that the car doesn't float like a DS on long-wave undulations but seems to follow the overall contours of the road very comfortably without ever getting jerky on minor irregularities; hump-backs can still catch the system out because the front wheels are slow to come down, but the rubbers absorb the shock very well. A combination of better damping and firmer springing in the system has given the car a sportier feel without the ride suffering. For a sports GT the ride is unequalled and there are very few saloons which rival it—it is most akin to that of the Jaguar XJ6. Around town it is harsher; low speed thump is noticeable on sharp ridges but there is little judder transmitted to the occupants even on cobblestones when the tyres sing gently.

Each front seat has no fewer than six controls; front and back of the cushion each have three alternative heights and there is a wide range of fore and aft adjustment. The seat back "breaks" some 6in. above the normal hinge line; reclining the upper half can vary lumbar support although the fully reclined position puts a prominent ridge into your back. Another control moves the soft headrest vertically or horizontally. The final control on the outer edge of the backrest automatically springs the seat forward on its runners to allow easy access to the rear; a gentle push slides the seat back to its original settings.

Another driving position variable is the steering wheel, which slides in and out and up and down and takes the various column stalks with it—an excellent arrangement. With such seating versatility anyone can get comfortable—until we were used to the car we preferred to sit as high as possible and look down on the wide bonnet for accurate placing through narrow town gaps. Our only criticism is that the seats do not give enough side support; they are comfortably shaped and padded for straight line driving but the shoulders are not held at all—it might be easier to steer if you were held more firmly.

The back seat is rather cramped for large adults with the lowish roof and only just enough room for legs between the seat back and rear seat—plenty of width though. Forward visibility is good but to the rear the view is hampered by the blind spots behind the angular rear side windows which hinge open with a knurled screw. The wiper stalk gives an intermittent slow wipe, or a continuous fast wipe (we would have liked another speed in between) but the wipers are effective and stay on the screen at speed.

1 spare oil. 2 oil filler cap. 3 distributor. 4 dipstick (behind air cleaner). 5 water filler cap. 6 hydraulic fluid reservoir. 7 screen washer reservoir. 8 front suspension struts. 9 twin coils. 10 hydraulic pressure reservoir. 11 hydraulic pump

We anticipated that the multiplicity of lighting would give a daylight effect but the QI lights were disappointing with their yellow bulbs; maximum safe speed with the main beam and the two spots was only 85 mph at the most on roads without cats eyes, dropping suddenly to a mere 60 mph on the separate dipped lights—dipping switches off main and spots (if on) returning to all four. The swivelling spots keep deliberately slightly ahead of the steering to give quite remarkable illumination on twisty roads. Experience with the DS21 Pallas with white bulbs showed that the system is potentially better than any other, but a combination of yellow bulbs and the full width cowl reduces the output to more mundane levels.

The intake for the heater is positioned on the bonnet deliberately to avoid ram pressure so the volume control operates in conjunction with a fan to ensure that the output doesn't vary with speed; two other slides control temperature by thermostat, and direction variation. Fresh air comes through eyeball vents at each end of the facia as well as the large grilles in the centre which have separate volume and distribution controls. Altogether you have very good control of the atmosphere—and full air conditioning if you want at extra cost.

Fittings and furniture

All dials on the main binnacle are oval, like the steering wheel. On the left is a housing for the left eyeball outlet (left-hand-drive car), speedometer and rev counter visible through the single-spoke wheel, and an "all systems go" collection of no fewer than 14 warning lights and tell-tales. You only worry if the red ones come on, for water temperature, hydraulic pressure or engine oil pressure with a large central one lighting in sympathy for any red light. There is also a check button to make sure these four are working. Each light is clearly marked so it isn't too hard to sort out what is happening.

Under the oval clock on the right of the nacelle are three rectangular gauges for water temperature, fuel and oil temperature. To the left of these are three or four push-in buttons for parking lights, heated rear window and interior light with an optional one for fog lights, but the main controls are all within fingertip reach on the stalk. The near stalk on the left controls non-self-cancelling indicators, flashers (push away) and a rather weak horn (pull towards you), while the further left-hand stalk operates the wipers and screenwasher. On the right is the usual Citroen lighting stalk; unscrew it 90° and you get side or dipped lights (using an axial movement as well), a further 90° and you get dipped or main with the spotlights controlled by a button on the end. Surprisingly it is quite simple to work all this out and use them without thinking, so the ergonomics must be sound.

On the console are electric window lift switches, cigar lighter and ashtray plus the optional radio complete with electric aerial and three speakers. There is a glove locker on the passenger's side, pockets in each door and in the rear for oddments. There are three keys—one for starter/steering lock/ignition, one saying "Bouchon" for the petrol filler and a third with the Citroen chevrons for doors, glove locker and boot. We didn't have our cases in France but all our test kit and some luggage fitted in the boot quite easily.

The interior of our car was trimmed in carpet and leather and extremely tastefully finished.

Servicing and maintenance

One look under the bonnet would be quite enough to put the home mechanic right off the thought of doing his own servicing. All the things that he needs to reach like dipstick and the various filler caps are accessible; even the sparking plugs are easy to reach. There is also a place for a spare litre can of 20/50 oil.

Wheelchanging follows the usual Citroen pattern using the ride height adjuster. The SM has five slots for this, one for normal motoring, two ground clearance ones, plus the two extremes for wheel changing in conjunction with the adjustable stands for propping the car up while the appropriate wheel retracts.

The SM isn't yet available in Britain but it is hoped that some should be for sale in April; Citroen mechanics are currently being trained in its servicing which is required every 5000 miles. ∎

WE DRIVE ...

Alfa Romeo Montreal and Citroen SM

Michelin's Foreign Car Test Day, held on the Silverstone track, gave a rare opportunity to gain driving impressions of two cars strange so far to Britain.

AT last, we got to drive Alfa's Montreal: even though it was no more than a brief ride round Silverstone. The car in question, brought along for the Michelin Test Day last week, was a left hand drive example, still proudly bearing its Milanese number plates.

Getting installed was no problem; the Montreal is no converted racer, but a very civilized GT. It certainly sits low on the ground, but one can drop gracefully into the driving seat and start to take stock of the situation.

For me, the driving position is not good. The Italian nation and I have agreed to differ about what constitutes a normal ratio of arm to leg length. In the Montreal, as in almost every one of their cars, I have to sit with my knees well bent, and splayed on either side of the steering wheel. For the rest, I can hardly quarrel with the way the cockpit is laid out. It is difficult to be dogmatic without driving a car like this a long way, but there were no obvious idiocies in the minor controls or the instruments. Visibility in all directions was better than I had expected.

The engine started without any churning, and it seemed that the exhaust note was very subdued, and the induction even more so. There was a slight suggestion of mechanical noise from the engine bay.

The clutch was moderately heavy, but the gearbox, in true Alfa tradition, light and precise. The gate is in the pattern more usually associated with Porsche, with first gear on its own to the left and back, and the other four in a normal H-pattern. I was told that first gear would, in any case, only be needed for leaving the paddock; and so it turned out.

For all its racing ancestry, the engine lacks nothing in torque low down, and I was able to change up to second while ambling down the pit road under the eye of the marshal. Still feeling my way, I held the inside all the way to Copse, and found that (in third gear by now) I arrived at it just a little faster than expected. This is some measure of the smoothness and relative quietness of the Montreal.

The steering did not feel quite so impressive; not as light, and I thought not as precise, as in the smaller Alfas. In many ways, I was reminded of the contrast between the Fiat Dino and 124 Coupé, and indeed there was a good deal of similarity between the Dino and the Montreal where steering and handling are

concerned. If the Montreal was hustled into a corner the steering became a good deal heavier, leading to the feeling that the car was understeering. If one studied the line the car was taking and the steering angle applied, this was found not really to be so. The Montreal does understeer, and very consistently (more so than the small Alfas), but it does not do it to excess. It is the self-aligning torque from the massive tyres, presumably, which makes the steering progressively heavier and rather spongy. In the circumstances, Alfa have done a very good job of filtering out road shocks from the steering—a car which is bad in this respect can give its driver a hard time round Silverstone.

Performance was most impressive; there is no doubt that the Montreal was one of the fastest cars on hand, and given sufficient driver practice, might well have proved the fastest of all. The gear ratios were wrong for the track, and round Stowe and Club in particular one had the feeling that third was too low, and fourth too high. Fifth was really too high to use anywhere on the circuit, unless one made a point of taking it on the straight before Woodcote. The latter corner could be taken very nicely in fourth, and I ran out of courage here at an indicated 95mph or so. The rev limit shown was only 6,500, and as in all Alfas it was easy to take the delightfully smooth engine past this point unless one kept a wary eye on the rev counter.

The ride was remarkably soft, without making the car feel at all unstable. Through the corners, it could be felt leaning hard on its suspension, yet without any great impression of roll. Pouring on more power made it feel very stable indeed, although just occasionally the car would lurch diagonally as it crossed a camber change. In a straight line, it gave a remarkably comfortable ride.

In many ways, driving the Montreal was a remarkable experience. It showed that it is possible to reach an extremely high standard of performance, handling *and* ride with a car of basically conventional layout. Alfa, in fact, seem to have done it again.

Jeffrey Daniels

CITROEN'S (typically) highly remarkable 2.6-litre vee-6 Maserati-engined high-performance front-wheel-drive hydro-pneumatically, independently suspended self-levelling power-steered power-braked SM high-performance coupé—a verbal mouthful only slightly near as full of complication as the car itself—first appeared at Geneva in 1969. By 21 January this year we managed to gather enough information to publish a full description and cutaway drawing; last week, at the Michelin Foreign Car Test Day at Silverstone, we briefly drove a left-hand drive model.

As will be remembered, one of the more unusual features of the SM is its power-assisted rack and pinion steering, which has power-assisted self-centring which

increases in effect as road speed rises. Anyone interested in suspension and steering and the effects of their design on a car's behaviour and who hasn't driven the SM must have wondered how much of a good thing such ingenuity is; I certainly did.

Racing driver Dave Brodie was "supplied" by Citroen Cars to demonstrate the car for two laps before handing over for each journalist's three laps. Before we left the paddock Brodie put the stationary car on to full lock, then let go of the slightly elliptical wheel, which promptly turned itself back one revolution to the straight ahead; a welcome provision when manoeuvring. We circulated twice, neatly but fast, then I took over.

At low speeds the steering is on the light side, even for power assistance. After a fair bit of experience of DS Citroens, the distinctly racing-cum-Italian driving position—small dismeter'd wheel at near full-arm's length—seemed strange in a Citroen. Flooring the throttle produces a pleasingly loud-ish thrum from the engine, and a satisfactorily large amount of acceleration, to me surprising in such a relatively heavy car (28¼ cwt). The gearchange looks odd but works very precisely and smoothly, though it is a bit heavy.

The perhaps surprising truth about the steering as far as I was concerned during such a short drive is that I found it completely natural and was even unconscious of it. This is partly because of the car's perfect straight stability; it runs arrow-true. And, although *for once* a manufacturer has taken the obvious advantage of power assistance to provide beautifully high-geared steering—only two turns lock to lock—as intended by its designers the car is both marvellously "swerveable" and yet not at all twitchy. Not wanting to alarm Mr Brodie or to frighten myself. I did not try to see what happened anywhere near the car's clearly high limit of cornering power; but it is clearly an ultimate understeerer, but by no means too much so too soon. The perhaps high-ish level of engine noise makes it fairly obvious that one is going fast, but that is all. Staying in fourth rather than using the overdriving fifth, an indicated 110 mph came up on the elliptical speedometer down Hangar Straight—a speed I didn't exceed in many other cars that day—and one seemed to have no trouble lapping smoothly yet fast. Smooth Silverstone is no place to test ride, but through Abbey, a kink which has many cars lurching oddly if taken fast enough, the SM was as steady as a rock.

The styling grows on one. Three-quarter-rear vision isn't as bad as I had thought it would be; the interior has a bizarre singularity that is mainly pleasing. Typically odd quirks of Citroen design. hit you between the eyes; open the ingenious if not roomy enough glove locker and a thing like a small bag of sherbet with a straw lights up the interior. The button brake presents no problems to anyone educated with enough DS experience. I left the car more than ever keen to get to know it properly.

Michael Scarlett

Cornering attitudes for two new thoroughbreds, Citroen SM (left) and Alfa Romeo Montreal

AUTOTEST

CITROEN SM
(2,670 c.c.)

AT-A-GLANCE: Fastest front-drive car ever, with Maserati vee-6 engine. Very brisk performance, poor fuel consumption. Excellent power steering with novel servo-centring. Very powerful, fade-free brakes. Good ride, superb handling. Fine standard of finish. Small boot. Technically the world's most advanced car.

MANUFACTURER
SA André Citroen, 133 quai André Citroen, Paris 5e. France.

UK CONCESSIONAIRES
Citroen Cars Ltd., Trading Estate, Slough, Bucks.

PRICES
Not yet fixed, but expected to be about £5,500 (inc. P.T.) for right-hand-drive version.

PERFORMANCE SUMMARY
Mean maximum speed	135 mph
Standing start ¼-mile	16.9 sec
0-60 mph	9.0 sec
30-70 mph through gears	8.8 sec
Typical fuel consumption	18 mpg
Miles per tankful	360

IT has taken quite a long time for the new and very exciting Citroen SM to filter through to us for road test. The car was announced at the Geneva Salon in March 1970, several months before it was ready to go on sale. By the autumn of last year they began to appear on the French roads in private hands and one was imported here for the concessionaires. Now they occasionally crop up with British licence plates and our test car came to us hot from the Michelin foreign car test day at Silverstone. Right-hand drive versions are expected to be available after this year's Motor Show.

It is fair to say that the SM breaks with convention in almost all its features. It is a front-drive car (like all Citroens have been for the past 27 years) powered by a Maserati vee-6 engine driving through a five-speed manual gearbox. It has hydraulic suspension, very advanced power steering with servo-centring, pressurized power brakes, anti-dive front suspension geometry and a futuristic shape which looks as if it has come straight out of a stylist's sketch book. Even the interior is heavily stylized, with an oval steering wheel matched by oval instruments, a facia which would do credit to a sculpture exhibition and hammock-type seats padded with deep

Above: In some ways the SM bears a family resemblance to the earlier big Citroens, yet the styling is original and exciting, as well as aerodynamically efficient. The inner lamps are steerable, and all six are self-levelling. Inset: The drooping waistline gives back seat passengers a better view, and the back window panel doubles as the boot lid

Right: The cockpit is a mixture of styling and proper ergonomics which turns out to be quite effective in practice. The seats are very comfortable, with headrests which can actually be used as such.
Bottom: The back seat, also very comfortable, is more capacious than it seems, and the front seats tilt and slide forward for access. Bottom right: The spare wheel takes up a large part of the luggage space

The scene of complication under the bonnet becomes little better when it is studied. The engine itself lives right at the back, with part of one cam cover visible here; most of the rest is 'plumbing' for the various powered systems

square-section rolls fitted individually into an outer frame. A lever on one side of the backrest alters the rake and a matching lever on the other side allows the back to tip and the whole seat to slide forward for access to the rear seats.

The four-cam Maserati engine is unusual in having a 90 deg included angle between its cylinder banks; it was derived from a vee-8 on which this layout gives perfect balance. On a vee-6, 90 deg between cylinder banks gives unequal firing impulses and unbalanced secondaries and you definitely feel this when you start the engine and drive it in the lower half of the rev range. It is noticeably rougher than a straight six or a vee-8, but still better than many fours including Citroen's own. At higher revs it becomes much smoother and at 5,000 and above it is better than many sixes and some vee-8s. What roughness there is lower down is well insulated, but it comes through as a high-frequency harshness felt by one's contact with the pedals, gearlever and steering wheel.

There are three twin-choke Weber carburettors to take care of the induction and cold starting can be easily accomplished by several prods on the accelerator instead of using the choke. As soon as it has fired properly, the engine runs evenly and without flat-spots or spitting back. It is fairly quiet mechanically with no tappet thrash or camshaft chain whine, the main noise being a deep induction "thrum".

Brisk performance

The throttle has quite a long and sensitive movement, but there was some stiction in the combination of cable and rigid links on the test car and the idling often stuck at about 1,500 rpm instead of the more normal 750 rpm.

Power output is 170 bhp (DIN) at 5,500 rpm with a red sector on the rev counter from 6,500 to 8,000 rpm. The instrument proved dead accurate when we checked its calibration and we respected the 6,500 limit when taking performance measurements. The upper gears are equally spaced, with bottom slightly closer to second; this gives very progressive steps under full-bore acceleration and a useful overlap of torque between all ratios.

French law favours engines under a capacity of 2.8 litres in regard to the tax paid annually, so despite being something of a luxury sports car the SM comes under this limit with a swept volume of 2,670 c.c. The kerb weight is close to 30cwt (not far short of a Jaguar XJ6) so the performance, while being decidedly brisk, is not in the ultimate GT class. Nonetheless the 0 to 60 mph time of 9sec and the 0 to 100 mph time of 24.3sec are all the more impressive.

There was enough clutch bite for wheelspin getaways from rest together with some tramp if too many revs were used as well. First gear shot the SM up to nearly 40 mph, second to just short of 60 mph and third on to nearly 90 mph. Fourth was good for 115 mph and in top we measured 135 mph in both directions on an almost calm day. At speed the SM has true arrow-like stability aided by the very sophisticated servo steering mechanism and fundamentally secure front weight bias.

At the kerb with a half-full tank, the SM has over 60 per cent of its weight on the front wheels. This means an individual tyre load of about 1,000lb at this end, so power steering is an obvious essential. On the SM it not only magnifies the driver's effort on the wheel in the usual way, but provides servo return to the straight ahead position, this latter function varying with the speed of the car.

All this is very novel, but the effect is much the same as on any lesser car with good

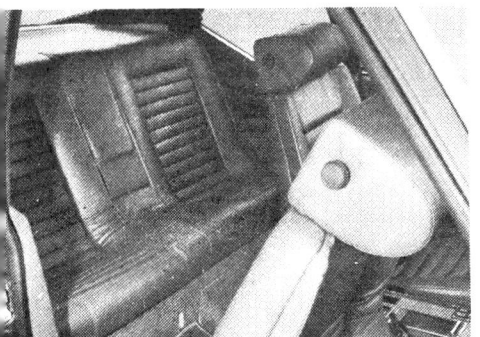

ACCELERATION

SECONDS

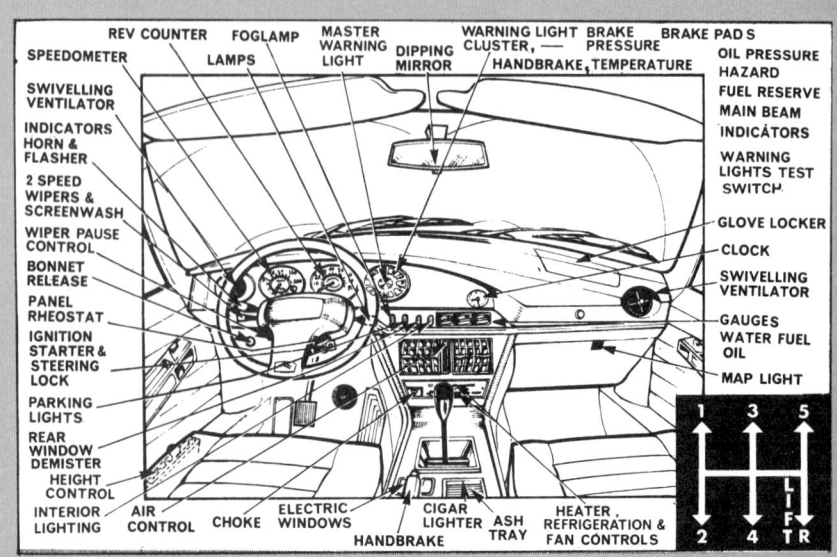

SPEED MPH TRUE INDICATED	TIME IN SECS
30	3.4
32	
40	5.0
43	
50	7.0
54	
60	9.0
64	
70	12.2
74	
80	15.3
84	
90	19.1
94	
100	24.3
104	
110	30.3
115	

SPEED RANGE, GEAR RATIOS AND TIME IN SECONDS

mph	Top (3.32)	4th (4.24)	3rd (5.78)	2nd (8.49)	1st (12.78)
10-30	—	—	—	4.4	3.1
20-40	—	8.5	5.7	3.5	—
30-50	11.2	7.7	5.2	3.6	—
40-60	11.0	7.5	4.8	—	—
50-70	11.6	7.7	5.2	—	—
60-80	11.4	8.2	6.0	—	—
70-90	12.6	8.6	—	—	—
80-100	14.2	9.4	—	—	—
90-110	—	11.9	—	—	—

Standing ¼-mile
16.9 sec 93 mph

Standing kilometre
30.2 sec 110 mph

Test distance
700 miles
Mileage recorder
3.5 per cent
over-reading

PERFORMANCE
MAXIMUM SPEEDS

Gear	mph	kph	rpm
Top (mean)	135	217	6,000
(best)	135	217	6,000
4th	115	185	6,500
3rd	84	135	6,500
2nd	57	92	6,500
1st	38	61	6,500

BRAKES

(from 70 mph in neutral)
Pedal load for 0.5g stops in lb

1	25		6	35
2	30		7	35
3	35		8	35
4	35		9	35
5	35		10	35

RESPONSE (from 30 mph in neutral)

Load	g	Distance
20lb	0.38	79ft
30lb	0.64	47ft
40lb	1.02	29.6ft
Handbrake	0.27	112ft

Max. Gradient 1 in 4

CLUTCH

Pedal 40lb and 5in.

MOTORWAY CRUISING

Indicated speed at 70 mph	. . . .	74 mph
Engine (rpm at 70 mph)	. . . .	3,100 rpm
(mean piston speed)	. . . .	1,525ft/min.
Fuel (mpg at 70 mph)	. . . .	27.2 mpg
Passing (50-70 mph)	. . . .	5.2 sec

COMPARISONS

MAXIMUM SPEED MPH

Jensen Interceptor	. . . . . . (£6,138)	137
Citroen SM	. . . . (£5,500)	**135**
Porsche 911T	. . . . . . (£3,671)	129
BMW 2800	. . . . (£3,499)	124
Triumph Stag	. . . . . . (£2,326)	116

0-60 MPH, SEC

Jensen Interceptor	. . . .	6.4
Porsche 911T	. . . .	8.1
BMW 2800	. . . .	8.9
Citroen SM	. . . .	**9.0**
Triumph Stag	. . . .	9.3

STANDING ¼-MILE, SEC

Jensen Interceptor	. . . .	15.0
Porsche 911T	. . . .	16.0
BMW 2800	. . . .	16.4
Citroen SM	. . . .	**16.9**
Triumph Stag	. . . .	17.1

OVERALL MPG

BMW 2800	. . . .	21.4
Triumph Stag	. . . .	20.7
Porsche 911T	. . . .	17.9
Citroen SM	. . . .	**16.0**
Jensen Interceptor	. . . .	12.9

GEARING (with 195/70 VR-15in. tyres)

Top	. . . .	22.6 mph per 1,000 rpm
4th	. . . .	17.6 mph per 1,000 rpm
3rd	. . . .	13.0 mph per 1,000 rpm
2nd	. . . .	8.8 mph per 1,000 rpm
1st	. . . .	5.9 mph per 1,000 rpm

TEST CONDITIONS:
Weather: Fine but cloudy. Wind: 0—8 mph. Temperature: 13 deg. C. (56 deg. F).
Barometer 29.3 in. hg. Humidity: 40 per cent. Surfaces: Dry concrete and asphalt.

WEIGHT:
Kerb weight 29.5 cwt. (3,298lb—1,500kg) (with oil, water and half full fuel tank.)
Distribution, per cent F, 62; R, 38. Laden as tested: 32.7 cwt (3,648lb—1,660kg).

TURNING CIRCLES:
Between kerbs L, 35ft 5in.; R, 35ft 11in. Between walls L, 38ft 3in.; R, 38ft 9in.
Steering wheel turns, lock to lock 2.

Figures taken at 7,000 miles by our own staff at the Motor Industry Research
Association proving ground at Nuneaton.

CONSUMPTION

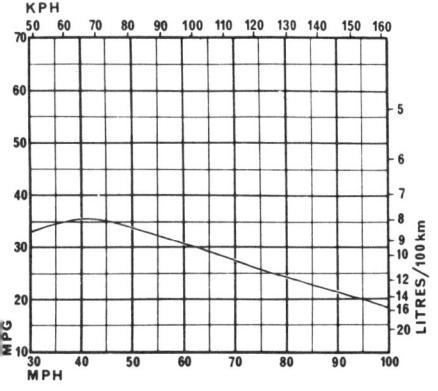

FUEL
(At constant speeds—mpg)
30 mph	33.0
40 mph	35.4
50 mph	33.5
60 mph	30.1
70 mph	27.2
80 mph	24.4
90 mph	21.6
100 mph	18.6

Typical mpg 18 (15.6 litres/100km)
Calculated (DIN) mpg 24.7 (11.4 litres/100km)
Overall mpg 16.0 (17.6 litres/100km)
Grade of fuel   Premium, 4-star (min. 98 RM)

OIL
Miles per pint (SAE 20W/50) 350

SPECIFICATION FRONT ENGINE, FRONT WHEEL DRIVE

ENGINE
Cylinders . . .	6, in 90 degree vee
Main bearings .	4
Cooling system .	Water; pump, thermostat and twin electric fans
Bore	87mm (3.42 in.)
Stroke	75mm (2.95 in.)
Displacement .	2,670 c.c. (163 cu.in.)
Valve gear . . .	Four overhead camshafts, chain driven
Compression ratio 9.0-to-1 Min. octane rating: 98 RM	
Carburettors .	3 twin-choke Weber 42 DCNF
Fuel pump . . .	Bendix electric
Oil filter	Full-flow
Max. power . .	170 bhp (DIN) at 5,500 rpm
Max. torque . .	170 lb.ft (DIN) at 4,000 rpm

TRANSMISSION
Clutch	Diaphragm spring, 8.7 in. dia.
Gearbox . . .	5-speed, all-synchromesh
Gear ratios. . .	Top 0.81
	Fourth 0.97
	Third 1.32
	Second 1.94
	First 2.93
	Reverse 3.16
Final drive . . .	Hypoid bevel, 4.375 to 1

CHASSIS and BODY
Construction . .	Integral steel hull with bolt-on front wings; aluminium bonnet.

SUSPENSION
Front	Independent, trailing arms hydropneumatic struts interconnected and self-levelling
Rear	Independent, trailing arms, hydropneumatic struts interconnected and self-levelling

STEERING
Type	Rack and pinion with speed-sensitive power assistance
Wheel dia. . .	15 x 13.7 in.

BRAKES
Make and type .	Disc front and rear
Servo	Pressurized hydraulics
Dimensions . .	F 11.8 in. dia.
	R 10.1 in. dia.

WHEELS
Type	Pressed steel, 5-stud fixing, 6in. wide rim
Tyres—make . .	Michelin
—type . .	XVR 70-series radial ply tubed
—size . .	195/70 VR-15 in.

EQUIPMENT
Battery	12 Volt 70 Ah
Alternator . .	65 amp. a.c.
Headlamps. . .	Six-lamp system, self-levelling, coupled to steering, 110/220-watt (total)
Reversing lamp .	Standard
Electric fuses . .	12
Screen wipers .	2-speed with variable interrupt device
Screen washer .	Electric
Interior heater .	Fresh-air blending, air conditioning
Heated backlight	Standard
Safety belts . .	Extra
Interior trim . .	Leather seats, pvc headlining.
Floor covering .	Carpet
Jack	Pillar
Jacking points .	4, under body sills
Windscreen . .	Laminated
Underbody protection (type) .	Tectyl treatment only

MAINTENANCE
Fuel tank . . .	19.7 Imp. gallons (no reserve) (90 litres)
Cooling system .	23 pints (including heater)
Engine sump . .	12.5 pints (7 litres) SAE 20W/50 Change oil every 3,000 miles. Change filter element every 6,000 miles.
Gearbox and final drive . .	3.9 pints SAE, Change oil every 12,000 miles
Grease	6 points every 3,000 miles
Tyre pressures .	F 32; R 29 psi (normal driving)
Max. payload. .	800 lb (363 kg)

PERFORMANCE DATA
Top gear mph per 1,000 rpm	22.6
4th gear mph per 1,000 rpm	17.6
Mean piston speed at max. power . .	2,700
Bhp per ton laden	104

STANDARD GARAGE 16ft x 8ft 6in.

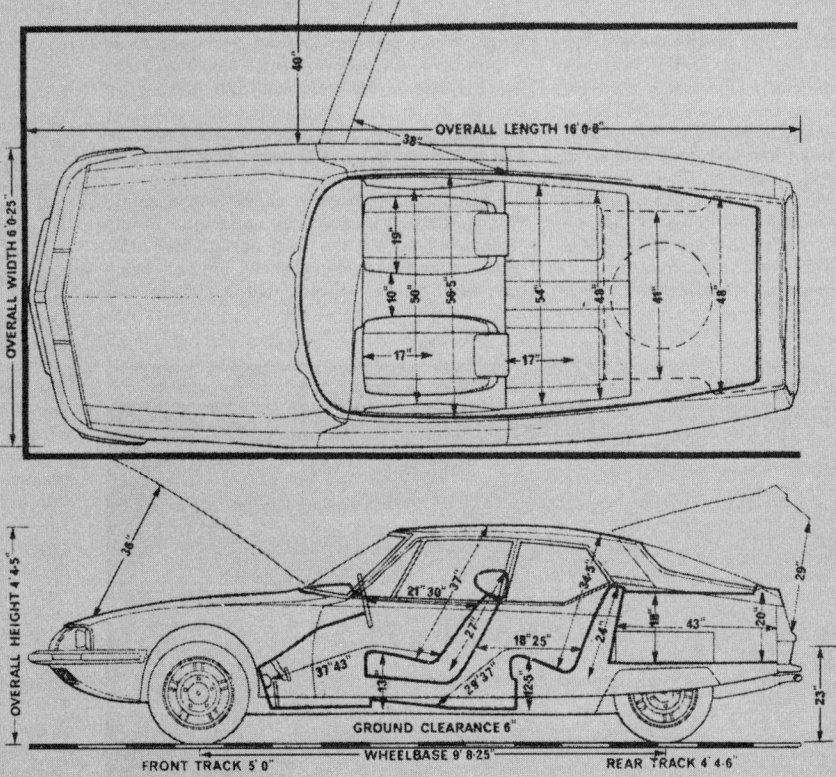

SCALE 0.3in. to 1ft
Cushions uncompressed

CITROEN SM
AUTOTEST . . .

fundamental steering geometry incorporating plenty of castor. Where it is superior is in completely eliminating what would otherwise be phenomenal understeer in such a powerful front-drive car, and in permitting extraordinarily high steering ratios which would otherwise make the SM exceedingly twitchy at speed.

With just two turns from lock to lock the steering is sensitive and it takes a driver new to the car about 50 miles before he can relax at the wheel and not overdo the small movements necessary to follow the road. From then on, though, the true benefits really show through and the SM becomes as nimble on the open road as a much smaller sports car like the Lotus Elan. Seldom is more than half a turn of lock required, even for tight roundabouts or sharp junctions into minor roads. On a sweeping route we use regularly to avoid the congested A5 it was easy to hustle this big left-hand drive car through the twists and kinks at high speed with supreme confidence and masses of cornering power in hand. Similarly we were able to take the banked MIRA bends at near 120 mph and flash to 130 mph down the straights, something we would not think of attempting in many other cars. It rode round the high-speed track like a train, unaffected and undeflected by the ripply surface and sudden camber changes.

In many ways the steering feels like one of the experimental American systems (like the Ford of Detroit "wrist-twist" system we tried in 1967) and in terms of feed-back from the road surface it is somewhat dead. This prevents the wheel kicking when the front wheels hit a sharp bump or pot-hole and it was uncanny how the SM stormed over a very un-level crossing with absolutely no "fight" from the front and no pattering at the back.

The ride is characteristically Citroen, yet much less so than on any other model. The same kind of hydro-pneumatic struts and accumulators are used as on the D models and the new GS, but attitude changes are much less in general. The front end rears up noticeably under full power acceleration, but perfect anti-dive geometry prevents the plunge which normally follows under heavy braking. High-frequency shocks are completely absorbed in the system, yet the usual Citroen low-frequency pitch and float is also pleasantly absent. There is some bump thump when hitting small obstacles like cats' eyes and although this is worse than on cars like the Jaguar XJ6 and Peugeot 504, it is still well insulated and never really intrudes.

Roll angles when cornering fast are much less dramatic than on the other Citroens but with this much power and quite high roll stiffness it is relatively easy to pick up the inside front wheel and get it spinning. On one of the open bends of MIRA's No. 2 road circuit we were able to leave a broad black line of rubber on the road all the way through at about 50 mph in second. Despite this the SM did not run wide and displayed no apparent understeer.

On wet surfaces there is much less traction, but still enough to get the car quickly off the mark when required. With front drive the effects of wheelspin do not affect the stability, so when traction is broken it does not really matter.

Brakes are operated by pressurized hydraulics and worked by the D-type Citroen rubber button. On this model an angled plinth puts the pedal almost in line with the clutch and accelerator and for the first time it is now possible to heel-and-toe when making downshifts. The brakes are very light to use, only 40lb effort being enough to bring the car to a rapid stop at over 1g retardation. There was very slight initial fade from 70 mph, but the linings soon stabilized. After about the third stop in our fade test they became harsh and caused the front wheels to judder badly as the car came to rest. This did not affect the stopping power and was largely a result of their location, at the front, on the inboard end of quite flexible drive shafts.

The handbrake is worked by a massive lever on the central tunnel and could not hold the car on anything steeper than a 1-in-4 gradient. The clutch was hard put to cope with a restart on this gradient, slipping badly and making nasty smells.

Being geared at 22.6 mph per 1,000 rpm in fifth gear, the SM is not a very flexible car around town. At 30 mph in fifth the running becomes very uneven and one seldom gets out of fourth gear except on a motorway. Our steady speed fuel measurements show that more petrol is actually being drawn in at 30 mph than at 50 mph, so it is not surprising that the rich mixture presents problems. This characteristic undoubtedly accounts for our low overall consumption of only 16 mpg and also explains why the DIN standard touring figure (calculated from 5th gear consumptions) is so much better. Driving with less verve with more out-of-town journeys, an owner would probably average nearer 18 mpg with 20 just within bounds if he took in some long motorway mileages. With a total capacity of 20 gal, the fuel tank permits a useful range of around 300 miles.

Ergonomics have been carefully considered in the cockpit, despite the apparently strong stylist's influence in the detail design. Two main dials for road and engine speed are set within easy sight of most drivers, with a third matching oval containing a cluster of warning lights complete with a test button to check the circuits. Under this on the right of the wheel within fingertip reach is a row of pushbuttons for fog and parking lights, heated backlight and the interior roof lamp. A stalk on the left of the steering column works the two-speed wipers and electric washers, with a variable-pause interrupter adjustment hidden under the column surround. Indicators are not self-cancelling, but the audible warning is loud. Pushing the indicator lever flashes main beams and pulling it sound the horns in two stages, for town and country.

On the right of the column is a lighting knob which is turned for switching on side and headlamps, pushed for dipping and pressed in to switch on quartz-iodine auxiliary long-range beams. These latter are steered by the front wheels and all the lamps are levelled to compensate for attitude changes of the car.

Front seats are extremely comfortable and they have been tailored to suit the semi-reclining sports car driving position. Integral headrests fit snugly into the nape of the neck, and their height and angle can be adjusted. The seats themselves slide up angled ramps as they come forward and they have their own three-position height adjustment at front and rear edges.

The back seat is larger than it looks at first glance or in a photograph and it will take two adults quite well. There is a central folding armrest and ashtrays each side. Each of the front doors has a deep pocket under its armrest and there is a small glove locker in the top of the facia.

Climatic control

Electric windows are very slow to operate, but with refrigeration included in the specification there is seldom any need to open them. Heater controls are integrated with those for the air conditiong, a single temperature slide selecting either hot or cooled air, backed up by a variable-speed booster fan. The "fridge" has the ability to pull the cockpit temperature down rapidly, even when the car has been parked in scorching sun.

The back window lifts up for access to the boot, like on the Jensen, but the luggage space inside is very disappointing. Most of it seems to be taken up by the spare wheel and it would be difficult to get more than two average suitcases in there besides.

Opening the huge flat bonnet reveals a sight which is truly awe-inspiring as all the mechanical complication is there for inspection. In fact, when you break the individual systems down to their elements, it is not hard to work through each in turn and a trained Citroen mechanic should be able to get at everything vital quite easily. Routine attention to oil and water levels is perfectly straightforward.

The big question which hangs over a car like this Citroen is whether all the expense and complication are worth it. After the experience of this test our conclusion is that they are because it is this aspect of the design which makes the SM so outstanding. Getting back into other cars afterwards makes them, not the Citroen, seem odd and difficult (especially in regard to the steering) and we feel that for a large and heavy car in this class it sets new standards of handling and stability. The engine is something of a compromise, but very sporty in its characteristics and well suited to the car. Performance is good, economy disappointing, styling effective and finish excellent down to the finest detail. If European co-operative design could produce more cars of the calibre of the SM, we would be backing it to the hilt and campaigning for Britain to be right in there with them. □

Like the DS series, the SM has variable ride height. When it is set normally, the ground clearance looks good for a car of this class, while it is possible to go down (bottom left) or up (bottom right) to either extreme

I feel this tremendous compulsion to tell you uncategorically that the Citroën SM is the best car in the world. But that would immediately send you right down on my back to explain why, and no one has ever told me just what makes any car the Best Car In The World. The SM is neither the fastest, nor the cheapest, nor the most expensive, nor the most beautiful, nor the least attainable, nor the most status rendering automobile in the world. Yet it has to be the most advanced car from the safety-engineering standpoint and if one is to be properly analytical about it, that should make it the best in the world. It certainly is one of the most fascinating to drive.

It had just begun to rain when I picked up the SM from Citroën in Paris. I was given a short orientation drive, as will everyone who buys one. It is such a different feeling car that you should get a short course before striking out on your own. Right off, the most fascinating feature about the car is the steering. In town, it's a dream, because of the very fast 9.4:1 overall ratio in the power rack-and-pinion unit and it only takes one complete turn of the steering wheel to take the front wheels from a full right lock to a full left lock. It needs only 34.5 ft. to turn a full circle. As a comparison, the quick Porsche 914 has a ratio of 17.7:1, needs 2.5 turns lock-to-lock and has a turning diameter of 36.1 ft. So you slip easily through traffic, being careful that the quick ratio doesn't fool you into clipping a curb. This light, quick system would be dangerous on the freeway where a muscle spasm could mean a lane change, so they've added a centrifugal steering regulator that runs off the back of the transmission and as the speed increases, so does steering effort. Bobweights inside the regulator bring pressure on a slide valve that regulates pressure in the power steering unit, so as you accelerate on the freeway, you can move the wheel from side-to-side and feel the tension increase with speed. As if that weren't enough, the steering has a self-centering system that returns the wheels to the straight ahead whenever you let go of the wheel, even at a standstill.

Next on the interest scale, is the Maserati engine that powers the SM. It's a dual-overhead-cam V6 of 163 cubic inches and puts out 180 SAE horsepower at 6250 rpm. It has a light alloy block and head, a 4-main bearing crank and carburetion is three 42DCNF Webers. The engine has an oversquare 87mm bore and 75mm stroke, though short stroke engines are supposedly thought of as dirty smog engines. But

the figures don't pass on the surprise in finding the engine not the finicky beast you expect dohc, Weber-carbureted engines to be. It was smooth and never gave a bit of trouble in response or starting. In fact, it felt in no more need of some mysterious accelerator-clutch reflex action than a common U.S. V8, and less than the Boss 302 or Chev Z/28-type engine. The car has front-wheel drive, like all Citroëns, the company figuring that layout offers the most in terms of safety and person packaging. Brakes are four-wheel discs, operated by a rubber bulb between the clutch and accelerator. I thought that was novel, but didn't appreciate, until we got the car on a test track in the U.S., the novelty of the entire system. The all-synchro 5-speed Citroën transmission was smooth and not the jumble one always fears a 5-speed will be.

Suspension is four-wheel independent, with anti-roll bars front and back. There is, of course, the famous Citroën hydropneumatic suspension that will automatically maintain an even ground clearance. You can, as with all such Citroëns, pick the height you care to be from the ground with the system.

Of course, one reason why all French cars ride well is their excellent seats and the SM is no piker. The seats are infinitely variable for fore-aft movement and seatback rake; combined with a steering wheel that allows both up/down and in/out movements with one control lever, the car could easily fit about 98 percent of the people in the

world over the age of 18. There is a speedometer and tach and a huge cluster of idiot lights surrounding a red master disaster "STOP" light on the dash. Gauges for water and oil temperature and fuel level sit just above the ventilation air conditioning outlet and controls. The back seat is a bit cramped, but no worse than, say, a big Chevrolet, and the seats dip down enough to the rear to at least make you feel like you have more room than you do. Finish is excellent and the sealing stood up perfectly to several downpours.

Way up on the interest list, but a sure victim of the U.S. safety standards, is the headlamp system. Along with the center-mounted license plate, the Cibie lights reside under glass just above the bumper and have three lamps on each side — a dipped lamp, a wide main beam and a long-range lamp. All are quartz iodine. In addition to just being a very superior system, the long-range lamps swivel just slightly ahead of the steering, lighting wherever you are going and the whole unit is mounted on a device that keeps them level with the road despite added loads or what have you. The effect at night on a winding road is awe inspiring, almost like bringing the daylight with you. The man (or men) who devised the laws that keep that system out of the U.S. have done us all an injustice.

Styling is, of course, a matter of personal taste, though you somehow get the feeling that Citroën really did de-

Citroën's Super Machine

For years Citroën made slow, ugly, interesting cars. Now they've made a fast, beautiful, fascinating car/By John Lamm

Citroën

sign the car this way because it is more efficient and they don't seem to care; as they state, "the shape of the SM makes no concession to fashion." How true, but it does pack that Maserati engine and front-wheel-drive system up front, four adults surprisingly comfortably in the middle and a full 20.67 cubic feet of luggage space in back — most large American sedans have about 12-15 cubic feet. To give you a size comparison, the SM's wheelbase is 116.17 inches, while a Torino Cobra runs 117 inches. Overall length is: SM, 192.64 inches; Torino, 206.2 inches and weights are SM, 3,370 lbs.; Torino, 3,586.

That was the car in France, where it is like a small god to the average 2CV driver. But what happens to the SM in the U.S., where drivers are used to high-powered cars, where the roads are too smooth to use that Citroën suspension to its full advantage and the speed limits too low to make use of the Maserati engine? You just start appreciating the car for different reasons. It

quickly becomes perhaps the world's greatest freeway car, ready to deal with long normally-boring sections and traffic jams. It's the car least inclined to make you bored with driving to work. In the midwest they'll love it for its traction in rain and winter and for the way it will smooth out roads that have been deeply scarred by the thawing and freezing of early spring.

We got ours shortly after the Los Angeles Auto Expo, where it had been shown as a European model. For our testing, though, it magically became an Americanized version — externally at least. First hint and the most disappointing, was the way they had to muck up the front end by removing the glass from the headlamps and then replacing them with round all-American headlamps. It's still an interesting, relatively good-looking front end, but a zero compared to the European edition. The engine was still a European version, though it had passed U.S. tests.

Our first test of the car was with people. The results were very favorable. We parked the car behind the main Petersen Building and the phone calls started, everything from "What is it?"

to "Can I drive it?" Every place we glided with the car, people rubbernecked and stretched to see it. The two leading comments were, "What kind of car did you say it was?" and "But Citroen used to make such ugly cars." Only one person ever told me she didn't like the looks; about twenty persons, many driving Mercedes and Lincolns, wanted to know where they could buy one. Interestingly, though, the most stares came from Porsche drivers.

Our second test was mechanical, to answer that other very popular question, "What'll she do?" Briefly, she'll do very well, thank you. Since this is no ordinary car, we could do no ordinary test, instead dusting off all the test equipment *Sports Car Graphic's* former tech editor Paul Van Valkenburgh had devised to really delve into a car's performance. First there's aerodynamic drag, which can roughly be equated to "streamlining" or how much air a car disturbs while running down the road (in this case at the mean speed of 100 mph). That disturbed air has a drag effect, like the car towing so many extra pounds of weight. In the SM's case, there are 231 pounds of drag at 100

Top: European SM front is beautiful, with six Cibie lamps, turning road lights under glass. Uncovered U.S. version is monument to our asinine lighting laws. Above: SM has constant 6.1-inch normal ground clearance but you can manually change that to one of five possible heights. Extreme up and down are for jacking.

SPECIFICATIONS

Engine	Maserati V6
Bore & stroke — ins.	3.4 x 3
Displacement — cu. in.	164.4
HP @ RPM	180 hp (SAE) @ 6250
Torque: lbs.ft. @ RPM	172 ft.-lbs. @ 4,000
Compression Ratio/Fuel	9:1/Premium
Carburetion	3 Weber 2 bbl (42 DCNF)
Transmission	Citroen 5-speed
Final Drive Ratio	4.37:1
Steering type	Power-rack and pinion
Steering Ratio	9.4:1
Turning Diameter (curb-to-curb-ft.)	34.5 ft.
Wheel Turns (lock to lock)	1
Tire size	195/70 VR 15 Michelin X
Brakes	4-wheel disc
Front Suspension	Indept., single upper and lower arms, anit-roll bar, hydropneumatic system
Rear Suspension	Indept., single trailing arm, anti-roll bar, hydropneumatic system
Body/Frame Construction	Unit
Wheelbase — ins.	116.4
Overall length — ins.	192.6
Width — ins.	72.2
Height — ins.	52.1
Front Track — ins.	60.1
Rear Track — ins.	52.2
Curb Weight — lbs.	3370
Fuel Capacity — gals.	19.7
Oil Capacity — qts.	6.2

PERFORMANCE

Acceleration

0-30 mph	3.7 secs.
0-45 mph	5.6 secs.
0-60 mph	8.6 secs.
0-75 mph	13.3 secs.

Standing Start ¼-mile

Mph	84.66 secs.
Elapsed time	16.76 secs.

Passing speeds

40-60 mph	5.0 secs.
50-70 mph	5.7 secs.

Speeds in gears*

1st	mph @ rpm	43.5 @ 6500
2nd	mph @ rpm	61.2 @ 6500
3rd	mph @ rpm	82.9 @ 6500
4th	mph @ rpm	111.6 @ 6500
5th	mph @ rpm	102.9 @ 6500

Mph per 1000 rpm (in top gear) 20.5

Stopping distance

From 30 mph	28 ft.
From 60 mph	129 ft.

Average gas mileage 20.2 mpg
*Speeds in gears are at shift points (limited by the length of track) and do not represent maximum speeds.

mph. As a comparison with cars of similar cost and interior space, the Jensen Interceptor II has a drag of 385 pounds, while the slightly larger Mercedes 280SE coupe has a drag of 450 pounds. This drag factor relates directly to better gas mileage and greater top speed for less horsepower.

Next item on the read-out sheet is acceleration. The favorite benchmark is, of course, 0-60 which the SM manages in 8.6 secs. As a comparison, that puts it into a class (roughly) with the Datsun 240Z (9.1 secs.), and the Mazda RX-2 Wankel (9.1 secs.). Quarter-mile times ran from 16.76 secs. (84.66 mph) to 17.14 (82.79). The interesting point about the Maserati V6, though, is the amount of low-end power that is available, especially in consideration of the engine's overhead cams, Weber carburetors and other pieces that usually mean a more peaky engine with plenty of power way up the rpm scale, but with limited power at low rpm.

Along with above-average seats and suspensions, French cars have always been a bit ahead of the game with brakes, the SM carrying the whole process still another step ahead. Basically there are the four discs, a equalizing/modulating device and accumulator. Under normal circumstances, if you hopped on the brake bulb in a panic situation the nose dips and the modulator will hold the brakes right to wheel skid (1g in this case), then ease up momentarily. Like an anti-skid system it will grip, ease up, grip, ease up, bringing you to repeated non-lockup stops. As a safety measure, there's an accumulator that stores up enough pressure for 40 panic stops with a dead engine. Even that fail-safe device has a back up, the handbrake, which will supply one last ditch chance to stop.

Finally to the skid pad. There was one serious limit to the car's pad performance, the tires. With the car's inherent front-wheel-drive tendency to strong understeer in the 200-foot circle, the tires began to smoke, then chunk. Even with that limit, the SM managed to generate .704g to the right, .712 to the left. On the road course, the SM showed only a trace of its fwd heritage, with above-average handling, but even that wasn't its real forte. Take it to a rough road, with dips, ruts and railroad crossings and when the rest of the cars have had their ends skid and chatter right off the road, the SM will be quietly motoring away.

Now don't think you can get all this for nothing. In fact, the SM will sell for around $10,500 in the U.S. Compare it then to a $10,000 Eldo or Mark IV and they look like pikers. To ease the pain, there will be a Borg Warner automatic coming in shortly after production starts and a 4-door will be close behind. The future looks good for the SM. That front end seems a natural to accept a safety bumper and somehow you know that Citroën will make that Maserati engine conform to smog laws, right up to fateful 1976 — maybe even later. In Paris I had asked Monsieur Jean-Paul Cardinal of Citroën if they could do it, perhaps having to redesign that chassis platform to make room for catalytic reactors and afterburners. He said that if a redesign was necessary, they would do it, but perhaps they might have a new answer to the problem and could use the existing chassis. You could scoff at a lot of manufacturers if they said that, but don't ever scoff at Citroën. They build the SM. /MT

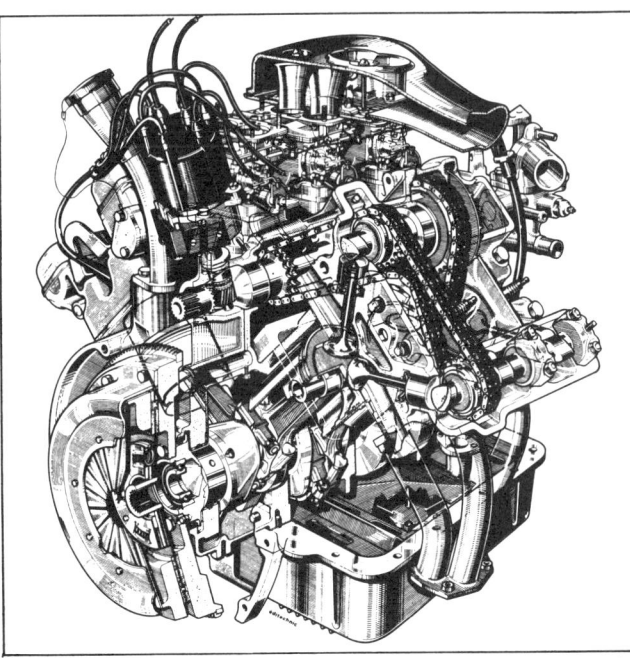

Above: SM's heart, a docile Maserati V6 with low end torque. Right: Only possible styling fault is slightly garish taillamp. Below: Fascinating interior has full instrumentation; good visibility; soft, fully adjustable, comfortable seats.

Despite its appearance, the Citroën SM is much more than a GT version of the DS. It has been designed from first principles.

controllability, especially at speeds above 120 mph. In countries where rapid travel is regarded as an essential part of commerce and administration, the cruising speed of orthodox cars is limited not by laws but by chassis deficiencies. That is why you see so many cars travelling at 105 mph or so, for the drivers find higher speeds too fatiguing. The SM makes motoring in the 120 to 130 mph band a safe and relaxed business, which means that there is a fantastic reserve of controllability at more moderate velocities.

This is brought about by developing the suspension and roadholding of the car to the ultimate degree, and then controlling it by a steering gear with entirely new characteristics. All four wheels are independently sprung on the well-known Citroën principle of hydro-pneumatic self-levelling suspension, anti-dive geometry being incorporated to avoid any change of attitude when the big, power operated discs are used to the full. By placing the front discs inboard, no compromise need be accepted in the steering geometry and the suspension members are freed of torque reaction.

Front-wheel drive is essential for the kind of stability that is required and this means that 60 per cent of the weight must be borne by the front wheels, which carry tyres of very large section. Such a setup would entail either unacceptably heavy steering at low speeds or hopelessly low gearing—probably both—if orthodox methods were used. To apply power assistance to such a design would result in a transatlantic-type vehicle with hopelessly vague steering at high speeds and far too many turns of the wheel to make skid correction possible.

The Citroën solution is so radical that drivers of modern big cars must learn to drive all over again, and will take 50 miles or so to become used to the sensation. Drivers of light vintage cars with high geared steering will jump straight into the SM and feel at home, for the controllability resembles that of a Type 35 Bugatti. The gearing is indeed similar, for there are only two turns of the Citroën steering wheel between two remarkably sharp and taxi-like locks. There is very strong power assistance at low speeds, which progressively diminishes as the car goes faster. Most important, there is a built-in self centring effect in place of castor action—if one stops the car with the wheels on lock they will slowly move into the straight ahead position. Connected with the suspension and steering by hydraulic means are the headlamps. All six of them move up and down automatically to keep the level of the beams absolutely constant, irrespective of suspension travel, and the two long-range quartz-iodine projectors turn with the steering, throwing the light on to the car's intended path round a corner instead of on to the outside hedge.

The transmission to the front wheels is through the excellent five-speed gearbox that has for some time been available as an extra on the DS. In France, for tax reasons, it is desirable to keep the engine size below 2.8 litres, and a V6 Maserati unit was chosen, with four chain-driven overhead camshafts

Citroën SM — "like a good deed in a naughty world"

ROAD TEST/John Bolster

At a time when a reactionary design philosophy is the curse of most motor manufacturers, the Citroën SM is like a good deed in a naughty world. The typical popular car of today may be styled in the modern fashion but under the tinware it bears a distressing resemblance to the vehicles that go from London to Brighton on the first Sunday in November. The Citroën SM has been designed from first principles in the space age and owes nothing to the horseless carriage.

The SM might be regarded by the uninitiated as a GT version of the DS. True, it contains the advanced features of the DS which make that machine such an excellent high-speed touring car, but it embraces new solutions which result in entirely unaccustomed standards of stability and

The hammock-type front seats are fully adjustable, as is the familiar one-spoke steering wheel.

and three twin-choke Weber carburetters. It is in a 90-deg Vee instead of the 60-deg angle that is necessary to give even firing intervals with six-cylinders, but this disadvantage is accepted because the boring machines at the Maserati factory are for V8 engines and it would be uneconomic to re-equip the works with a new set of machines for this comparatively small production. The engine gives a lot of power for its size, with a net output of 170 bhp.

The car in which all this machinery is mounted is a two-door 2 plus 2 coupé of arresting appearance and highly efficient aerodynamic shape. The standard of construction and finish are of the very highest. The hammock-type front seats have adjustable headrests and the steering wheel can be instantly regulated, both up-and-down and fore-and-aft. These seats fold up and slide forward in one movement giving unobstructed access to the rear seat. This is yet another advanced feature, for it makes a two-door car the equal of a four-door in passenger convenience, especially as some four-door vehicles have rather narrow apertures. In contrast, the luggage boot is largely occupied by the spare wheel, and is surprisingly meagre.

When I took over the Citroën SM for a week, I decided to make the best use of it. Having an appointment in Milan, I abandoned the flying machine without regret and set off for the Townsend Ferries at Dover, where so many of my better journeys begin. The SM was already attracting attention, but in France the interest was redoubled and was to follow me throughout the trip. As "my" car had left-hand drive, I found it more at home in its own country, and already I was completely acclimatized to the steering. Cutting across country, I hit the *Autoroute du Nord* at Arras in pouring rain, which eventually reached almost cloudburst proportions.

The greatest problem was to overtake other Citroëns, for a DS21 travelling in a pillar of spray is a formidable obstacle. The Michelin tyres cut through the carpet of water magnificently but eventually I was warned by sudden wheelspin at 100 mph, that the dreaded aquaplaning had begun. Most rear-drive cars would have skidded horribly or even swapped ends at this juncture, but the SM remained completely stable and I merely lifted my foot to restore traction.

In spite of the filthy conditions, the big Citroën was slipping round Paris on the *Boulevard Périphérique* in well under three hours from Calais and, after a welcome pause *chez* Jabby Crombac—his house is called *Brands Hatch*—the SM was off down the *Autoroute du Sud*, where violent storms failed to move her from her path. The rain and darkness slowed traffic almost to a standstill; then suddenly we broke into sunshine, and the Citroën worked up to 130 mph whenever traffic permitted.

The night was spent in the Beaujolais country at Solutré, after which we had a miserable journey through Bourg and Nantua, cursed with interminable halts and crawling past road repairs. The Maserati engine disliked this and begun to run unevenly, but after the Mont Blanc tunnel one is soon on the Autostrada. Across the Plain of Lombardy, the SM cleared her throat and a good long

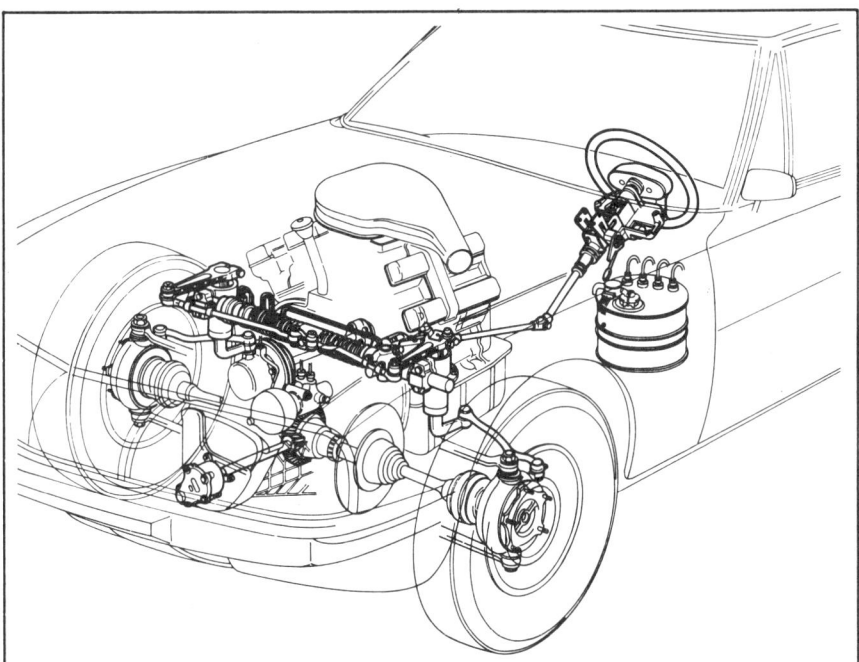

A cutaway showing the front-wheel-drive transmission and steering geometry of the SM. The suspension is excellent and the brakes (discs inboard at the front) powerful.

burst at 130 mph cleaned the plugs for the rest of the trip.

Unbearable heat in Italy was followed by another even more spectacular storm on the homeward journey. By the time I hit the Autoroute at Macon, the sun was shining and I expected to put up a 110 mph average. Alas! The road was full of holiday traffic and caravans galore were mixed up with lorries. Everybody made way for the flying Citroën, but the speed differential was so great that I seldom dared employ the maximum. Nevertheless, the average was highly satisfactory and I was able to stop for a leisurely lunch to avoid arriving too early at Calais. After the Channel crossing, the ingenious lights had a thorough testing under English conditions.

After 2,000 miles in a hurry, I know much more about the Citroën SM. The steering is by far the best yet, and must cause all other designers furiously to think. This is the first car with complete stability at speed which can also dodge like lighting in an emergency. It is impossible to feel the power assistance increasing and decreasing the response to the wheel seeming absolutely constant, which is the case with no other car.

The suspension is excellent, though not as soft as that of the DS. There is no wallowing and remarkably little roll, but above all there is no way of telling from which end of the

car the power goes on to the road. If ever a car had neutral steering characteristics, this is it, and the cornering power is extraordinarily high for a heavy car. Wind noise and road noise are extremely low, with the exception of the bang which occurs when a wheel drops into a hen's nest, which is what the French call big potholes. The suspension permits unusually long travel to all four wheels and I never felt the bump stops come into action, even under the most extreme conditions, yet the ride feels harder and the whole character more sporting than that of the DS. Like the DS, the brakes are immensely powerful and virtually immune from fading the anti-dive geometry of the suspension avoiding any nose-down attitudes. However, the hand-brake is somewhat inadequate, in spite of its well-placed lever.

The engine gives plenty of power, but the uneven firing impulses are noticeable at low speeds. It can both be heard and felt in the middle ranges, but from 5500 to 6500 rpm it becomes outstandingly smooth. The excellent gearbox is there to be used, and I never engaged fifth gear below 100 mph when in a hurry. Because this is a substantial car with an engine of moderate size, lazy driving does reduce the performance, and sporting handling pays dividends. Though the power-operated brakes have the well-known Citroën button pedal, one can easily use heel-and-toe.

The SM is the first car with complete stability at speed which can also dodge like lightning in an emergency.

Again like the DS21, the SM goes on and on gathering speed when you think it has reached its limit. It is still accelerating quite hard at 120 mph, but to get over 130 mph calls for a very long straight, though it seems happy to continue indefinitely at such speeds.

The luxurious interior complements the excellent ride. Perhaps a short driver would find it difficult to judge the width for this is a wide car and the scuttle is rather high. The electric windows are slow to open and close, which lets the other driver get away before you have maligned his sister in your impeccable French. For the optional air-conditioning I have the highest possible praise. In a searing heat-wave it kept the interior of the car perfectly cool, even when set to run on the lowest notch. Of all the luxuries, this is the one that I would choose. I must also extol the lights, which are so accurately focused at all times that they don't dazzle people on the other carriageway.

As usual, however, the dipped beam could do with a few more watts.

After a week of driving the SM, I found that the steering of ordinary cars needed too much attention and effort. This Citroën is a complicated car, but all its complexities are justified by results, and its price is moderate for what it offers.

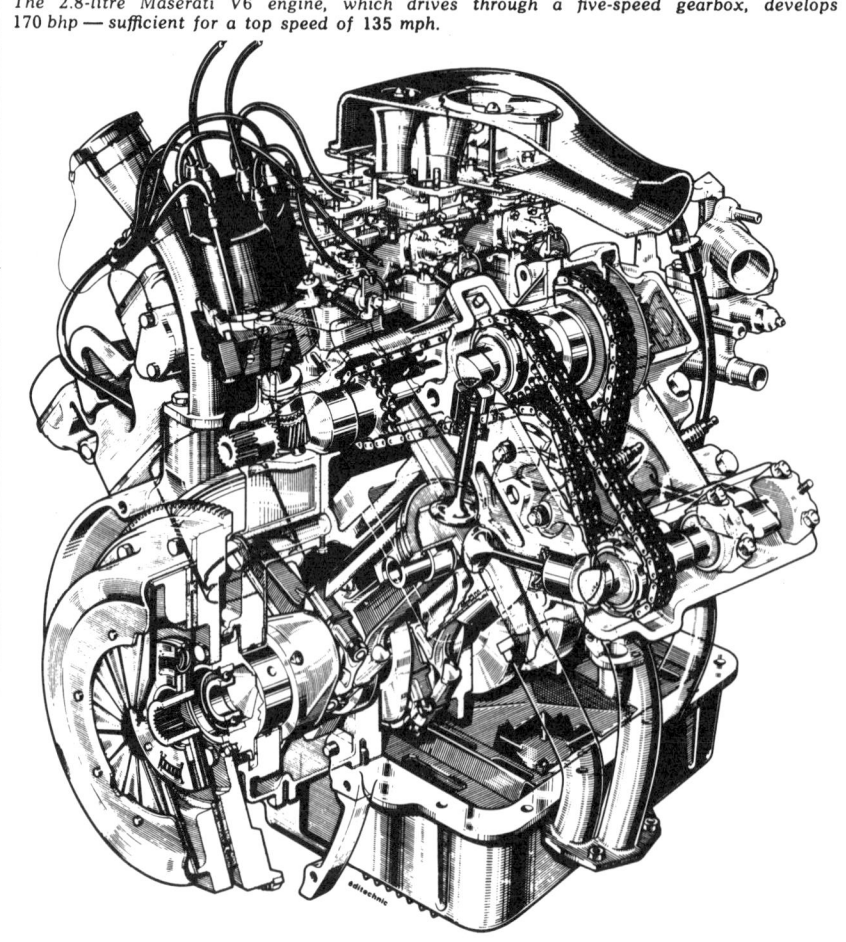

The 2.8-litre Maserati V6 engine, which drives through a five-speed gearbox, develops 170 bhp — sufficient for a top speed of 135 mph.

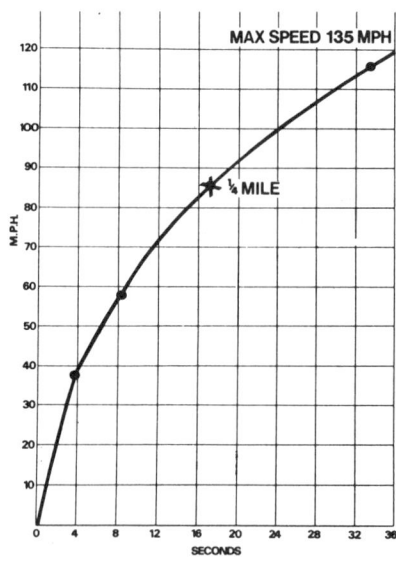

SPECIFICATION AND PERFORMANCE DATA

Car tested : Citroën SM 2-door 4-seater coupé, price £4689. Extras on test car : Air conditioning £206, leather upholstery £186—all including tax.

Engine : Six cylinders in 90° V, 87 mm x 75 mm, 2670 cc. Four chain-driven overhead camshafts. Compression ratio 9 to 1. 170 bhp (net) at 5500 rpm. Three twin-choke Weber carburetters.

Transmission: Single dry plate clutch, 5-speed all-syncromesh gearbox with central change, ratios 0.81, 0.97, 1.32, 1.94 and 2.93 to 1. Hypoid final drive, ratio 4.375 to 1. Open driveshafts to front hubs with homokinetic joints.

Chassis: Combined steel body and chassis with aluminium bonnet. Hydropneumatic self-levelling independent suspension all round with wishbones in front, trailing arms behind, and anti-roll bars at both ends. Power-operated disc brakes all round, inboard in front. Bolt-on disc wheels fitted Michelin 195/70 VR-15in tyres.

Equipment : 12-volt lighting and starting with alternator. Speedometer, rev counter, water temperature, oil temperature and fuel gauges, heating demisting and ventilation system with heated rear window. 2-speed windscreen wipers and washers with variable interrupter. Flashing direction indicators. Reversing lights. Extra : Air conditioning, radio.

Dimensions : Wheelbase 9 ft 8.25 ins. Track, front 5 ft, rear 4 ft 4.46 ins. Overall length 16 ft 0.6 in. Width 6 ft 0.25 in. Weight 1 ton 9.5 cwt.

Performance : Maximum speed 135 mph. Speeds in gears : fourth 115 mph, third 85 mph, second 58 mph, first 37 mph. Standing quarter-mile 16.8s. Acceleration : 0-30 mph, 3.4s, 0-50 mph, 7.1s, 0-60 mph 8.9s, 0-80 mph, 15.6s, 0-100 mph, 24.2s.

Fuel consumption: 15 to 20 mpg

A Totally New Driving Experience

Featuring a unique hydropneumatic suspension, the Citroen Maserati SM is in a class by itself. This Franco-Italian creation is also a surprisingly frugal luxury car.

In July of 1970 there started down a small assembly line at Citroen's Paris plant a chassis bearing Serial No. 00SB000 3 which soon became the first production unit of what is undoubtedly one of the most significant Grand Touring cars *in terms of overall concept* produced to date. The styling was fresh and new, at the same time having a vague familial resemblance to the DS Citroen, and the technical specifications made fascinating study for those interested in such things.

Known as the Citroen Maserati, or in the latest factory literature, Citroen SM, the car is the happy result of the marriage of S.A. Automobiles Citroen and Officine A. Maserati S. p. A. For those who may have wondered why the large French concern acquired controlling interest in the small (but world famous) Italian car maker the answer is now clear: For the first time since such nameplates as Bugatti, Talbot et al disappeared from the active list, France now has a first rate GT car.

A Maserati type C 114-1 dohc V-6 driving the front wheels and hydro-pneumatic all-independent suspension would by themselves be enough to set the SM apart from the run of the mill GT car. But just how different a car it really is can only be appreciated by driving it. You can't just get into one and drive away without having first been checked out by someone familiar with it. And it takes at least a week of driving it before it quits springing surprises on you. Not that it has a lot of idiosyncrasies; it doesn't have any in fact. It's that it is so totally different from any other car — even the DS 21 — that it's like learning to drive all over again.

To begin with, you can't see the ignition lock when seated in the normal

33

Citroen's double chevron symbol, displayed at right rear of hood, also serves as grille for heater/air conditioner fresh air intake.

driving position. You have to find it alongside the bulbous steering column, then figure out the key orientation totally by feel. Once underway you involuntarily set up a zig-zag course because of steering overcontrol. Hydraulically assisted, it is *very* quick with only 2 turns lock to lock. But overcontrol is no problem at higher speeds because the steering automatically stiffens up so that progressively more pressure is required to turn the wheel a given amount. It takes a few miles of driving before you learn to steer smoothly at all speeds.

The next routine to be mastered is the operation of the levers — two on the left and one on the right — that sprout from the steering column. Between them they switch the head lights/parking lights, select the beam, turn signals, operate the horn (soft and loud tones), and windshield wipers/washers. Once we got them sorted out, we found these finger tip controls far quicker and easier to operate than the usual assortment scattered about the instrument panel and left toe.

The brake pedal isn't a pedal at all but rather a low rubber bulb. Because the actual travel is practically nil — it's more a matter of pressure — the feel is quite different from that of a pedal, but you quickly adapt to it.

After the strangeness wears off you

Large rear greenhouse window comes standard with heating grid to control misting problem. Rear quarter windows swing out; fronts operate electrically; front vents are immobile.

start to savor the general character of the car. The quick steering makes low speed maneuvering a breeze and masks the heavy understeering characteristic typical of front drive cars. From the feel of the steering, there is no indication whatsoever that it is a front drive car. Not even on extremely rough surfaces with the wheels steered to the limit is there any shock or motion transmitted back to the steering wheel.

Clutch pedal pressure was light, but the clutch action itself, as revealed during acceleration test, was smooth and positive. The moderately short throw 5-speed shift linkage had a nice, precision

feel, and unusually powerful synchronizers made downshifting almost as easy as upshifting. Together, the clutch and gearbox action made driving in traffic a much more pleasant experience than we were prepared for.

The 3 dual-throat Weber-fed Maserati V-6 performance was characteristic of what we have found in other Maserati passenger car engines: a definite upsurge of power starting at mid-range (3000 rpm in this case) but with amazing low speed smoothness and lugging ability to match. The impression you get is that the engine is considerably larger than it actually is. It also makes its presence known with a distinctly audible exhaust/power throb under load. This in what is otherwise a very quiet car can either be music to your ears or a source of minor annoyance, depending on how your taste runs. About the only other noise to intrude is an occasional patter from the Michelin X radials as they traverse certain types of pavement

Oval instrument bezels match oval 1-spoke wheel. Control stalks on steering column, marked with symbols on European model shown here, are marked in English on U.S. version. Steering wheel is fully adjustable.

This view lets the secret out of the bag: It's a Citroen. Narrowed rear tread gives characteristic snake hipped look.

Understeer has been the cornering mode of all front drive Citroens, with the SM no exception. U.S. front seen here takes sealed beams. European lighting, nixed by our laws, features 6 Cibie rectangular quartz iodides, 2 of which steer with the wheels to "see" around corners!

imperfections. Even so, the noise level is below that of most cars and far below that of other GT cars.

The air conditioner-heater system, suffice to say, is on a par with those of our domestic luxury cars which are the standard of the world. We were never aware when the compressor cut in and out, the engine having sufficient torque at low speeds to handle the extra load without faltering.

The quality of materials, design and workmanship of the standard all-leather upholstered passenger seats are such that we can't see how they could be significantly improved upon. And they are comfortable, too. The longer you sit in them, the more you appreciate what an asset they are for long distance touring. There are two levers on each of the front seats. Depressing the outboard ones allow the seat backs to tilt forward and the seats to slide forward on rails to ease access to rear seats. When pulled back, the seat then "remembers" and always returns to whatever rake and fore and aft position it was previously set. The inboard levers allow the seat to be reclined or set at whatever rake is desired. There are also other adjustments for tilt and fore and aft position. The seatbacks are topped off with fully adjustable headrests that were obviously designed as part of the seat and not as an afterthought.

The SM was designed to seat four in comfort, which it does, although the

front passengers get the lion's share of the room. It is, however, more than just a 2 plus 2 design and is perfectly capable of accommodating two rear seat passengers on extended trips.

The instrumentation is all you could ask for — and then some. In addition to gauges for water and oil temperature and fuel level, there is a cluster of 13 warning lights surrounding a big red bullseye "STOP" lamp. The individual lamps are marked with symbols (some of which we never figured out) and warn of everything from low oil pressure to

excessive brake pad wear. Any critical condition that could lead to disaster causes the stop lamp to light which is absolutely impossible to ignore. A test button on the cluster permits checking of the critical warning lamps and the stop lamp.

And then there is the hydropneumatic suspension system with some highly practical as well as entertaining features. Citroen wrote the book on such a system when it came out with the DS 19 way back in 1955, but despite its demonstrated practicality and superiority, there are to this day no imitators. Due to a self-leveling feature, the ride height and feel never change regardless of load, quite an asset with any car. Also, by means of a lever beside the driver's seat, you can increase ground clearance from the normal 6.1 inches to a choice of 6.9, 9.1, or 10 inches for rough going. The following incident, related by a friend who had the opportunity to observe how French driv-

Ups and downs of hydropneumatic suspension, controlled with lever beside driver's seat, can be in 5 positions, with extreme ones used in jacking.

Stops were straight line and short. What wheel locking that occurred was always the fronts and always during the last few feet of a panic stop.

ers use their Citroens, illustrates the advantages of this:

"I was following a DS on a French country road when we came upon a stretch with the pavement torn up for resurfacing. We were doing about 60 mph. He put his suspension in a high position and never slowed down one bit. I had to slow to a crawl because it felt like the wheels were going to be torn off my Humber Hawk. I never saw the DS after that."

A situation never arose where we could put the feature to such a practical test, but amused ourselves with it in traffic. When alongside another car at a traffic signal we'd raise or lower it if we caught the driver staring at us. The startled reactions we sometimes got alone made hydropneumatic suspension worthwhile.

There is also a low position of the suspension that's used for wheel chang-

ing only. (The bullseye comes on if you try to drive with it in this position.) You put the suspension in the highest position, put the jack stand in place, then put the suspension in the low position which causes the wheels to lift off the ground. Thus the suspension does all the work of jacking for you.

The Citroen AM-FM multiplex stereo system installed in the SM is remarkable for its fidelity in the higher frequency range without sacrificing low range. The domestic units we're accustomed to listening to tend to boom the bass and cut out the highs entirely. The Citroen system reproduces brilliant highs right up to the limits of the human ear.

The SM is pleasant enough in town and on the freeway, but you just can't fully appreciate what the car can do for you until you try maintaining a good clip on narrow winding secondary roads with less than the best surfaces. While there are cars that can outdo the SM in absolute cornering power, we would choose the SM over them every time for bac country work. It corners well enough, and the comfort keeps you fresh hours longer. The suspension soaks up bumps that would make the

average GT car harsh and unpleasant, and the responsive steering and powerful brakes have enough reserve to cope with the unexpected.

The brisk performance of the SM together with amazingly good gas mileage provide one of the more pleasant surprises we've had recently. Of course, our test car had the European version engine without an air injector pump for emissions control which reduces both mileage and performance. But even if the pump knocks several miles per gallon off the numbers we recorded, the SM will still give excellent fuel economy by GT car standards. It may be argued who cares about gas mileage in a car of the SM's price class. The answer is those in countries where fuel prices are very much higher than in the U.S. and those who do not wish to be bothered with frequent stops for refills. With the SM's fuel capacity and economy you need never stop for fuel more often than you do for food or sleep, and for a Grand Touring car, that's the way it should be.

Three factors contribute to the SM's fuel economy: 1) The Michelin X steel-belt radial tires have very low rolling resistance. 2) The aerodynamically ef-

Jack is simple adjustable stand; suspension does the lifting.

Rear window, linked to trunk lid, hinges upward to reveal large, 20-cubic-foot trunk.

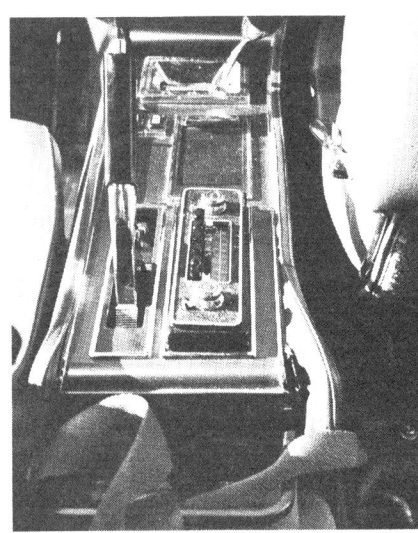

Citroen AM-FM multiplex stereo radio nests in unusual position beside parking brake at rear of center console.

ficient body shape requires less power to push through the air at a given speed than squarish shape cars of equal size. 3) The gearbox has widely spaced upper ratios. Citroen could have crammed 5 close ratios in the box for more impressive acceleration, but they characteristically chose economy and durability instead. Both 4th and 5th ratios are actually overdrives with wide spaces between 3rd and 4th and 4th and 5th. For example, on shifting from 4th to 5th at 70 mph, the engine rpm drops from 4000 to 3100 and internal engine friction, which is proportional to the square of the rpm, is cut nearly in half.

We seldom make extensive com-

ments about style, believing it's something that speaks for itself. But this being a Citroen and a GT car selling in a price range where styling can make the difference between failure and success, technical features notwithstanding, some comments are in order. As Citroen well knows, the DS styling is far from everybody's cup of tea, especially in this country. Although the SM bears enough resemblance to the DS that you can tell they belong to the same family, the SM is evidently a winner judging by the comments it elicited during our test. It attracted a great deal of attention wherever we took it, which is itself a favor-

able indication. People simply do not gather around a car they consider ugly. An indirect compliment came from a service station attendant who declared, "It's the first Citroen I've seen that I can stand to look at."

All of which opens the door to some speculation about the future of the design. Although not merely a DS with different exterior sheet metal, the chassis is similar enough in design details and construction techniques so that if produced in equal quantities, the cost of manufacture would not be significantly different. And there's no reason why the DS engine and gearbox, or something like them, can't be used. The DS's front drive predecessor had a production life that spanned 21 years and a world war. The DS itself is now 17 years old. Could it be that the SM, with somewhat less exotic power and driveline components and interior furnishings, will soon replace the DS and the Maserati powered version is being used to test the water?

If Citroen entertains any serious marketing plans for its regular line of cars in this country, such a move would make sense. In an attractive package, the good riding, exclusively Citroen hydropneumatic suspension would have tremendous appeal here. Citroen has carefully maintained direct branches on the east and west coasts over the years despite scant sales volume, and it could be that in the SM lies the key to the realization of their ambitions. Just as this was written, the first small batch of SM models reached these shores. But Citroen had already been besieged from would-be dealers from all over the country wanting to handle the car. As of then, Citroen was holding off, fearing

that an impending resumption of the dock strike would hinder the supply.

Production lead times being what they are, auto makers are rapidly coming down to the wire on the time designs for the 1975 models must be finalized. That's the year really stringent emission standards are supposed to take effect. Just as domestic car makers, up to their ears in thermal reactors and catalytic converters, are giving every indication that they may balk at the new regulations because they're unable to meet them, Citroen has cooly hinted that they may have a different solution to the problem.

An SM with an easy to make clean Wankel engine, perhaps? Now *there* would be a dream machine to end all dream machines! ●

Citroen power plant is a 162.9 cu in. DOHC Maserati V-6 with 3 dual-throat Weber carburetors.

CITROEN MASERATI SM COUPE

SPECIFICATIONS AS TESTED

Engine* . . . . 162.9 cu in. dohc V-6
Bore and stroke . . . . 3.43 x 2.95 in.
Compression ratio . . . . 9.0 to one
Horsepower . . . . 180 at 6250 rpm
Torque . . . . 172 lb-ft at 4000 rpm
Transmission . . . . 5-speed, manual
Final drive ratio . . . . 4.375 to one
Steering** . . . . 2.0 turns, lock to lock
Turning circle (curb to curb) . . . . 41.3 ft
Brakes** . . . . 4-wheel hydr. disc
Suspension . . . . . . hydro-pneumatic, front & rear
Tires . . . . 195/70 VR 15 Michelin X
Dimensions (ins.):

Wheelbase . .	116.1	Front track	60.1
Length	192.6	Rear track	52.3
Width	72.2	Ground clearance . .	6.2
Height	52.1	Weight	3153 lbs

Capacities:

Fuel	24.0 gals	Oil	6 qts
Coolant . . .	14.0 qts	Hydraulic sys. . . .	6 qts.
		Trunk	20 cu ft

*European version without air injector pump for emissions control
**Power assisted

PERFORMANCE AND MAINTENANCE

Acceleration: Gears:
  0-30 mph . . . . 3.5 secs—1st
  0-45 mph . . . . 6.7 secs—1st-2nd
  0-60 mph . . . . 10.1 secs—1st-2nd
  0-75 mph . . . . 14.6 secs—1st-3rd
  0-¼ mile . . . . 16.9 secs at 82 mph
Top speed (est) . . . . 130 mph
Stop from 60 mph . . . . 149 ft
Average economy (city) . . . . 18.2 mpg
Average economy (country) . . . . 25.7 mpg
Fuel required . . . . premium
Oil change (mos/miles) 3000
Lubrication 3000
Warranty (mos/miles) . . . . . 12/unlimited mileage
Type tools required . . . . metric
U.S. dealers 125

RATING

	Excellent (91-100)	Good (81-90)	Fair (71-80)	Poor (60-70)
Brakes	92			
Comfort	96			
Cornering	91			
Details	94			
Finish	94			
Instruments . . .	96			
Luggage	92			
Performance . .		90		
Quietness		90		
Ride	94			
Room		90		
Steering	91			
Visibility		90		
Overall	93			

BASE PRICE OF CAR

(Excludes state and local taxes, license, dealer preparation and domestic transportation): $11,805.
Plus desirable options:
$n/a 3-speed Automatic
$11,805 + Total

ANTICIPATED DEPRECIATION:

(Based on current Kelley Blue Book, previous equivalent model): n/a 1st yr. n/a 2nd yr.

n/a—not available

Citroen SM Technical Report

Citroen engineering ushered in "tomorrow" back in 1955 . . . and is still doing it.

by John Ethridge

Beautiful as the skin of the SM may be, it's somewhat saddening to realize that it hides so many brilliant technical achievements! Citroen can't do like Bulova did with its Accutron electric watch — build a denuded model to sell to the public, so come along for a photo-journalistic look-see under the sheet metal of this most unusual car. Students of the DS design will see much that is familiar and will certainly agree with Citroen's contention that they've surpassed even themselves in reaching a higher degree of perfection.

1

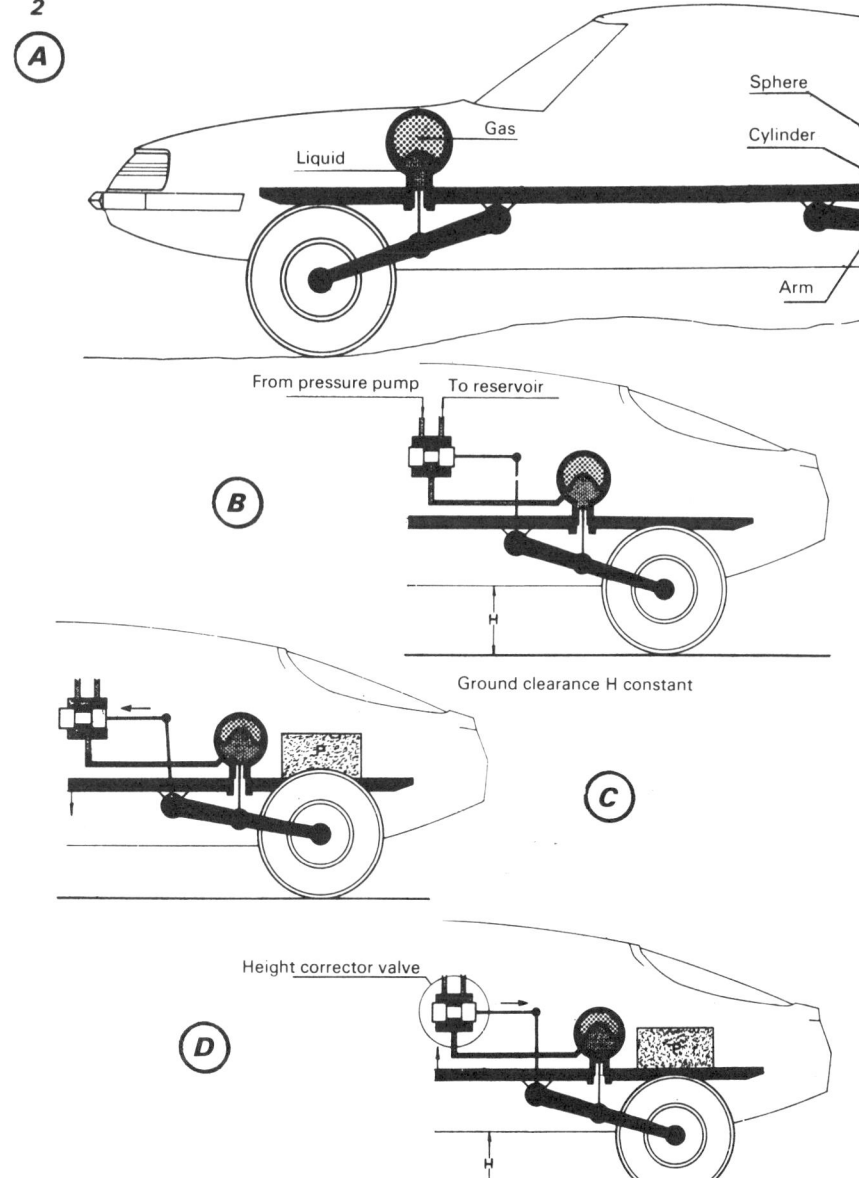

2

Ⓐ

Sphere

Gas

Liquid

Cylinder

Piston

Arm

From pressure pump

To reservoir

Ⓑ

Ground clearance H constant

Ⓒ

Height corrector valve

Ⓓ

1. SM packages weightiest components up front over driving wheels. Springing is via a highly sophisticated hydropneumatic system with constant level, adjustable riding height features.

2. A) Hydropneumatic springing is basically pistons linked to suspension arms pushing against columns of liquid which in turn push against rubber diaphragms contained in spheres to compress trapped gas.
B) Load leveling is accomplished by linking the suspension arms to slider (or spool) valve in such a way that liquid is either admitted to or bled from the cylinder above the piston to compensate for varying loads so that ground clearance H remains constant.
C) Adding load P to trunk causes rear to sag as gas in sphere is further compressed and actuating valve so that more liquid under pressure is admitted to cylinder.
D) When correct height H is reached, valve goes into neutral position so that liquid is neither admitted to or bled from the cylinder.

3. *Maserati 90° V-6 aluminum engine weighs only 308 lbs, abounds with unusual features. Chain drive for the 4 camshafts is via an intermediate shaft located approximately where the camshaft would normally be in a domestic pushrod V-8. Directly driven off the intermediate shaft are the water pump and distributor, while the oil pump is driven directly off the end of the crankshaft. (An extension shaft coupled to the intermediate runs forward of the engine to drive the hydraulic pump, refrigerant compressor, alternator and air injector pump which are all chassis mounted.) The crankcase is split horizontally at the crankshaft centerline so that the 4 main bearing caps are integral with a deep box-like structure, making for an extremely rigid, robust lower end. A sump bolted to this structure holds the engine oil which is circulated through a filter and cooler.*

4. *Engine and gearbox bolt together in rigid, compact unit. Main caliper is seen at left of inboard disc. Smaller dark caliper at top right of disc is for the hand operated parking brake.*

5. *SM 5-speed all-synchro gearbox is of such generous proportions that designers obviously made provision for possible future increases in power and torque. The synchronizers are of large diameter and, therefore, very powerful. Dark mechanism on bell housing is slave cylinder for hydraulically actuated diaphragm clutch.*

6. *Shown here and in engine/ gearbox photo is a governor that bolts to the end of the gearbox and drives from the tail of the pinion shaft to sense car speed. It is hydraulically connected to the power steering system so that required steering effort on part of the driver increases with speed, thus making the very quick steering safe and controllable at high speeds.*

7. *Steering is rack-and-pinion assisted by main hydraulic system. Steering effort governor is shown forward of front axle near centerline of car in this phantom view.*

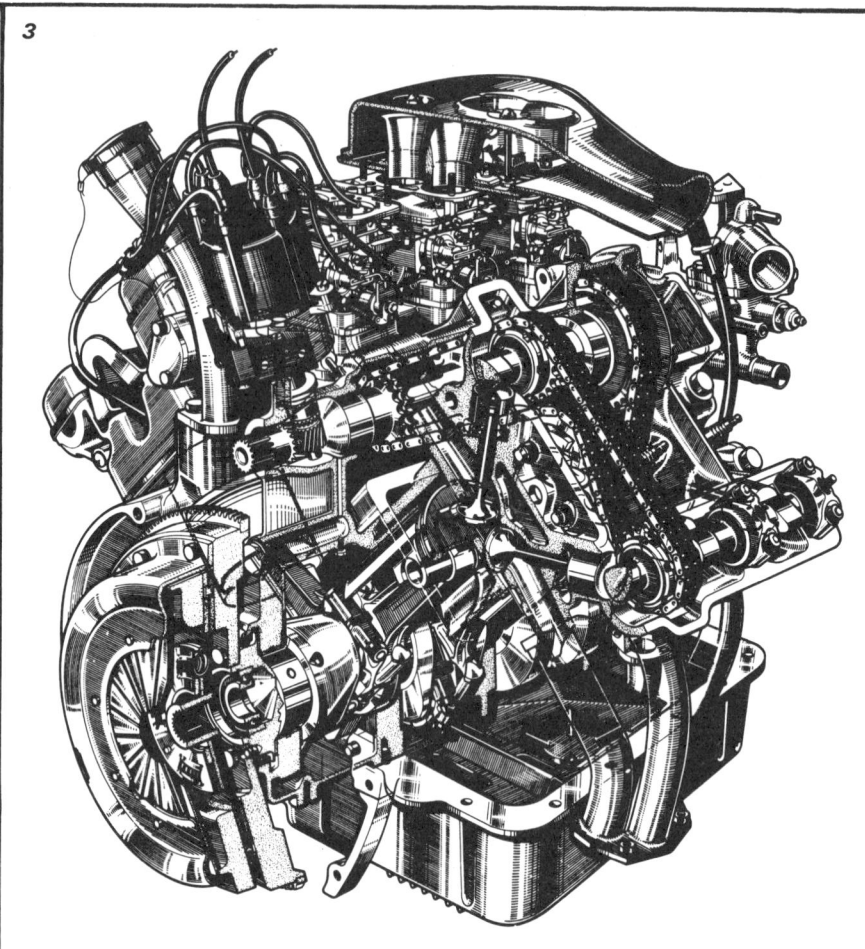

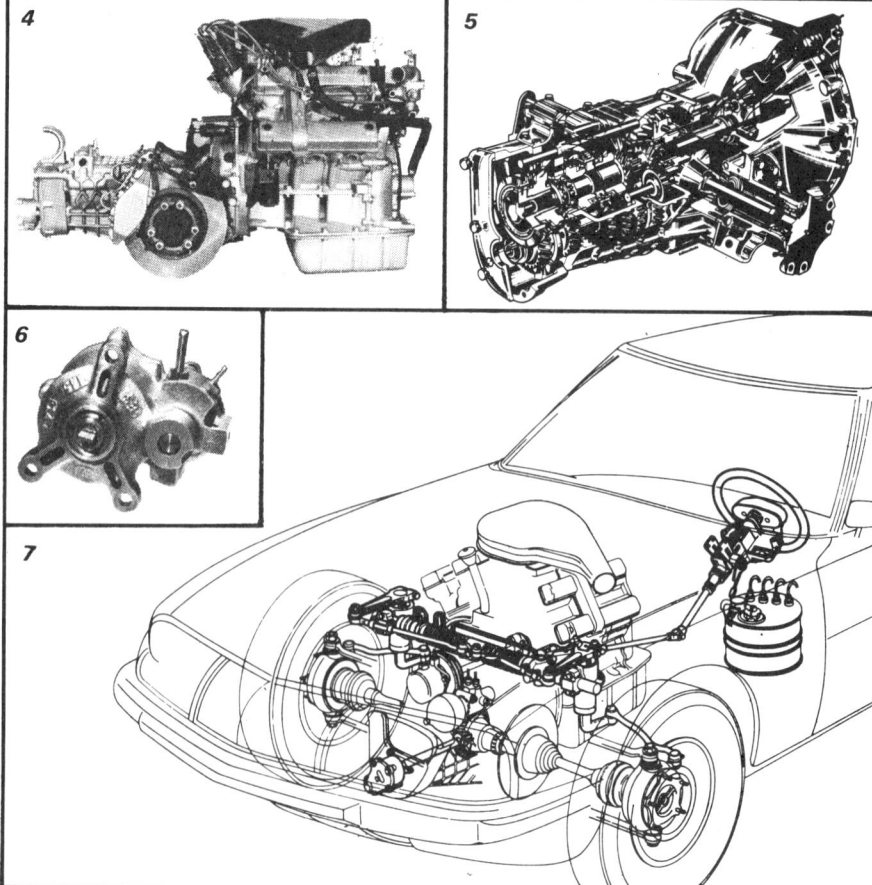

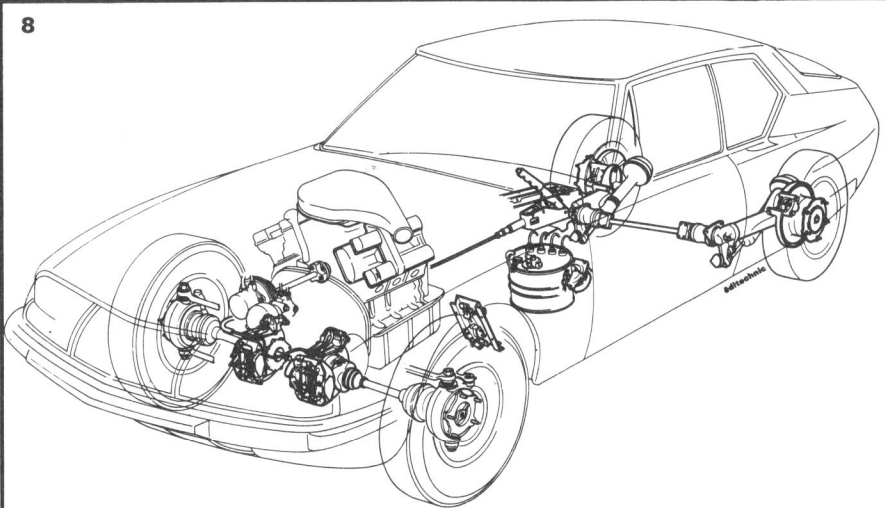

8. 4-disc brake system derives hydraulic power from main system but has own accumulator which reserves enough hydraulic energy for 30-40 stops should main system fail. System incorporates modulator/proportioner that takes into account rear suspension load to control rear braking effort to prevent lockup and skids.

9. Removal of access cover in belly pan reveals front discs, engine clutch and flywheel. Tubes seen coming from discs hubs on either side protect disc by draining any gearbox oil that may seep past the side seals safely to the ground.

10. Twin ducts bring cooling air from scoops under nose to front discs which do bulk of stopping work.

11. SM front suspension pieces look somewhat like those of DS except they are reversed in direction. (Front of car is toward right in picture.) Known as a trailing arm arrangement the SM suspension is superior to the DS leading arm setup because of its anti-drive action under braking.

12. Front suspension arms pivot on bearings. Front stabilizer bar, seen emerging from U-bolted bracket on lower pivot is linked to bell crank on upper arm. Also acting on bell crank is hydropneumatic "spring," the corrugated boot end of which is visible here.

13. Hydraulic pump (1) is a 7-piston wobble plate design driven at half engine speed and is capable of supplying 51.2 cubic inches of fluid per minute at 600 engine (idle) rpm. Pump rotates all the time when engine runs, but pumps intermittently according to the demands of the system. Main accumulator/pressure regulator (2) stores 0.4 quarts of fluid pressurized by compressed gas acting on diaphragm in sphere. The pressure regulator cuts in the pump when the pressure in the sphere falls below 2176 psi and cuts it out when pressure reaches 2539 psi.

14. Rear suspension is single trailing arm with stabilizer bar (not visible here) interconnecting right and left pivots. Hydropneumatic unit is seen parallel to exhaust pipes. Hydraulic line on arms leads to disc caliper, hidden by splash cover.

15 & 16. Diaphragm spheres, installed hand tight, are readily removable for replacement or inspection if the suspension is put in the lower position and, in case of the pressure regulator sphere, bleed valve is opened. The rubber diaphragms, so an experienced Citroen mechanic informs us, are subject to deterioration and failure according to time in service, not number of miles car is driven.

17. Drum-like cannister with tag warning against the use of anything but Total "LHM" green liquid holds 5.75 quarts of the stuff and is the central hydraulic system reservoir. LHM is a highly refined light mineral oil, and Citroen says you can use automatic transmission fluid in a pinch, if you later drain and refill with the proper liquid. Citroen used to use something more like ordinary automotive brake fluid but switched its domestic cars in 1966 and U.S. export models in 1969 to mineral oil because of its far superior lubricating and anti-corrosion qualities. They recommend draining and refilling every 24,000 miles.

18. Air pump (left of suspension sphere) runs off toothed belt, supplies air to injectors just downstream of exhaust valves and, under deceleration, to intake passages between the carburetors and intake valves to lean out mixture. Anti-evaporative fuel systems are also installed on U.S. models.

19. Twin multi-blade molded plastic thermostatically controlled fans contribute to SM quietness, brisk acceleration, handle total cooling chores, including extra load imposed by standard air conditioning.

20. Heater/air conditioning evaporator "climatization" unit appears to be more accessible than ones on domestic cars, should service ever be required.

21. SM is of unitized construction with many bolt-on external panels. Design is extremely efficient in terms of strength and stiffness to weight. Under 3200-lb weight is feather light for car of this size with so much equipment. ●

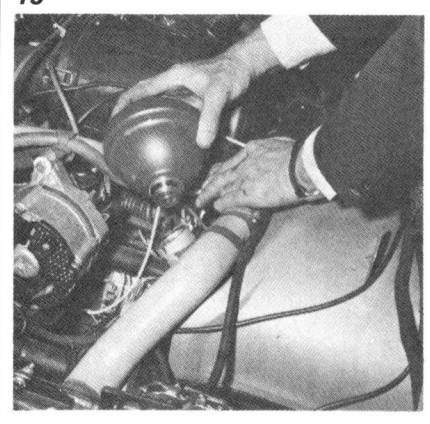

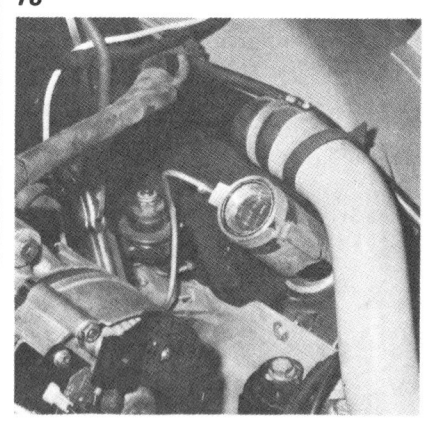

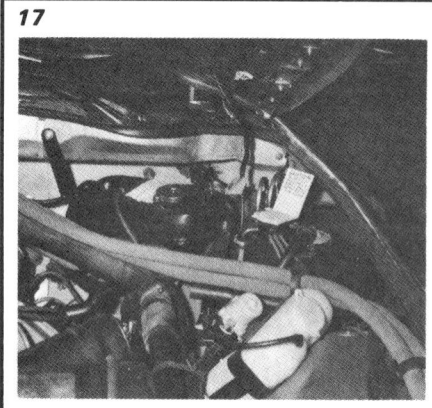

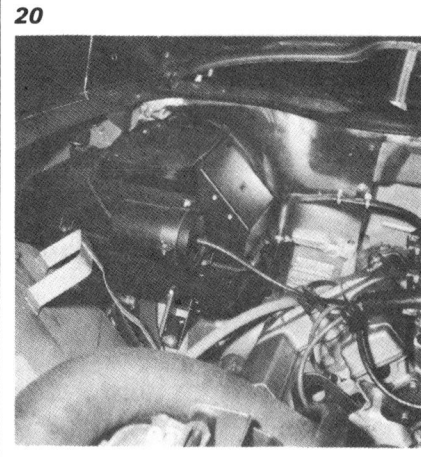

CITROEN SM

The Citroen SM is one of those landmark cars. Not because all cars are going to be like it in the future—nobody really has the nerve to copy Citroen even when they're right—but because it breaks new ground, does so in a thoroughly original manner that only Citroen could conceive, and still turns out to be a well worked-out, rational car that's delightful to drive, ride in or even talk about.

The SM doesn't replace any existing Citroen model. The D and DS sedans continue in production along with smaller models that aren't sold in the U.S., and there's a new, small GS sedan that is equally fresh and original and will, we hope, soon be sold over here too. The SM, however, is Citroen's flagship—a sleek, fast, luxurious 4-seater priced at over $11,000 in the U.S. and offered for the delectation of well-to-do enthusiasts who don't mind being different. It's a long car, fairly heavy, its front wheels powered by a newly developed Maserati V-6 engine of 2.7 liters and 180 bhp, embodying Citroen's well proven hydropneumatic suspension system and a central hydraulic system that powers suspension, steering and brakes.

No Citroen in recent memory has been in debt to any other car for styling inspiration, and the SM is character-istically unique. But whereas recent Citroen family cars have been weird to the point of putting most people off (while endearing themselves to a select group), the SM has an aggressive potency that is more universal in appeal. Several of the editors found its form disconcerting, but our resident styling expert and the general public are much impressed. The shape is strongly influenced by aerodynamic studies (successfully, as the attainable maximum speed reveals) which have dictated a broad, low, softly-penetrating nose and a much narrower, abruptly terminated rear end. The difference between the ends of the car has brought the most criticism, and certainly the last foot, with the angular rear bumper and the awkward bulge for the license light, is decidedly unattractive. The front, though it has lost two of its six lights (the ones that turned with the wheels) and the streamlined glass covers to U.S. regulations, has suffered less than many European designs in this respect and is still effective. When the suspension is "down" the SM has an unmatched road-hugging appearance which is both futuristic and rational. Whether you like it or not, the styling is a true landmark too. We don't like the rear end, and the wheel covers are less than we'd expect on an $11,500 car, but otherwise—*formidable!*

Almost everything about the SM is different or noteworthy in some way. All Citroens take getting used to, and the SM is no exception. Its steering, the most radical thing about it, takes the most acclimation. To begin with, it's the quick-

est steering on a passenger car since the days of tillers—the 9.4:1 ratio means about half the wheel-twirling of a Datsun 240Z. But that's only the beginning. The power assist to the rack-and-pinion steering gear varies with wheel position and car speed. As the steering wheel is moved away from center position, power assist increases, so that it helps you most in a parking maneuver. But with steering so quick a driver might be likely to put the car into the bushes at high speed, so Citroen engineers made the power assist decrease with increasing car speed. Finally, the steering's return action is also powered and this *increases* with speed. There's enough of this return action that with the car at rest and the engine idling the wheel will return to center position when released.

To become accustomed to all this new stuff, a driver has to spend a lot of time in the SM. The first inclination *is* to overdo it, particularly at low speeds. The steering feel is good, though it must be artificially supplied by the hydraulic system, but until acclimated the driver has to consciously avoid turning the wheel too much either going into a corner or coming out. As speed builds up the power-assist decrease more than takes care of things and at 60-80 mph through sweeping bends and tighter turns we felt more at home with the SM. At still higher speeds, over 100, it seems that a lot of attention is again needed.

Most SM owners, we think, would spend more time behind the oval steering wheel and drive fewer other cars than

we did, so they probably would get the benefit of what has to be the most maneuverable luxury car there is. The super-quick steering has another effect: to mask the always strong understeer of front-wheel drive. It may be that steering like this could only be used in a fwd car; in vigorous cornering the final understeer is always there to "save" you in case you do put in too much lock. In this respect the SM is typical fwd, extra power fed in by the throttle producing more and more understeer. But cornering power is high on the big Michelin XVR 70-series tires: over 0.72g is impressive for a 3250-lb luxury car, especially with fwd as the front tires have to do much more than half the work.

Only a couple of real deficiencies show up in the steering: if one tries to turn the wheel rapidly with the car at rest the power assist doesn't keep up with the demand, and its hydraulic system is likely to squeal loudly. San Francisco people will be glad to know that it is possible to leave the front wheels cramped over, by holding the steering wheel over while shutting off the engine.

If anyone thinks the Citroen's extreme suspension complication isn't worth the trouble, let him take a ride. There is no better-riding car in the world than the SM. At anything over 30 mph it is like the proverbial cloud and will traverse big bumps and dips at speeds and with aplomb that leaves passengers awestruck. This is nothing new to Citroen, as the same can be said of the DS sedans, but the SM is better. Its "springs" are stiffer than the sedan's, and this together

CITROEN SM

with the stiffness of the high-speed tires means a bit of clumpity-clump over tar strips and the like at low speeds. But the DS is also notable for some rather irritating ride motions, and the SM dispenses with these for the most part. Its front suspension geometry allows a degree of squat on braking that nicely matches that of the rear (yes, the rear does squat on braking!), so that the whole car hunches down but remains essentially level. On acceleration there is a lot of "speedboat" effect with the front end rising dramatically but gently. And the automatic leveling system, with little if any time-delay built in, compensates when any of this is going on so that, for instance, after you've rolled to a stop the car is initially high and then comes down. Still, we found more satisfaction from the great competence of the suspension than irritation from its odd motions. As on the DS there is a manual height control, with the normal central position plus a "high" and two lower settings. The high position makes the ride amusingly stiff and is useful for off-road operation or for tire changing; we can't think of any good use for the lowest position, but we did occasionally amuse ourselves by running the car up and down when stopped by other cars at a traffic light. With how many cars can you do things that make you laugh out loud?

A characteristic Citroen mushroom pedal actuates the SM's fully hydraulic-powered brake system. It's higher off the floor than the DS's mushroom and closer to the throttle, to allow simultaneous use of it and the throttle for smooth downshifting. Such a "button" for brakes makes the new SM driver think he'll have to learn braking all over again, but in reality he hardly notices it when driving. There is a

difference in feel, though: effort is very light and we think braking action isn't thoroughly proportional to pedal effort. The SM has disc brakes all around, and they squeal a good deal of the time; but they are quite fade-free and will stop the car in 182 ft from 60 mph or 300 from 80 with good control on dry asphalt pavement.

Aside from the steering the SM is more conventional in controls than the last DS we drove, having a 5-speed, manual, central-shifter gearbox rather than the DS's odd semi-automatic with column shift. This gearbox, by Citroen, is one of the finest 5-speeds we've ever encountered even though the box is a great distance from the shift lever. The lever moves easily and precisely in a cylindrical bar that slides from side to side as one moves the lever laterally, though the bar makes a clanking noise on some shifts; there's no gearbox noise and the ratios seem perfectly chosen for the engine.

As we understand it, Maserati (now a subsidiary of Citroen) developed the SM's V-6 engine very quickly from an existing V-8 design they had. It's a 90° unit with dual overhead cams on each bank and an unusual auxiliary driveshaft that runs the cams via central sprockets and chains (not at the end of the engine) and continues forward to a bank of auxiliaries about 2 ft ahead of the engine. The engine makes a mixture of intriguing sounds: at idle it has a typical V-6 roughness, seeming to misfire; at low speeds, up to about 4000 rpm, it sounds for all the world like a Corvair; and as the revs climb toward its 6500-rpm redline it takes on the character most appropriate to it—that of a highly tuned engine of racing ancestry. It's by no means smooth or quiet, but we think most enthusiasts would delight in the noises it makes, especially in the upper rev reaches.

The car we tested was not a U.S. version even though it had the quad headlights; thus our comments about engine behavior may not apply to the emission-controlled unit U.S.

CITROEN SM

customers will get. In the test car, however, the engine was most impressive: tractable and strong even at low revs and generating far more performance at high revs than 2.7 liters, 180 bhp and 3250 lb led us to expect. The unit revs freely and power is just beginning to fall off at the redline.

In the acceleration tests the front wheels tended to tramp if we tried to spin them and we got some ominous noises as they finally settled down, so we resorted to clutch slip to get the performance figures. They are impressive nonetheless, and the top speed of 135 mph has to be a testimony to both the output of the Maserati engine and Citroen's advanced aerodynamics. Name another car, if you can, that will achieve 135 mph on 180 bhp in luxury and quiet! The quiet, by the way, is also notable at ordinary cruising speeds, thanks to the long-legged 5th gear. But there is some wind noise to spoil it.

We haven't been fans of Citroen interiors; on the DS the feeling is one of too much padding and softness. The SM is quite another story. It's upholstered in rich-looking leather and vinyl, and the seats are well padded but not too soft. There were some quality slips, however, both inside and outside the SM we tested. Front seats offer a range of adjustment not often found: for longitudinal position, back angle and the angle of the entire seat assembly. Inboard levers allow adjustment of the backs, whereas outboard ones release both the backrest and seat track so the seat can really be moved out of the way for entry into the rear seat and then returned to the preset position. The oval steering wheel also tilts and telescopes, so just about any driver can get comfortable. The head restraints really work, being close to the neck and also adjustable. Rear seating is less satisfactory, with limited headroom and legroom—a bit disappointing in so long a car.

Those who savor traditional round instruments won't find solace in the SM. Nothing is round! The three dials, outboard air outlet surrounds and smaller clock face all match the oval of the steering wheel. On the speedometer are given ultra-conservative stopping distances, from four speeds, which the SM easily beats. The crowning glory of this group, however, is the righthand dial, which contains no less than 13 warning lights for various functions, different colors denoting their importance. The three red ones—for engine oil pressure, coolant temperature and central hydraulic pressure—if activated are accompanied by a large center red light showing the word STOP and furthermore can all be tested by a button right in their midst. If a driver blows something up on the SM it's almost bound to be his fault.

The controls are nearly all unusual, but generally they work nicely. There are three stalks ahead of the steering wheel for lighting, signaling, wiping and washing; strangely enough the directionals are non-canceling and just as strangely we didn't find this to be a bother. The horn is a 2-stage affair with a meek little city beep available on light pull of the stalk and powerful air horns when it is pulled harder. The four pushbuttons to the right of the wheel, for various lighting functions, are difficult to find at night, just when you need them. Air-conditioning and heat-ventilation controls are nicely integrated and the air conditioning seemed effective as long as it worked, but it failed soon after we collected the test car. The radio is set into the rear of the console, between the seats, and is thus quite wrong for driver control; a passenger should tend to it.

There are vision problems. Several bits of chrome—along the window ledges, under the instrument panel and at the shift lever—cause glare at times, there is considerable distortion in the oddly shaped rear window, there is quite a blind spot at the left rear roof support and the rearview mirror is positioned too high. Electric window lifts are provided for the door windows, but the rear side windows can only be moved outward slightly by handscrews.

Citroen aerodynamics decree that the body be tapered toward the rear in plan view, and Citroen chassis engineering puts the wheels close to the rear corners. The trunk suffers. It's long and rather deep, but narrow and intruded upon by the spare tire. Nor is its finish particularly attractive.

Everything considered, the Citroen SM is one of the most delightful, satisfying and entertaining cars we've ever driven. We've often remarked that Citroen seems to do things differently just to do them differently, but in the case of the SM the novelty and mechanical complication really pay off. Whether the complication will manifest itself later as big repair bills is open to question, but it does not seem (from what reader feedback we have had) that the DS's hydraulic system has been unusually troublesome. And the SM's complication is, it would seem from inspecting the marvelous array of devices in clear view under its hood, at least fairly accessible. It really is a sight, with the compact engine stuffed back against the firewall, the transmission ahead of it and all the auxiliaries and two suspension spheres in a neat row up front.

If you have $11,500 to spend, like to drive and thrive on novelty, don't fail to try the SM.

PRICE

List price, west coast......$11,482
Price as tested, west coast.$11,482
Price as tested includes standard equipment (power steering & brakes, self-leveling suspension, tinted glass, rear window heater, leather upholstery, air conditioning, AM/FM radio)

IMPORTER

Citroen Cars Corp.
40 Van Nostrand Ave.
Englewood, N.J. 07631

ENGINE

Type................dohc 90° V-6
Bore x stroke, mm.....87.0 x 75.0
   Equivalent in....3.42 x 2.95
Displacement, cc/cu in...2670/163
Compression ratio..........9.0:1
Bhp @ rpm..........180 @ 6250
   Equivalent mph..............142
Torque @ rpm, lb-ft..172 @ 4000
   Equivalent mph..............90
Carburetion..three Weber 42DCNF (2V)
Type fuel required: premium, 98-oct
Emission control..none on test car

DRIVE TRAIN

Transmission..5-speed manual in unit with final drive
Gear ratios: 5th (0.757).....3.31:1
   4th (0.971).............4.25:1
   3rd (1.30).............5.68:1
   2nd (1.94).............8.48:1
   1st (2.92)............12.80:1
Final drive ratio..........4.38:1

CHASSIS & BODY

Layout....front engine/front drive
Body/frame...........unit steel
Brake type...11.8-in. disc front, 10.1-in. disc rear; actuated by central hydraulic system
   Swept area, sq in..........348
Wheels........steel disc, 15 x 6J
Tires..Michelin XVR 195/70 VR-15
Steering type..rack & pinion, variable power assist
   Overall ratio............9.4:1
   Turns, lock-to-lock.........2.0
   Turning circle, ft.........34.5
Front suspension: unequal-length lateral arms, hydropneumatic springing with automatic leveling, anti-roll bar

Rear suspension: trailing arms, hydropneumatic springing with automatic leveling anti-roll bar

ACCOMMODATION

Seating capacity, persons....2+2
Seat width, front/rear.2x19.0/52.0
Head room, front/rear...38.0/35.0
Seat back adjustment, degrees..30

INSTRUMENTATION

Instruments: 260-kph speedometer, 8000-rpm tachometer, 99,999 odo, 999.9 trip odo, coolant temp, fuel level, oil temp
Warning lights: oil pressure, hydraulic pressure, coolant temp, generator, reserve fuel, brake lining, directionals, lights on, high beam, rear window heat, hazard flasher

MAINTENANCE

Service intervals, mi:
   Oil change...............3000
   Filter change............6000
   Chassis lube.............3000
   Tuneup..................9000
Warranty, mo/mi....12/unlimited

GENERAL

Curb weight, lb...........3270
Test weight................3640
Weight distribution (with driver), front/rear, %....61/39
Wheelbase, in.............116.1
Track, front/rear.......60.1/52.2
Overall length............192.6
   Width..................72.3
   Height.................52.1
Ground clearance.....(normal) 6.1
Overhang, front/rear....39.5/37.0
Usable trunk space, cu ft......9.4
Fuel tank capacity, U.S. gal...19.7

CALCULATED DATA

Lb/bhp (test weight)........20.2
Mph/1000 rpm (5th gear)....21.8
Engine revs/mi (60 mph).....2750
Piston travel, ft/mi........1350
R & T steering index........0.69
Brake swept area sq in/ton....210

ROAD TEST RESULTS

ACCELERATION

Time to distance, sec:
   0–100 ft.................4.0
   0–250 ft.................6.5
   0–500 ft.................9.7
   0–750 ft................12.5
   0–1000 ft...............14.9
   0–1320 ft (¼ mi)........17.4
Speed at end of ¼ mi, mph...84.0
Time to speed, sec:
   0–30 mph.................3.4
   0–40 mph.................5.1
   0–50 mph.................6.8
   0–60 mph.................9.3
   0–70 mph................12.0
   0–80 mph................15.5
   0–100 mph...............25.9
Passing exposure time, sec:
   To pass car going 50 mph....6.5

FUEL CONSUMPTION

Normal driving, mpg........15.9
Cruising range, mi.........310

SPEEDS IN GEARS

5th gear (5950 rpm).........135
4th (6500)................115
3rd (6500).................82
2nd (6500).................57
1st (6500).................38

BRAKES

Panic stop from 80 mph:
   Max. deceleration rate, % g...84
   Stopping distance, ft........300
   Control................good
Pedal effort for 50%-g stop, lb..30
Fade test: percent increase in pedal effort to maintain 50%-g deceleration rate in 6 stops from 60 mph..................nil
Parking: Hold 30% grade?.....no
Overall brake rating.....very good

HANDLING

Speed on 100-ft radius, mph..32.9
Lateral acceleration, % g....0.722

SPEEDOMETER ERROR

30 mph indicated is actually..27.0
40 mph....................36.0
60 mph....................55.0
70 mph....................65.0
80 mph....................74.0
90 mph....................83.5
100 mph...................92.0
Odometer, 10.0 mi...........9.8

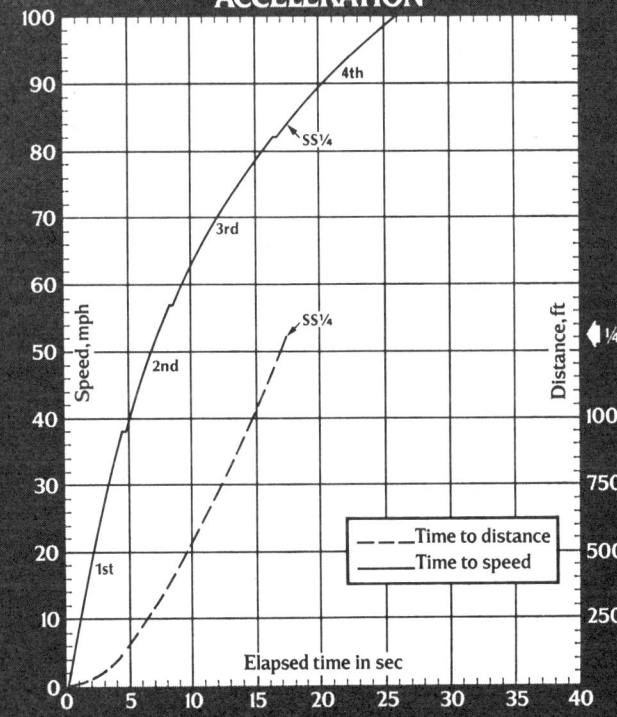

ACCELERATION

Speed, mph (vertical axis); Distance, ft (right axis); Elapsed time in sec (horizontal axis)

- - - Time to distance
——— Time to speed

¼ mi

CITROEN SM

A FINE COMBINATION OF FRENCH COMFORT ß ITALIAN PERFORMANCE

By David B. Lamb. Photos by John Plow

When Detroit decides it's time to introduce a new model, designers along with marketing people sit before a sheet of clean paper and proceed to copy all that's successful in other brands. If it appears stylish compacts are experiencing a tremendous upsurge in sales, then that will be the model Detroit produces. The pattern is often the same; be conservative and always do the expected. This is due in part to an accounting philosophy which dominates the Motor City. A philosophy which dictates greater returns can be realized from small, safe changes than from gambling on innovation. As a consequence, American automobiles tend to be bland and monotonous as each manufacturer markets his particular version of the Master Plan. Often, Detroit will sample the public in an effort to determine what it is they would like to see in an automobile. Since the average guy on the street is far from being an automotive technologist, he usually indicates a refinement of existing designs. The end result is a well-made, straightforward package with sales in the millions.

Citroen, on the other hand, does not rely upon the public to tell them what vehicle they should produce. They turn instead to a staff of contemporary technicians who come up with a package capable of meeting the highest technical demands. As such, Citroen is a company following a different path from its counterparts on this side of the Atlantic. Mind you, sales are less since the average consumer finds the French cars too radical for his taste. But then Citroen never set out to design "average" automobiles.

Take the matter of styling. In Detroit, it is the stylists who command the highest status within the hierarchy. In many cases the external shape of the American automobile takes precedence over the nuts and bolts problems which lie below the pretty skins. At Citroen the opposite is true. In the early stages of the SM's development for example, low drag and aerodynamic efficiency were placed near the top of the list. In effect this implied a functional profile versus styling for styling's sake which dominates the U.S. scene. The resultant shape of the SM is 'different' to say the least.

All surfaces lying 90 degrees to the car's direction of travel have been eliminated. Up front, where the American companies place a massive chrome-plated grill, there's nothing but a gentle sloping hood which extends from a rubber bumper to the base of the steeply raked windshield. Even the lights, which must be positioned upright for maximum illumination, have been modified for the sake of improved aerodynamics. In both the European and Canadian versions, six powerful Cibies are located behind a clear plastic fairing which conforms to the wind-cheating shape of the hood. Below the front bumper, in a belly pan which runs past the mid-way point of the engine, there's a grilled opening for the radiators. The sides are rounded, as are the windows for further drag reduction. The overall body shape is unusual, being wider at the front and tapering by eight inches less at the rear for better air penetration. Where one would

normally expect chrome strips, fake louvers and non-functional scoops, there's nothing but clean uncluttered metal, all of which contributes to a very low drag factor, and a controversial body shape.

The interior of the SM is in complete harmony with the futuristic outer body panels. At the front, two rolled and pleated leather bucket seats sit facing a way-out dash. Nothing is round. Four oval dials dominate the upper facia with an air inlet at the far left. Next is a speedometer, which incidentally has stopping distances marked for each speed on the dial. Accompanying the speedometer is an easy-to-read 8000 rpm tachometer redlined at 6250 rpm. Finally, a multi-purpose warning system sits at the far right, housing numerous color-keyed idiot lights along with universal coding. This oval theme is carried through to the steering wheel which is fully adjustable for height and depth. To the driver's right is a wide console with the chrome-plated five speed shifter protruding from the center. As the console sweeps up and blends into the base of the dash, air inlet and controls break up the smooth surface. At the very top of this area are three aircraft-type gauges for fuel, water temperature and oil pressure. Subjective though it may be, we couldn't help but feel the dash is too gimmicky.

Power for the SM is supplied by a V-6 Maserati engine displacing a modest 163 cubic inches. With the help of three dual-choke Webers, it manages to produce 180 horsepower at 6250 rpm and 171 lb. ft. of torque at 4000 rpm. Regardless of the small engine, the car is capable of a remarkable 140 mph top speed which says a great deal for the effectiveness of the body shape. The powerplant sits well forward in the engine compartment with only the front portion of the valve covers visible when the hood is popped. The remainder is buried beneath the overhanging firewall. Sitting ahead of the Maserati powerplant and hidden for the most part by the hydraulics is the five-speed gearbox. The unusual configuration of this unit is due to Citroen's reliance upon front wheel drive on all their models.

But it is the steering system which is most novel. The ratio is a fast 9.4:1 with a mere two turns from lock to lock. By comparison, the average sedan's steering is usually 20:1 with 4.5 turns lock to lock. At rest, and with such an abbreviated steering ratio, it would be impossible to turn the 195VR70 radials without some form of power assist. This the SM has, but with a number of interesting additions to normal servo assist units. This particular system has complete power assist when the car is stationary; so much so that when the wheel is released the front wheels return to the straight ahead position automatically. For those who prefer to cock their wheels when parking on hills, the system will leave the wheels as positioned, providing the ignition is turned off prior to releasing the steering wheel. Of course once underway, the driver requires feedback through the rim to keep the car from wandering and once again the Citroen hydraulic system accommodates the driver's needs. As the speed increases, so does the steering effort, making the SM feel as if it were on railroad tracks. There's no numbness or play in the wheel as speeds go beyond 70 mph. On the contrary, the car almost steers itself. On paper this might sound fine but in practice it takes a lot of time to get used to. For the first few hundred miles the driver feels neither comfortable nor competent.

The timing of our road evaluation couldn't have been better. A number of U.S. magazines have had the good fortune to test the vehicle before T&T, but every one had been conducted in a warm, dry climate. We, on the other hand, had an opportunity to drive the SM through miles of sloppy snow and cold temperatures. Though the other magazines had raved about the handling and all around performance, none had been able to evaluate the capability of the heater, cold weather starting or the SM's front wheel drive over glare ice.

We took delivery of the SM at Yonge Steeles Motors in Toronto and were given a quick cram course on the operation of the vehicle — such is the nature of this French automobile. After a demonstration of the steering and an explanation of all the gauges, we were left on our own. Entry is a bit awkward as a carpeted sill juts up to seat level, forcing the driver to fall, as it were, into the bucket seat. At first, these felt far too hard, but after a few hours we began to see we were wrong. Seats, it appears, are somewhat like beds, too soft and your back screams for relief. After long hours of driving we never had the slightest back trouble. However we did find starting on a cold morning to be a bit of a pain. One has to jiggle with the manual choke to find the right setting, then with the first turn of the key it usually fires. Unfortunately it won't run smoothly until the engine attains operating temperature. We also had a few beefs about the heating system. Long after the water temperature needle was up, nothing but lukewarm air came from the outlets. After fiddling with the controls for some time, we noticed the scoop on the right side of the hood was filled with a mixture of snow and ice. This was no doubt affecting things since super-cold air was entering the heater. Nevertheless, even after we removed the snow from the inlet, the air was never as hot as it could have been.

Our first trip around the block proved to be quite an adventure. As we turned the first corner, the SM nipped smartly around and proceeded to aim for the sidewalk at an amazing rate. Ever cool, we casually flicked the wheel only to find the car dart back across the center of the road. Needless to say, for the next few blocks we were more than a little gun-shy about the ultra-quick steering. After a while however, you do begin to feel more at home with the steering and start to appreciate the remarkable degree of control and

Rear seats were exact replicas of the fronts . . . a rare thing

Somewhere down there is a Maserati V6 engine, putting out 180 hp. at 6250 rpm.

Uniquely Citroen GT styling was an engineering exercise

Split photo shows the SM's ability to ride high or low, depending on the setting of the level controls.

precision it affords you. Traction in the snow is absolutely incredible. At stoplights for instance we could nail the throttle only to have the SM leap forward while other cars slithered and squealed for a grip on the slick surface. Mind you, if the clutch is dumped, the front end will rise noticeably, unloading the front wheels in the process, and leading to violent wheel hop. This latter phenomenon causes the whole front end to jump and sound as if the car is being driven over bare railroad ties. But it's an extreme condition and one that doesn't occur under normal conditions.

At idle the Maserati V-6 is a quiet engine, barely audible to the passengers. However once the needle starts to sweep across the face of the tach, everything comes alive with a delightful sound. Once it's passed 4000 rpm, the engine sounds almost identical to the Ferrari Dino 246 GT we tested last fall. By the time it reaches the redline, your flesh is covered with goose bumps. On the highway we were astounded by the SM's ability to track. Some of the roads we drove on were absolutely glare ice, yet it didn't affect the car in the least.

job done when you need them. Many times the spray from cars ahead would cascade across the windshield and the wipers would simply smear the mess even more. Also they seem to be designed for right hand drive which leaves a nasty space at the left of the windshield, blocking a good portion of the road in left hand turns. Even the washers don't help much as they are also aimed to the right side of the glass. Your passenger might appreciate it, but it's not sufficient for the driver, if you're travelling at the speeds the SM is capable of maintaining.

With many cars, BMW's for example, you feel at home immediately. Within a few miles some innate knowledge tells you just how far you can push the machine through corners. But with the Citroen it's just the opposite. At first there are so many things to adapt to, the entire experience can be disconcerting. However the longer you live with the car the more you come to like it. It might never be a big seller in Detroit terms, but it will certainly be classed as a high water mark in automotive technology.

When an SM passes you on the highway, there's no way you can confuse it with anything else

It got so we were pushing the car as hard as we could, simply to find the limits. But the faster the car travels the more steady it feels. During the first few hours we did feel stiff tugs coming back through the rim, which we later realized were signs of our overworking the system. Though the car performed flawlessly on the straights, we did run into a few problems through turns. We should hasten to add that we haven't had extensive experience in large front-wheel-drive machines, so it could well be a reflection of our driving and not the car's fault. Nevertheless, during the snowy periods, we found the SM constantly pushing to the outside of the corners. Being front wheel drive, more gas simply makes it understeer to the apex just that much quicker. As a result, we found cornering a frustrating experience, calling for a gentle touch with slight applications of the throttle. Mind you, through dry corners (what few we found) the car could be driven at very high speeds with not the slightest complaint from suspension or tires.

After driving for some time in miserable, wet, slushy conditions, we noticed that we weren't getting good illumination of the road ahead. When we pulled over to the side we discovered a great mass of frozen slush piled in front of the lights. Apparently, the bumper which projects beyond the plastic fairing was acting as a convenient ledge for the brown mess. With the lights recessed so far behind the plastic shield, the heat from the Cibies couldn't penetrate to melt the opaque-covering.

Another design feature that will have to be altered for Canadian driving conditions is the wiper system. Though they're equipped with airfoils for speeds in excess of 100 mph, they just don't get the

Trunk is on the minimal side; extra baggage goes in rear seat

Peter Robinson reaches for superlatives after a day in . . .

CITROEN'S super machine

From France's greatest technological genius comes a weird device so dedicated to the advancement of the car as an art form it shatters all previous concepts and ends up being a marvellous car into the bargain.

WHEN YOU ARE confronted by a car which is totally different, totally new and stunningly original it is very easy to become carried away and indulge in a technical essay which for all its big words and endless specification—only half of which the writer probably understands—fails dismally to describe the feeling and character of the car concerned. Such was my problem with the incredible Citroen SM. Revolutionary in the true sense of the word, complex, sophisticated and completely captivating, the SM represents a realm of motoring beyond the imagination.
It is a "cloud nine" car that is probably *the* motoring experience of the '70s. Certainly it makes a mockery of standards we have, until now, accepted as being the ultimate.

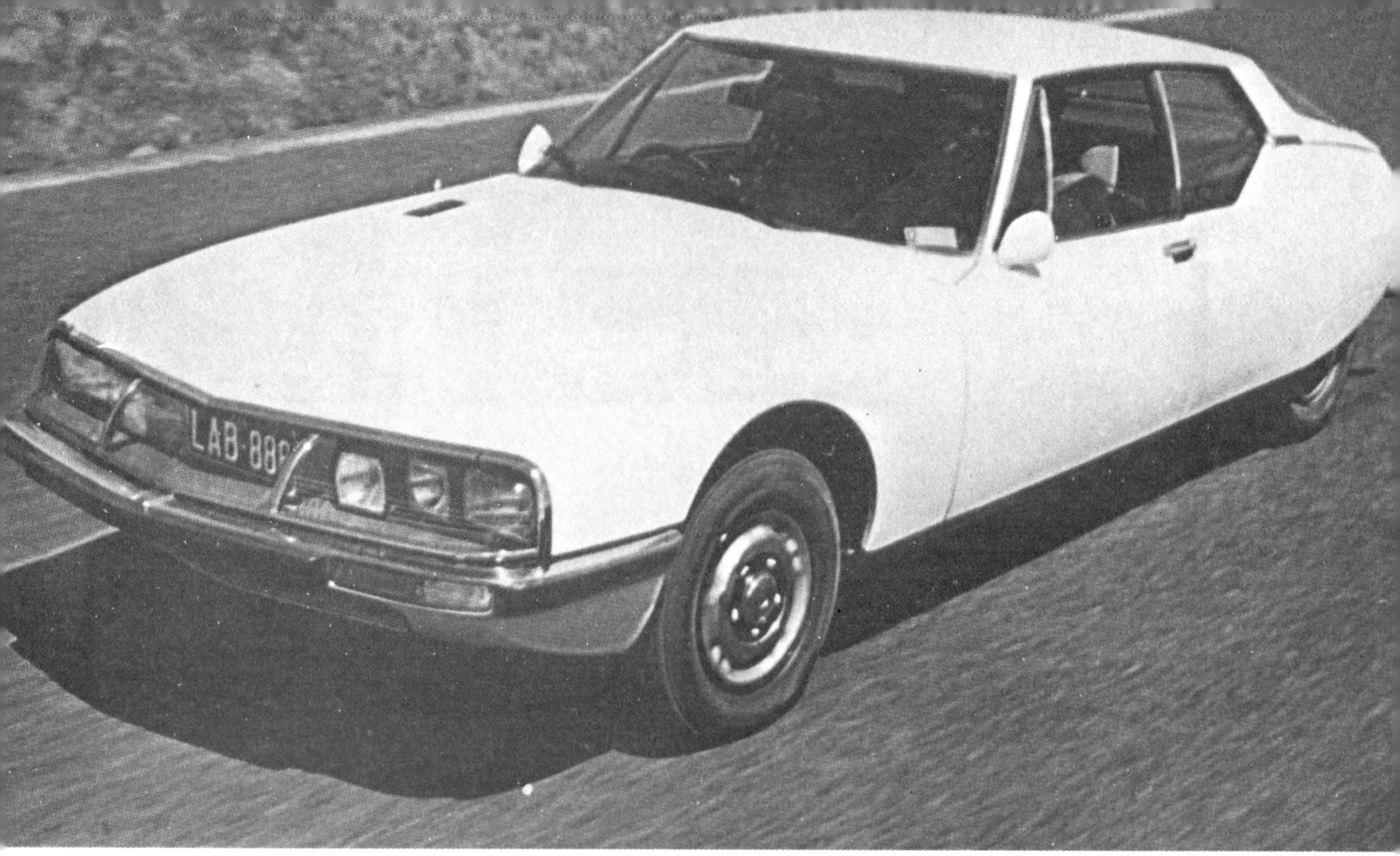

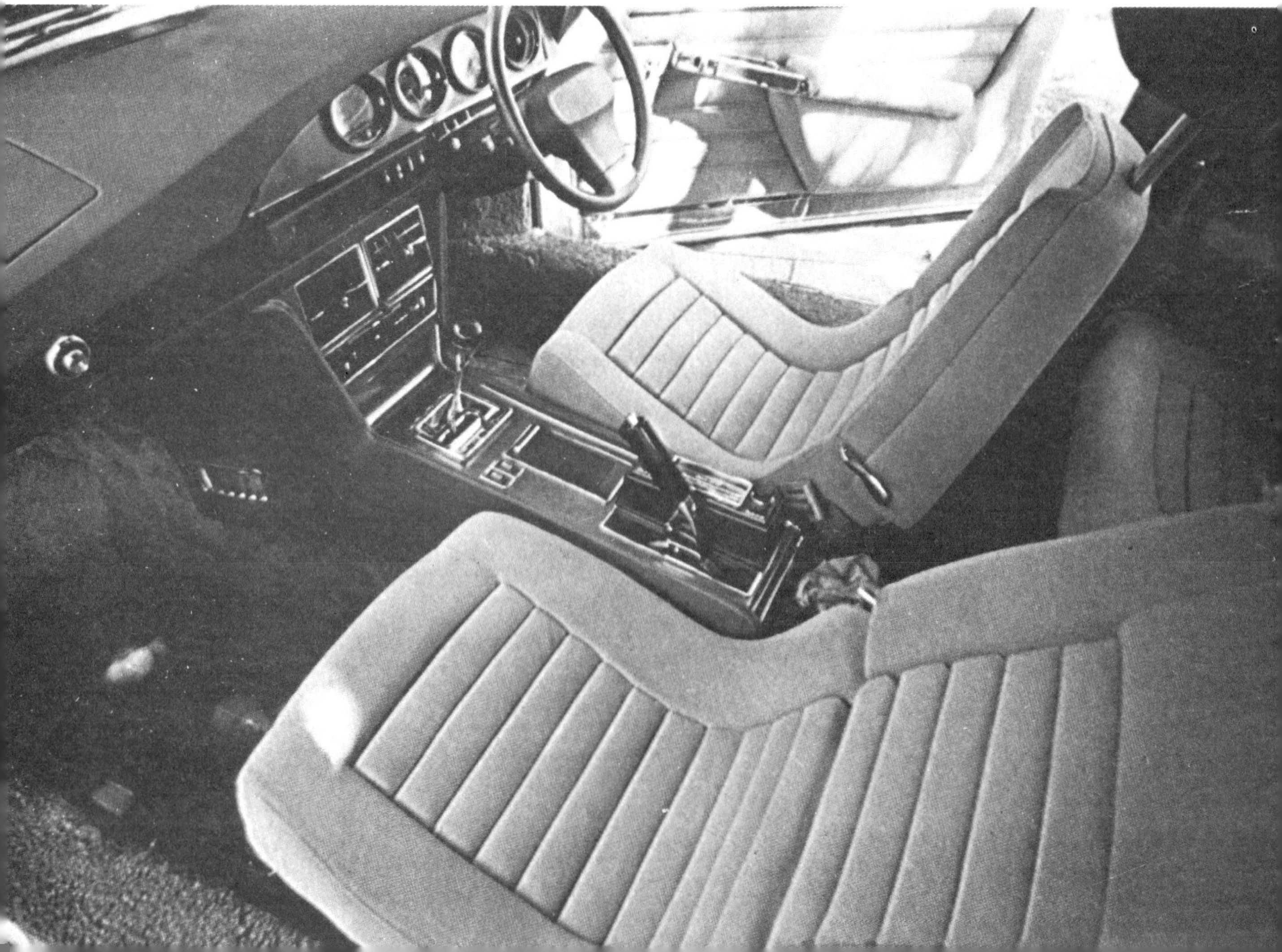

It confirms the sheer brilliance of the Citroen design team — the same people who in one year released the SM and the little GS sedan at opposite ends of the price spectrum.

If you come from a conventional car — meaning everything else — the SM almost requires the driver to take out a new licence but then all Citroens have been like that, one way or another. After a few minutes at the wheel the car moves in around you and inspires the utmost confidence and security.

Perhaps best of all the SM provides the driver with the precision and excitement of a Porsche or Dino while the passengers enjoy a genuine and completely comfortable and luxurious four-seater unaware of the pleasure the driver is extracting and the speed at which the car is travelling. It is this hitherto impossible combination of ideals that makes this Citroen a hallmark in the history of the car.

Below Left
Extravagant yet superbly comfortable and tasteful interior is highlighted by incredible seats. Squab adjustment starts six inches up the curved cushion.

Below
Beneath that confusion of plumbing lies a compact Maserati V6 engine located well back against the fire-wall.

CITROEN'S super machine

So much for creating the impression of greatness, now comes the justification.

Our SM, at the time the only one on the road in Australia although by now another will have been converted by Chapel Engineering in Victoria, belongs to a Melbourne man who ordered it in Paris after seeing one at the show in 1970. A painstaking and superbly executed conversion took four months and helps justify the car's price tag of $19,500. And now it is for sale because his wife finds it hard to drive around town.

We collected the car one Friday morning and spent the day driving the SM with a feeling of wonder which has still not faded away. Normally casually blase about high performance cars I shared with Mel Nichols an instant enthusiasm for the SM which grew with every mile.

Incredibly the SM lives in a garage with a Ford Thunderbird and Buick —

how it puts up with them is hard to imagine.

Driving down one of Toorak's quiet streets we spied the SM hiding behind a Holden and quickly agreed it looks far better in the flesh than pictures. It is a long, sleek and even beautiful from some angles — only the clumsy handling of the tail lights and the C-pillar seen from a three-quarters rear view gives the car a slightly heavy touch.

Vastly more important is the honesty and efficiency of the shape which so suit the character of the car. A shape so smooth it simply slips through the air, the SM tapers off towards a point at the tail for aerodynamic perfection. Like other Citroens it is neither in nor out of fashion but a piece of originality that stands on its own merits. Again it is the skill of combining the exotica with the practical which makes this car unique.

It is an oversimplification to say the SM is a development of the DS with a

Far Below
Visibility is one of SM's many plus safety features, with excellent brakes, roadholding and steering ensures it of high primary safety rating.

Below
Rear seats are just as comfortable as those in the front but lack adjustable headrests. It is a genuine four seater.

Maserati V6 engine and a new two-door body. The SM takes the concept of a high performance touring machine and tunes it to the nth degree making complete use of the advanced engineering which Citroen has used for almost 40 years. Together with this are a number of new features which on their own are unique but which are so superbly blended to complement each other that it is hard to imagine the SM any other way.

The Maserati engine is a compact, twin cam per bank, V6 of 90 degrees with the hard feel typical of many high performance Italian engines and emphasised in the SM because all other vibration and noise is so well masked. Response to the throttle is instantaneous from 3500 rpm, below that there is a hesitation revealing a lack of low speed torque. Not really surprising when you discover the engine is only of 2.7 litres capacity and producing 182 bhp at 6250 rpm and 172 lb/ft of torque at 4000 rpm.

At 3200 lbs weight the SM is obviously not going to be a super car with Phase III HO performance but all the same it is a very brisk mover and fully capable of using all its power in circumstances when other quick cars are virtually lifting off or even braking.

A standing quarter mile of 17.0 seconds is not especially quick but the SM is just gathering strength for it rushes on to 100 mph in only 24.4 seconds, 60 mph coming up in 9.5 seconds and overall fuel consumption is unlikely to drop below 20 mpg unless you continually thrash the car.

But it is the SM's supreme ability as a touring machine which overshadows the figures themselves. I still find it hard to believe but 120 mph cruising speeds are so absurdly quiet and comfortable they can be achieved without the passenger being aware of any sudden increase in noise level from half that speed. Conversations can be carried on in normal tones and although acceleration does drop off above 110 mph the SM will go on to achieve a top speed on the high side of 130 mph and from just 182 bhp that is rare indeed.

But even before you can get to these speeds you have to go through an acclimatisation course with the steering and, for that matter, the layout of the interior.

Wide opening doors reveal an interior of sumptuous luxury with a warmth achieved though the use of brushed nylon upholstery on the seats and doors and plush, deep carpeting almost everywhere else. From behind the small, oval, padded wheel with one thick, stylised spoke the car reinforces the atmosphere of mystery created by its appearance.

A drooping, almost sculptured dashboard with oval instruments is sunk beneath the long sweeping facia top with, over towards the centre, small subsidiary gauges and fits the jet-age image of the car. The information system includes an aircraft style illuminated warning set-up with a large central stop light and a series of telltale lights around its circumference. Then there is a console which flows down the centre of the car and holds the air-conditioning controls, gearlever and ashtrays among others.

Initially the seats feel too hard but apart from a slight lack of lateral support they are very close to being perfect with an incredible range of adjustment. This, together with a steering wheel which moves in and out

CITROEN'S super machine

and up and down with a single lever, makes finding a comfortable driving position simple.

The rear seats are exactly the same except they are non-adjustable and miss out on the headrests (these are soft and fully adjustable to suit all sizes). Although there appears to be a lack of knee and leg room in the rear the seats are so well padded I was quite content to ride as a back seat passenger for almost 100 miles and that alone makes the SM almost unique among modern cars.

The sophistication and refinement of the interior are complemented by a ride comfort close to that achieved with the S series sedans but with tighter, more precise handling.

And that brings us to the steering. Power assisted rack and pinion with an incredible 9.4 to 1 overall ratio for just two turns lock to lock it needs just over 34 feet to turn a full circle. It is so light and so quick most drivers will need a period of adjustment — a slight twitch is enough to cause a lane change. As speeds rise you can feel the tension in the steering increase so that there is more resistance to change the higher the speed. It is all artificially induced, of course. As if that is not enough the steering has a self-centring system that returns the wheels to the straight ahead when you let go of the wheel — *even at a standstill.*

In normal driving the steering wheel needs to be turned just an inch or so to move out and around another car and just a quarter of a turn for a right angle bend so it is incredibly sensitive and remarkable for its feel and precision.

The only problem is in acclimatising yourself to the point where you won't apply too much lock in either direction on wet roads, in the case of a slide, and that is something I'm not sure I'd trust myself to avoid. And the natural instinct to swerve violently in the face of a dangerous situation could obviously cause problems. But if you can develop your driving to avoid these — and that would probably not be too difficult as long as you didn't drive other cars — we have nothing but praise for the Citroen's steering.

The car runs straight at high speeds with a stability and unobtrusiveness that is remarkable.

And so it goes. The SM has front wheel drive, of course, but you'd never know from the quality of the gear change. First and second gear ratios are rather close — for a quick take-off — with a gap to third and fourth and fifth — both overdrives — ideal. A smooth and short change through a normal Alfa/Lambo pattern adds considerably to the driving pleasure and forms an almost sensuous relationship with the engine. It has that unique Italian aggressiveness which has the driver changing gears when it is far from necessary.

Fifth can be used around town but the engine is happier in fourth or third and these seem to be the gears most used in normal Australian driving. In Europe on the major roads and motorways the SM's long legs and truly superb suspension allow 110 mph cruising with only 5000 rpm on the tacho.

If you get tired of that you can return to secondary roads and enjoy the responsive handling of a thoroughbred in which normal understeer and oversteer just don't exist, partly because of the steering but also because of the hydraulic suspension and excellent Michelin XVR tyres which allow the car to reach such high "G" forces.

Braking is completely fade-free through the strange Citroen sponge which serves as a pedal and that requires a sensitive touch for progressive stopping. It has that wonderful feeling of just tearing out the road as it drags the car to a stop as quickly as is technically possible.

There is much more — the turning headlights, automatic height control, adjustable ground clearance, electric windows, finger-tip controls, superb finish, big and entirely usable boot, wonderful visibility even in the back and the absolutely complete equipment of the cockpit.

More important is the way the car insulates the occupants from the sounds and feel of the outside world and promotes a feeling of security I've never experienced in any other car.

The in-built safety, the originality, the absorption of road irregularities, the technical brilliance of this design leave you so enthused and so in awe of the talent it displays you find it hard to associate it with other cars. It also makes you feel rather sad at local engineering concepts. By Citroen standards they are primitive and ancient — and who is going to say Citroen is wrong and they are right?

I count myself lucky to have spent one day driving and riding in the truly fabulous Citroen SM.

Above
Oval theme is continued from steering wheel through to instruments and even eye-ball vent. Driving position can be perfect for everybody with vast seat and steering wheel adjustment.

Far Left
Sensational style matches staggering roadholding of SM. Quick steering means the wheel is turned in impulses rather than vast movements of the arms.

• What if Citroën is right? What if the SM really *is* the world's most advanced car? What if it is a prototype for every other manufacturer to follow. Will anyone really be able to tell? Because even if it is all of that, and more, it is undeniably a mystery ship.

And in order to even begin to understand it, you are forced to first realize your own prejudices about automobiles: how they should look, how they should feel, perhaps even what they should do.

And there is no subtlety in the way the SM makes that demand. Even if you think you've been sufficiently preconditioned by a decade of Citroën DS and ID styling, the SM's styling is unexpected. In fact, it probably would have been better to spend a few years with Arthur C. Clark and Stanley Kubrick to prepare you for the SM's lines.

At that, you still might not be ready for driving the SM, especially when you find that just a tiny twist of the one-spoke steering wheel will send the whole car into a banking attitude not unlike a Boeing entering its final approach pattern. The list goes on. Every response is new . . . even alien. And it's intimidating, *very* intimidating—so much so that new drivers

Citroën SM

It's unique, no doubt. But more important, it is a highly successful approach to over-the-road transportation.

should have an hour of pre-flight training in a simulator, because the first 100 miles are tense. The steering seems over quick; the brakes overly sensitive, and the body wallows. All you are really confident about is that nothing on the SM acts like a normal car. Your mind worries about the unexpected. What would you do in an emergency? Grab an armful of steering and put yourself into the wall? Or lock up the brakes and skid off helplessly into the surroundings? It's too awful to contemplate, yet your mind can't ignore it.

Then, after 100 miles of edging over every divider line and cringing at thoughts of what might have been, you begin to understand. Don't struggle with the steering wheel, light-finger it . . . just brush the brake button with your toe . . . *Trust*

the SM; don't overwhelm it by trying to make it do what *you* think a car should do, because the SM is happiest with as little help from the driver as possible. The steering centers itself. Directional stability is fantastic. Don't worry about it. And when you stop worrying, you can start to appreciate what the SM really is. You notice how comfortable you are, that you can sit behind the wheel for hours without going numb. That the suspension glides over pock-marked roads. That you ride so securely at 90 that you have plenty of attention left over to scan to the rear in search of cops. Of course, all this is subjective—some people will be more or less comfortable, or secure than others. But there are factors, like gas mileage, which are absolutes—impressive absolutes that cannot be denied. For instance, you can cruise at 80 mph and roll out 20 miles to each gallon. And at the same time have *better* acceleration than any of the new de-smogged luxury sedans from the popular factories. It's incredible. You begin to wonder . . . well . . . what if Citroën is right? And maybe Detroit, maybe *everyone* else, is wrong. Wrong about needing large displacement engines. Wrong about sharply-creased Art Center School fenders. Wrong about 6-way power seats that go from barely tolerable to agonizing. Wrong about short-travel suspension and weighty anti-sway bars—as wrong as Studebaker or Edsel—and yet somehow allowed to continue and prosper because they are in the majority while Citroën is a universe unto itself. Although a lot has been written about the car, no one knows much about the *real* car. We have the first smog-certified, fully U.S. street-legal Citroën SM in this country.

The SM is the kind of car a coven of out-of-work NASA engineers might design as a theoretical exercise. It's complex, extravagantly so in its powertrain and suspension, similar to everyday cars only in that it travels on four wheels. The basic laws of physics have figured prominently in its design. Isaac Newton understood the behavior of mass: that the more you have, the more force it takes to get it moving . . . and the harder it is to stop . . . and turn. Citroën engineers understand equally well. Consequently, the SM weighs 3310 pounds. And that includes a full tank of fuel, power steering, power brakes and air conditioning. The low weight means you can have good performance and fuel economy with a small engine. It is also easy on tires and brakes.

Small engines perform even better if they don't have to labor against air damming aerodynamics. Citroën has long been a believer in this axiom. And the SM clearly benefits. Its top speed over 130 mph and exceptional fuel economy are the obvious results.

As the underlying physical principles are simple, the Citroën's mechanical innards are complex. One look under the hood will be more than enough to send flat-rate mechanics into the washing machine repair business. As all of the big Citroëns, the SM employs front-wheel-drive. The engine is turned around backwards and located entirely behind the front trans-axle—in essence becoming nearly a mid-engine layout. That is the simple part. It starts getting complicated when you discover that there are two power output shafts. The transmission drives off the crank in the normal way, but all of the accessories are fed by a long shaft running forward from between the banks where the camshaft would be on a normal Detroit Vee engine.

Of course, the Citroën SM could hardly be expected to have a normal engine. And it doesn't. This one comes from Maserati, a company that merged with Citroën in hopes of brightening its financial picture. Besides bringing with it an exclusive name, there are several other predictable features

PHOTOGRAPHY: DOUG MESNEY

of any Maserati engine: It will have two overhead camshafts, hemi heads, a 2-bbl. Weber carburetor for each pair of cylinders, and both the block and heads will be cast from aluminum. In these areas, the Citroën's powerplant lives up to its heritage. You could not, however, predict that it would be a V-6. But never mind that. All of the Citroën representatives love it. It says Maserati right on top of the air cleaner—which is something they've never been able to point to before. They've already learned that such an escutcheon brings with it an ability to blot the sneer off the lips of skeptics. And they like to boast about the engine's compact dimensions, particularly about how short it is. "The heads are only twelve-and-a-quarter inches long," they throw out . . . and pause to let that fact sink in. Which is commendable for a package containing 163 cu. in., but it results from a monumental compromise in engine design, easily the most significant technical shortcoming in the whole car. To make a V-6 that short, there can only be room enough for three crankshaft throws—like three-quarters of a V-8—which means that, to be in balance, there has to be 90° between the banks. When that is the case, it follows that the firing order becomes uneven—the sequence alternates between 90° and 150° of crankshaft rotation. So the engine is rough. The exhaust sounds funny, and the engine feels spastic when under load at low speeds. It's made all the more noticeable by the phantom-like smoothness of the SM's other systems. A 2-inch longer engine would be a far happier, if less unique, solution.

While the Maserati engine flies brave and proud in the face of conventional engineering practice, it's nothing compared to Citroën's own suspension. Its basic layout is remarkable for

two reasons; there is no camber change as the wheels move through the entire range of their travel, and there are no rubber pivot bushings. Let's start with the geometry. In front, the linkage is made up of two equal-length control arms pivoting on sealed bearings. So the track-width changes slightly with wheel travel but not camber. The linkage is also designed for "center-point" steering, which means that a line drawn through the two ball joints of each wheel intersects the ground at the center of the tire's contact patch. The general idea is to cancel out front-wheel-drive effects in the steering—and it works. Absolutely nothing comes through the steering wheel. This design also requires that the front brakes be inboard if they are going to be of a useful size—or else the wheels must be offset toward the inside like those of a Toronado. Citroën chose inboard discs.

At the rear, the suspension is a very simple independent arrangement with a single trailing arm for each wheel. Its unique contribution to the SM's behavior is that it causes the rear to squat under braking. And since there is no anti-dive in front, under hard braking the car comes down nearly level, lowering its center of gravity and thereby reducing the normal weight transfer to the front.

So far, all of this suspension discussion has been directed toward geometry—the suspension medium itself is no less unique. It is a gas/hydraulic arrangement that provides varying rates, and automatic leveling regardless of the load. Hydraulic pressure is generated courtesy of an engine-driven pump, and its flow to the suspension unit at each of the four corners of the car is modulated by height-sensing valves. If

(Text continued on page 60, Specifications on page 61)

the car drops too low, more fluid is pumped to the required units to bring the car back to its proper ride level. The springing actually is accomplished by compressing a chamber of gas trapped in a dome above the oil. The height adjuster can also be operated with a lever just to the left of the driver's seat. With a flip of the wrist, you can have either a Southern California "low rider" or a high-clearance Baja special.

The SM's final piece of chassis trickery is the steering. It's a very quick (two turns lock-to-lock) rack-and-pinion that is not only power-assisted to help you turn, but after you've finished turning, it powers itself back straight ahead again. And since it seeks a true straight-ahead position, it makes for convenient cruising on interstate highways. So strong is its instinct that it even straightens out after you've parked and turned off the engine. The only way to curb the wheels, as is required on San Francisco hills, for example, is to hold the position with the steering column lock.

You might think this would be about enough wonderment for any one steering gear. Just remember that this is a Citroën that we're talking about . . . and prepare yourself. The steering effort also grows progressively higher as speed increases. The idea is to provide very quick steering that is not twitchy at high speeds. It works. The problem is that it's twitchy at low speeds before the effort gets stiff. This is not so much because the effort is low as that there is near-zero "feel." The SM is a car that you steer by position of the steering wheel, not by any sort of pressure feedback. Most power steering is the same way, but others provoke less path error because the ratio is slower. With the SM, there is also a problem of not generating enough assistance at very low engine speeds.—like when you park it.

All of this imaginative machinery is encased in a body just slightly larger than that of a Firebird. And like the Firebird, the SM is a 4-passenger car—although its rear seating space is more useful. But it's the two front seat occupants who get the first class accommodations. Their two buckets are firm, far more so than you'd expect in a French luxury car, and they not only slide back and forth, but also up and down, and tilt. The seat backs also partially recline—but from a hinge point located about halfway up the back. So that every driver can get comfortable, no matter how odd his dimensions, the steering column has an exceptional range of angle and length adjustment. Added to this is the ventilation system—the best of our experience. Air conditioned or fresh air (your choice) can be admitted through three vents, one on each side of the dash and one in the console. All these vents can be individually adjusted for flow rate and direction. The result is as much air as you want wherever you want it.

Like most of its internal machinery, the SM's low speed behavior is unorthodox. Under acceleration, the rear squats and the nose rises an extraordinary amount. Then, as you shift, the nose momentarily falls and the car pitches like a rocking horse. The motions are gentle enough that the driver forgets about them after his break-in, but they are sufficiently conspicuous for observers on the outside to comment upon it. At low speeds, small bump harshness comes through from the super-high speed Michelins; and on textured roads, road noise is high, particularly in the rear seat—but above 30 mph the SM glides effortlessly over every kind of road. Wheel travel is long enough that the suspension never bottoms out, and the independent arrangement on each wheel, along with low unsprung mass, keeps the wheels in contact with the ground no matter how rough the surface. And since there is very little roll stiffness, the body doesn't rock from side to side even when the road does. For rough road travel or stable high speed cruising, the SM has absolutely no competition.

After you've completed the 100-mile driver break-in period, the SM is enormously satisfying. The engine is eager to rev, although it does sound rather agricultural below 4500 rpm. The 5-speed shifter is light and very accurate, with none of the linkage vagueness that traditionally accompanies remote transmission layouts.

It's unlikely that you can forget about the suspension's self-adjustment for height, however, because the SM issues a stream of unsubtle reminders even when you're not driving it. After you shut off the ignition and step outside, just about the time you're fitting the key into the door lock, the car gives a sigh, like a mechanical camel, and sinks down to its knees. It turns out that the system is designed with a built-in time delay, and it takes that long to lower itself back down after the driver's weight is removed. As the pressure leaks down out of the hydraulic system—it takes several hours after the engine is stopped—the SM drops still lower. If you leave it overnight, you'll find it snuggled down against its jounce bumpers, at least four inches lower than when you left it. Within 20 seconds after you start the engine, it rises again, ready for another day.

It's this sort of behavior, in addition to its exceptional performance, that forceably separates the SM from all other automobiles. It's unique, no doubt. But more important, it is a *highly successful* approach to over-the-road transportation, and we think fairly priced at just under $12,000. Nowhere will you find more for less.   •

ACCELERATION standing ¼ mile, seconds

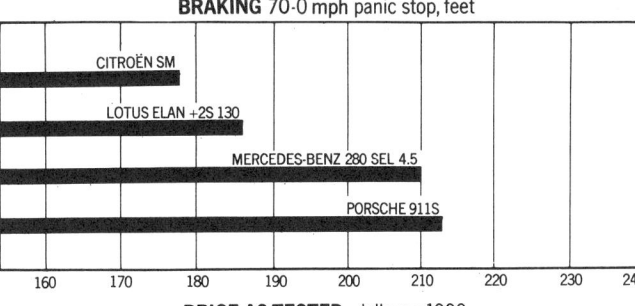

CITROËN SM
LOTUS ELAN +2S 130
MERCEDES-BENZ 280 SEL 4.5
PORSCHE 911S

13 14 15 16 17 18 19 20

BRAKING 70-0 mph panic stop, feet

CITROËN SM
LOTUS ELAN +2S 130
MERCEDES-BENZ 280 SEL 4.5
PORSCHE 911S

160 170 180 190 200 210 220 230 240

FUEL ECONOMY RANGE mpg

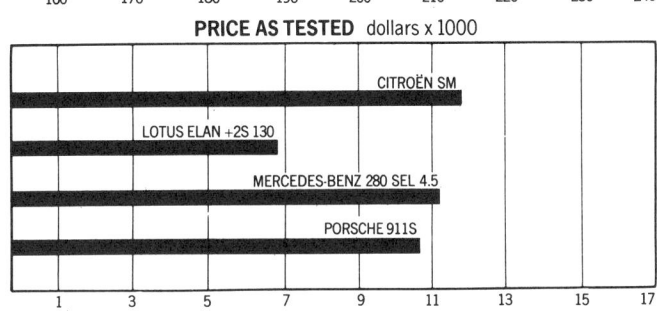

CITROËN SM
LOTUS ELAN +2S 130
MERCEDES-BENZ 280 SEL 4.5
PORSCHE 911S

6 10 14 18 22 26 30 34

PRICE AS TESTED dollars x 1000

CITROËN SM
LOTUS ELAN +2S 130
MERCEDES-BENZ 280 SEL 4.5
PORSCHE 911S

1 3 5 7 9 11 13 15 17

CITROËN SM

Importer: Citroën Cars Corporation
40 Van Nostrand Avenue
Englewood, N.J. 07631

Vehicle type: Front engine, front-wheel-drive, 4-passenger coupe

Price as tested: $11,968
(Manufacturer's suggested retail price, including all options listed below, dealer preparation and delivery charges, does not include state and local taxes, license or freight charges)

Options on test car: Base Citroën SM, $11,805; SM molding, $63; Dealer handling, $100.

ENGINE
Type: V-6, water-cooled, aluminum block and heads, 4 main bearings
Bore x stroke . . . . .3.32 x 2.95 in, 84.3 x 75.0mm
Displacement. . . . . .163 cu in, 2670cc
Compression ratio . . . . .9.0 to one
Carburetion . . . . .3x2-bbl Weber
Valve gear . . . . .Chain-driven double overhead cams
Power (SAE net) . . . . .170 bhp @ 5500 rpm
Torque (SAE net) . . . . .170 lbs-ft @ 4000 rpm
Specific power output . . . . . . .1.04 bhp/cu in, 63.7 bhp/liter
Max recommended engine speed . . . . .6500 rpm

DRIVE TRAIN
Transmission . . . . .5-speed, all-synchro
Final drive ratio . . . . .4.38 to one

Gear	Ratio	Mph/1000 rpm	Max.test speed
I	2.93	5.9	38 mph (6500 rpm)
II	1.94	8.9	58 mph (6500 rpm)
III	1.32	13.0	84 mph (6500 rpm)
IV	0.97	17.7	115 mph (6500 rpm)
V	0.76	22.6	115 mph (5100 rpm)

DIMENSIONS AND CAPACITIES
Wheelbase . . . . .116.1 in
Track, F/R . . . . .60.1/52.2 in
Length . . . . .192.6 in
Width . . . . .75.0 in
Height . . . . .52.1 in
Ground clearance . . . . .6.1 in (minimum)
Curb weight. . . . . .3310 lbs
Weight distribution, F/R 61.8/38.2%
Battery capacity . . . . .12 volts, 70 amp-hr
Alternator capacity . . . . .780 watts
Fuel capacity . . . . .24.0 gal
Oil capacity . . . . .7.4 qts
Water capacity . . . . .14.0 qts

SUSPENSION
F: Ind, equal-length control arms, hydropneumatic springs, anti-sway bar
R: Ind, trailing arms, hydropneumatic springs, anti-sway bar

STEERING
Type . . . . .Rack and pinion, power assist
Turns lock-to-lock 2.0
Turning circle curb-to-curb . . . . .34.5 ft

BRAKES
F: . . . . .11.8-in disc, power assisted
R: . . . . .10.0-in disc, power assisted

WHEELS AND TIRES
Wheel size . . . . .15 x 6.0-in
Wheel type . . . . .Stamped steel, 5 bolt
Tire make and size . . . . .Michelin XVR 195/70 VR-15
Tire type . . . . .Radial, tubeless
Test inflation pressures, F/R . . . . .31.3/28.5 psi
Tire load rating . . . . .1410 lbs per tire @ 36 psi

PERFORMANCE
Zero to	Seconds
30 mph	3.1
40 mph	5.0
50 mph	7.0
60 mph	9.4
70 mph	12.4
80 mph	16.7
90 mph	21.8
100 mph	28.2

Standing ¼-mile . . . . .17.1 sec @ 81.3 mph
Top speed (estimated) . . . . .135 mph
70-0 mph .178 ft (0.92G)
Fuel mileage . . . . .16-22 mpg on premium fuel
Cruising range . . . . .385-530 mi

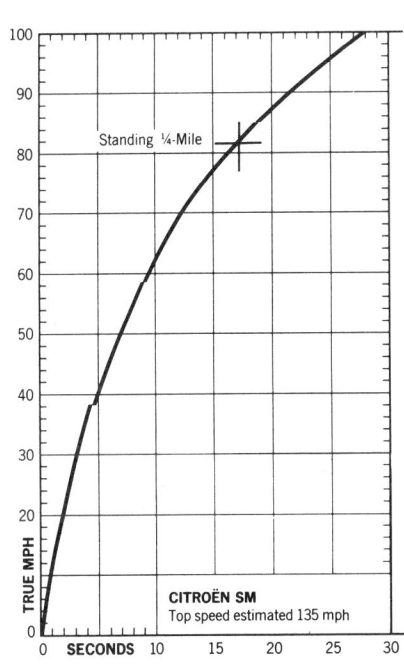

CITROËN SM
Top speed estimated 135 mph

Standing ¼-Mile

TRUE MPH

SECONDS

1972, 2·7 litre Citroen SM

THE CITROEN SM

The best of two worlds

ADVANCED.—The Citroen SM with FWD, hydropneumatic suspension, variable power steering, inboard front brakes, V6 Maserati engine, and 5-speed gearbox. Of the six headlamps the inner pair turn with the steering, and the perspex cover over the lamps and number-plate presents an unbroken nose-line to the wind.

THE PEOPLE behind the design and construction of Citroën cars are seldom, if ever, referred to by name, and in their own publicity material Citroën refer to "engineers in Citroën's research division". Little is heard about the research and development department of Citroën cars, and even less about the design department. The whole firm must be chock-ablock with brilliant designers and engineers, for Citroën cars have stood out on their own in the world of automobile design for as long as one can remember. You either believe in Citroën engineering or you are content with the standards of Dagenham, Luton or Detroit. If you believe in Citroën you will have accepted the "Traction Avant" in the mid-thirties, the DS series in the mid-fifties and you will certainly believe in the SM, which is surely going to carry Citroën through to the mid-eighties. When the DS appeared in 1955 there were those who detested its looks, were nervous about its road-ability, frightened of its apparent complication and refused to adapt their conventional driving style to the new-style demanded by the DS. These people shied away from the new Citroën and kept other, more mundane car manufacturers in business. Those who believed in Citroën approached the DS with an open mind, like I did at the time, and were truly staggered by what they discovered. Here was a car that was way ahead of all its competitors in the saloon car category and had remarkable powers of cornering, ride and average speed when driven enthusiastically. It was a triumph of production engineering, apart from a triumph of design, and some years later when testing another make of large front-wheel-drive family saloon I began to enthuse about it with the Editor when we stopped short and realised we had said it all in 1955, nearly ten years before, and all this new model was doing was catching up to where Citroën had started.

Not being a "family motorist" I never had any desire to own a DS Citroën, but always appreciated those who did, in all countries throughout Europe, and enjoyed many happy "dices" with enthusiastically driven ones in France or Italy. Over the years, when talking about cars and car design the DS Citroën would invariably crop up and we would try to visualize what Citroëns' replacement would be. Even in 1965, ten years after the introduction of the DS, we could not see any signs of what the next Citroën was going to be like, but having faith in Citroën engineering we were sure it was not only going to be exceptional, but as far in advance on engineering as the "Traction Avant" was and the DS was. As the decade of the seventies began the Citroën SM appeared and to Citroën believers it was no disappointment. An inkling had been given by the fact that Citroën had bought the firm of Maserati at the beginning of 1968, and though a certain amount of noise had been made about Wankel engine research, Maserati enthusiasts in Modena could be heard muttering about "French engineers crawling about all over the place" and some hardened Maserati workers left the firm as they could not stand the pressures being exerted by the French engineers. The Citroën for the seventies was powered by a Maserati engine which put the French firm in the high-performance category for the first time, for until then engines were not the most exciting thing about Citroën cars.

For the past two years I have been wandering about Europe "drooling" over the SM Citroën, at first only catching the odd glimpse of one now and then, and later as production got under way I was able to get closer to them. I can recall the first time I saw one parked by the roadside; I stopped and went back to enjoy being in the presence of such a beautiful looking piece of machinery. It was only recently that I was able to fulfil a great desire to drive one, and the two years of waiting have been more than worthwhile. In Great Britain Maserati cars are handled by Citroën at Slough, not far from London Airport, and last year I went there to borrow a Maserati Indy and the poor man who was lending me the car had an awful job getting me into the Indy, for on the other side of the garage was a Citroën SM. I just felt that one car was the end of an era and the other the beginning of a new era, and I had no regrets for the passing of the old and could not wait to experience the new.

Even in the exotic automobile surroundings of Monte Carlo and Nice the Citroën was beginning to make everything else look obsolete or peculiar and when I saw one among Lamborghinis and Ferraris I had to tell myself that it was not a one-off "dream car" or small production model, like the Italian cars, but was in mass-production. Last year, in a Letter from Europe, I mentioned how I had a little dust-up at 125 m.p.h. in my E-type Jaguar with a Citroën SM on a French Autoroute, and how it impressed me; that was the first time, and there have been others since. This year Mike Hailwood has been using a Citroën SM for motoring about Europe, he being one of the rare breed of Grand Prix drivers, like Niki Lauda and Ickx, who enjoy motoring for its own sake. The fact that Hailwood was still using his SM at the end of the season spoke volumes for the car, for he is not one to tolerate something he does not like and can afford to have any car he wants. The aura of the Citroën SM was growing all around me and when Citroën finally let us have one on loan for two weeks I could hardly wait to get in it. In spite of the glowing things that knowledgable colleagues said of it, I was fully prepared to be bitterly disappointed, especially when other people said how they did not like it. To say that the SM lived up to all my expectations, and more, is to understate the case. It rates at the very top of my list of desirable cars, even above the Dino Ferrari, which I rated as the ultimate in sports cars. The SM is even more than that, it is the ultimate in serious motoring, and by that I do not mean a dash up the road and back, or making a high average from A to B, or extracting the maximum enjoyment from driving. It is all of those things, but above all a car to live with, day in and day out, a car to use all day and everyday, under every type of going, fast or slow, but essentially for motoring with a capital M.

Having rated the SM that high I should now justify it, which will not be difficult, especially as I have long been Citroën biased as far as design and engineering are concerned. As regards the looks of the SM our full-page colour photograph in the October issue will determine whether you like it or not. Citroën say "The bodywork has been designed in a wind tunnel and has literally been sculpted by airflow.

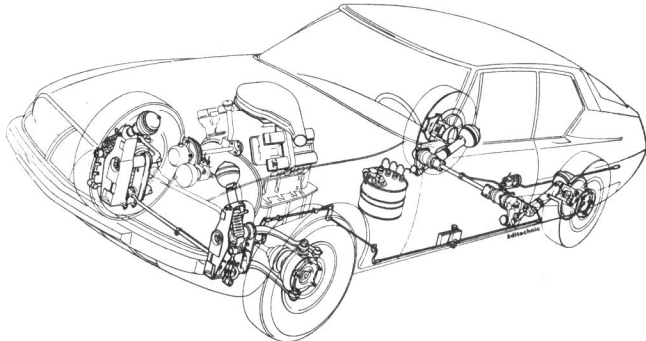

The Citroen SM suspension layout and hydropneumatic system, power being derived from a seven-plunger pump driven by an open jack-shaft from the front of the engine, with a large hydraulic reservoir on the left of the engine compartment.

Its profile of glass and steel has been freed of sharp edges and flat and angled surfaces which are important contributory factors of resistance to forward movement". They go on to say "Conceived by the styling department of Citroën's research division from functional data, the shape of SM makes no concession to fashion. Its aesthetics have been rationalised and are the direct result of study of logic and reason." Some people "nit-pick" about this detail or that detail, others compare it to a Dino Ferrari or a Jaguar, but I think this is pointless. There are many very beautiful looking cars and for me the SM is one of them. Mechanically you either look upon the SM as a nightmare, and drive off in your *Crootmobile*, confident in its sound and proven engineering," or you open up all the apertures and regard the engineering with a glow of satisfaction. Everything that Citroën pioneered and developed on the DS has gone into the design of the SM, and more besides. Needless to say all four wheels are independently sprung, on a trailing-link geometry, and suspension is by the proven hydro-pneumatic, self-levelling, constant ride-height system perfected on the DS. Brakes are power-operated discs all-round, the front ones being mounted "inboard" on each side of the 5-speed gearbox, for the SM is front-wheel-drive, as all Citroën's have been since the mid-thirties. The power-operated brakes have two independent circuits and braking effort distribution according to the load carried. Steering is also power-controlled and the self-centering action is achieved by the same hydraulic power source, and this power control

The compact 90-degree V6 Maserati engine which powers the SM, driving the front wheels through the 5-speed and reverse Citroen gearbox. Note the large calipers on the inboard front brakes, and the subsidiary handbrake calipers. At the front of the gearbox is the speed control for the steering power application.

varies according to the car's speed. The hydraulic power system also controls the battery of six headlights, keeping them level no matter what the load in the car is, or the attitude angle of the car under braking and acceleration. The heart of the car is the Maserati engine, especially designed and built by Maserati for the SM. It is a V6 of 90-degrees with bore and stroke of 87 x 75 mm. giving a capacity of 2,670 c.c. (French taxation has a savage demarcation line at 2.8-litres), and it develops 170 b.h.p. DIN at 5,500 r.p.m. and 170 ft./lbs. torque at 4,000 r.p.m., with a usable peak of 6,500 r.p.m. There are four overhead camshafts, chain driven, and a four bearing crankshaft, and with an overall length of 12¼ in. it can be appreciated that the bottom end is rigid. The car on loan had three downdraught Weber 42DCNF carburetters, but fuel injection is also available. All the engine castings are light alloy and the cylinder heads are identical and therefore interchangeable, and this neat and tidy looking power unit is mounted well back from the front wheels, almost under the windscreen. In front of it is the Citroën 5-speed and reverse gearbox, with very large disc brakes on each side, with additional calipers for the handbrake and above it an open jack-shaft from the front of the engine drives the power pump for the hydraulic systems, and the alternator. The oil reservoir for the hydraulics is on the left of the engine compartment and this supplies the self-levelling suspension, the steering, the brakes and the headlight control.

Although the SM looks like a 2-seater GT car, it is actually a 4-seater with more than room for legless dwarfs in the rear, for having all the mechanism "up front" means plenty of depth in the rear and with the front seats fairly high off the floor pan, there is good leg room in the back. It is not a 4-seater in the saloon car idiom, like the DS, but is a 4-seater in the GT idiom. The front seats adjust in all directions except sideways, and the headrests adjust up

and down and fore and aft so that they can be used, and are not just tiresome adornments waiting for the car to have a head-on collision. The scuttle is assymetrical, with all the dials and controls on the driver's side and the small oval steering wheel can be adjusted up or down and in or out. The whole column-surround adjusts with the wheel, so that the disposition of the various column control stalks remains constant to the wheel rim. The left-hand operates two controls, a short one which moves up and down for "winkers" and at the same time can be pushed forward to flash the headlights or pulled backwards to sound the horn. The longer stalk is for the wipers, position one being for intermittent wipe, starting off with 8 or 10 quick wipes and then one every now and then and position two gives continuous wipe, while pulling the stalk towards you actuates the squirts. At the right-hand finger tip is the lamps control, like all Citroëns, switching side, heads, dip and spot lights all on one control. You push the lever forwards for dip and this can be done with the knuckle of the second finger, and returned with the same finger. The driver has a tachometer and speedometer in front of him and slightly to the right is an all-important circular dial divided into fourteen segments, thirteen of them indicating that all is well with some auxiliary. These cover oil pressure, alternator output, fuel reserve, headlamps main beam, indicators right and left, front brake pad wear, water temperature, hydraulic brake pressure, handbrake "on", rear window heater, sidelamps and "hazard" warning. The fourteenth segment is actually a button, which you press to check that all the vital indicating bulbs are alright. In the centre of this dial is a master lamp, that shines bright red with the word STOP in the middle of it if anything is not functioning. When you switch on the ignition this sinister red lamp glowers at you until you start the engine and oil pressure, alternator, and hydraulic pressures start functioning. If it does not go out you switch off and call a Citroën mechanic. Similarly, if it should come on while you are motoring you stop at once because it means something has gone wrong. Having all this lot in one dial makes it very easy to check everything. In the centre of the scuttle is a clock, dials for water temperature, oil temperature and fuel tank contents, and below are simple, but comprehensive heater and cold air controls, while between the seats are the handbrake and controls for the electric windows. Also there is one of the nicest controls in the whole car, the gearlever. It is incredibly rigid and positive and a joy to use, for the five ratios are beautifully matched to each other and to the torque characteristics of the engine. The lever movement is long, but delightful to use and you change gear continuously for the sheer pleasure it gives. The lever is spring-loaded to the centre of the large gate, opposite positions for 3rd and 4th. To the left are 1st and 2nd and to the right are 5th and Reverse, 5th being a proper ratio and not a Motorway overdrive. It's position is to the right and forward, while 4th is central and back, and bearing in mind this is a left-hand drive car, the change from 5th to 4th at any speed under 100 m.p.h. is sheer joy. If the SM is built with right-hand steering this pleasure will be lost. Using 6,500 r.p.m. in the gears the SM gets up and goes in a fashion that caused more than one passenger to say "Citroëns are not supposed to go like this." The Maserati engine is a typical Italian thoroughbred, not smooth and silent, like a V12 Jaguar, but harsh and eager and becomes happier as the r.p.m. rise until it is humming round like a dynamo, like a Dino Ferrari or a Porsche 911. As you change gear at 6,500 r.p.m. the power is right on in the next gear, and so on up into 5th. The gearing is my idea of perfect for road use, for the SM will pull 6,000 r.p.m. in 5th gear (130 m.p.h.) so that you have 500 r.p.m. in reserve for "overwinding" downhill or with a following wind on an Autoroute. Normal relaxed cruising is 5,000 r.p.m. (106 m.p.h.), while high cruising is 5,500 r.p.m. (117 m.p.h.) and Citroën claim an all-out maximum of 220 k.p.h. (136 m.p.h.). It is a car that is just as happy at over 100 m.p.h. as it is at under that figure, and driving hard it gave 19 m.p.g., though less use of the r.p.m. and the gearbox would give 22 m.p.g.

Anyone who would query the "ride" in the SM would show their ignorance of basic design and like the DS, the hydro-pneumatic controlled self-levelling suspension makes you wonder why other designs still mess about with coil-springs, torsion bars, and leaf springs. On the left of the driver's seat is a control for raising and lowering the static setting of the suspension, which is very useful for anyone living in the country up a rough track and this control is also used for lifting the car up onto its jack when changing a wheel. The cornering ability of the SM is incredibly high, aided by 195/70-VR-15X Radial tyres by Michelin, and on dry public roads it was not possible to find the limit of adhesion. In spite of all the mechanism at the front and the wide bonnet, forward vision was terrific, making the car very easy

INTERIOR VIEW.—The driving compartment of the Citroen SM is spacious and comfortable with a rigid central gear-lever positioned for use. The oval steering wheel and column surround adjusts up and down or in and out, as a complete unit. The "glove locker" on the scuttle is nothing more than that. Warm air is deflected onto the feet from the central grille.

to drive at all speeds, while rear vision in the mirror was remarkable bearing in mind the almost horizontal rear window. A very satisfactory feature was the fact that the rear of the car is eight inches narrower than the front, a very desirable feature if you enjoy driving fast and close. The whole car is so full of interesting features that you could spend an enjoyable morning in it, without even driving it; such things as two-position "keeps" on the long, wide opening doors, the hinged rear-window that gives access to the luggage compartment with its cover to conceal everything when closed, the oddments container in the arm-rests, the warm-air vents to the rear passengers' feet, the swivelling spotlights that turn with the steering, the outer one shining on the centre of the corner and the inner one looking across the apex to the exit of the corner, the warm-air feed to the inside of the perspex box containing the lights, to prevent misting, and many more interesting "engineered" rather than "stylised" features.

I have left until last the Citroën steering, for in their own words "It is at least as big a step forward as the hydropneumatic suspension was when the DS was introduced in 1955." As the SM was designed as a GT car, for covering the ground from A to B very quickly, under all conditions and types of going it was felt desirable to have very high geared rack-and-pinion steering. This was done with a ratio of 9.4:1 (compared to 14.7:1 for the DS) which gives one turn of the wheel from straight-ahead to full lock, and as full-lock gives a turning circle of 34 ft. 6 in. between kerbs, it can be appreciated that steering wheel movements for all normal motoring are very small indeed. With the large Michelin Radial tyres power steering was essential, but Citroën engineers were not prepared to accept power control of the high geared steering for high speeds, so they designed an ingenious hydraulic system that gives full power steering when static, so much so that the wheels return to straight-ahead under their own power, when stationary, to minimal power at high-speed so that the steering is precise and accurate. This control is driven from the front end of the gearbox and varies in relation to the speed of the car. It is interesting to read the Citroën engineers' reasons for high geared steering "greatest ease of manoeuvring on winding roads, or in all instances where it is necessary to avoid an obstacle quickly, or whenever it is necessary to make a rapid correction to the trajectory of the car, as a result of the effect of an external force, such as a gust of wind, passing a large vehicle quickly, or the beginnings of a skid." They go on to say "it is an essential element of safety, for how many accidents have been caused because drivers were not able to exert the necessary effort at the steering wheel, or because they could not turn the wheels quickly enough due to low-geared steering." This is what is called "primary safety thinking" and you hear similar talk at Porsche and Mercedes-Benz, and it is so much better than the Ralph Nader hysterics.

When stationary or when maneouvring at low speed, such as parking, the steering wheel can be turned with one finger, but the effort to move the wheels *increases* with the speed of the car *and* with the steering lock angle, the increase being greater when the wheels start

to leave the straight-ahead position, and *decreasing* towards the end of the lock. The wheel of the SM is essentially something on which to rest your hands, and *not* something to grasp and wrestle with. Anyone not used to high-geared steering, either from vintage car experience or motor cycle riding, tends to start off in a series of swoops as they hang on to the wheel, but if you relax and let Citroën get on with it the SM steering is superb. The faster you go the more rock-steady it becomes, and like a Porsche 911 or a Dino Ferrari it is so steady and quiet and fuss-free at maximum speed that you feel you could use at least another 50 b.h.p. On very fast curves it really is outstanding for you make no conscious effort to change direction, a slight pressure on one side of the steering wheel is all you need and you "think" it through 100 m.p.h. corners rather than steer it through. Obviously the SM is meant for fast motoring, but equally it is an enjoyable car to drive slowly and dawdle about in, pottering down country lanes or along winding roads. It has that rare quality of being a nice car to be in at any speed, from stationary to its maximum, and the interior fittings and comfort are such that it would be a pleasant car to spend 12 or 15 hours a day in on a long European journey.

If you are not appreciative of Citroën engineering then you could probably find lots of things to complain about on the SM, or if you approached it as a family "fug-box" you'd complain about the glorious noise of the 4-camshaft Maserati engine, or the fact that you had a gear-lever that had to be used, and you would have awful trouble fitting your roof-rack or stowing the pram or the collapsible boat, but if you look upon SM as standing for Serious Motoring, you would enjoy it. Driving the SM I found nothing to complain about, but passengers taken on "demonstration" runs complained about the lack of sideways support afforded by the front seat, the obvious cure being for the driver to corner a bit slower, or alternatively to clamp the passenger in with a full seat-harness. The use of the word Safety-Belt would be a misnomer, for safety is inherent in Citroën designing and part of the basic conception of cars like the SM, in which accidents are of secondary consideration, the primary one being to design a car which is capable of avoiding an accident. I am sure Citroën engineers believe that the way towards safety is to avoid accidents and make sure the car will help the driver to do this at all times. Safety, performance and comfort were the three major aims behind the design of the SM, and there is no doubt that these have been achieved. Such perfection in design does not come easily or cheaply, and in Great Britain, as sold by Citroën Cars Ltd., of the Trading Estate, Slough, Buckinghamshire, the SM costs a minimum of £5,136, and by the time you have added to its "living quarters" with such things as leather upholstery, radio, air conditioning etc., the price could rise to nearer £5,700. On the road, taxed, insured, with all the extras and a full tank of petrol (20 gallons) there would not be much small change left out of £6,000, but you would have the ultimate in Motoring, and a real "Car of the seventies", that will no doubt carry through to the eighties while Citroën engineers work away at the next one and other manufacturers try to keep pace or struggle to catch up. It was one of the few cars I was really reluctant to return to its owners.—D. S. J.

REARWARDS.—The Citroen SM has a very distinctive tail treatment, the shape of which pleases all followers of Professor Kamm's theories on aerodynamics. The whole rear window hinges up about its forward end to give access to the deep boot.

The cornering power is very high indeed and the car can be flung through quite sharp bends in spite of its substantial size and weight.

Improved torque and traffic manners from Citroën's injected SM

Only the luggage boot lacks capacity if four people are carried.

When the Citroën SM first became available in this country, I took one on a most memorable long-distance test drive through France and Italy. My experiences were chronicled in an extra lengthy road test report, which appeared in AUTOSPORT of September 23, 1971. The machine proved itself a marvellous *grand routier*, with the best steering and high-speed stability of them all, compared with which lesser cars seem crude and almost dangerous.

In its original form, the V6 Maserati type engine had three twin-choke Weber carburetters, but the unit has now been re-designed to incorporate Bosch electronic fuel injection, with injectors aiming downwards into the ports, close to the valves. The installation looks highly complex, with rather a lot of loose wires about under the bonnet area, and a bit of tidying up would not come amiss later on. The object is not to obtain a spectacular gain in maximum power, though a useful 8 bhp is added, but to increase the torque in the middle ranges and improve traffic manners.

Most important, the new engine passes the strict European anti-pollution requirements. It also overcomes the dirty habit of plug fouling, to which the carburetter version was occasionally subject in slow traffic. The improved torque has enabled an even higher overdrive fifth gear to be incorporated in the transmission.

Naturally, the very advanced technical features of the chassis remain. In brief, an engine-driven pump, with hydraulic accumulators, supplies the power to operate the self-levelling independent suspension, the steering, and the disc brakes, which are inboard at the front.

The steering is the most revolutionary feature of the car as it is very high-geared—almost as quick as that of a racing single-seater. Since the preponderance of the weight is on the driven front wheels and the section of the tyres is very large, nothing less than fully powered steering will do at low speeds. As the car goes faster, the power is reduced and eventually the driver is on his own, getting the full sensation of the road through the very direct steering.

People accustomed to slow and soggy steering may take a long time to become accustomed to the SM. It is worth persevering, however, for this is the only car which combines true stability in a straight line with the ability to dodge instantly—it must therefore be the safest car in the world. Personally, I was quickly at ease in the first

The steering wheel is adjustable in both directions and the interior is beautifully appointed. Below, the V6 Maserati-type engine has now been redesigned to incorporate Bosch electronic fuel injection.

it is the best yet. Not as soft as that of the Citroën DS, it nevertheless absorbs all the bumps and the car remains level whatever the surface, with no disconcerting dive under heavy braking. Road and wind noises are virtually non-existent. The complexity of the suspension is amply justified by results and the self-levelling ensures that the ground clearance is maintained when a full load of passengers and luggage is carried. There is also a lever to raise the car hydraulically when negotiating really rough country tracks. It would be fair to say that a car without self-levelling suspension is simply not modern.

I would like to cover this brilliant design in far greater detail, but space is limited. It is, however, essential to mention the six lights, which have their own self-levelling system, four of them also turning to throw their beams round corners, controlled by the steering. The seats are very comfortable, the steering wheel is adjustable in both directions, and the interior is beautifully appointed. Only the luggage boot lacks capacity if four people are carried. The heating is very effective, with plenty of fresh air ventilation, and refrigerated air-conditioning is an optional extra.

The object of my short test was largely to compare the fuel-injection SM with the carburetter version. First of all it is far better in traffic, never becoming lumpy or misfiring. There is a small but useful increase in performance all the way up the scale and the greater medium-speed torque is noticeable. The low-speed flexibility is exceptional for such a highly-tuned engine and I think that the fuel consumption figures have improved, though I cannot be precise because the conditions of the two tests were so different. For me, though, it is the functional, aerodynamic shape that appeals most and this is true beauty.

SPECIFICATION AND PERFORMANCE DATA

Car tested : Citroën SM 2-door 4-seater coupé, price £5478.09 including car tax and VAT.
Engine : Six-cylinders in 90 deg v, 87 mm x 75 mm (2670 cc). Compression ratio 9 to 1. 178 bhp (net) at 5500 rpm. Four chain-driven overhead camshafts. Bosch electronic fuel injection.
Transmission : Single dry plate clutch. 5-speed all-synchromesh gearbox with central change, ratios 0.7, 0.9, 1.3, 1.9, and 2.9 to 1. Hypoid final drive, ratio 4.375 to 1. Open driveshafts to front hubs with homokinetic joints.
Chassis : Combined steel body and chassis with aluminium bonnet, Hydropneumatic self-levelling independent suspension all round with wishbones in front, trailing arms behind, and anti-roll bars at both ends. Power-operated disc brakes all round, inboard in front. Bolt-on disc wheels fitted Michelin 205/70 VR 15 X tyres.
Equipment : 12-volt lighting and starting with alternator. Speedometer, rev counter, water temperature, oil temperature, and fuel gauges, clock. Heating, demisting, and ventilation system with heated rear window. 2-speed windscreen wipers and washers. Flashing direction indicators. Reversing lights.
Dimensions : Wheelbase 9 ft 8.25 in. Track (front) 5 ft, (rear) 4 ft 4.46 in. Overall length, 16 ft 0.6 in. Width, 6 ft 0.25 in. Weight, 1 ton 9.5 cwt.
Performance : Maximum speed 141.6 mph (see text). Speeds in gears : Fourth 115 mph; Third 85 mph; Second 58 mph; First 37 mph. Standing quarter-mile 16.0 s. Acceleration 0-30 mph, 3.4 s; 0-50 mph, 6.3 s; 0-60 mph, 8.2 s; 0-80 mph, 14.9 s; 0-100 mph, 23.1 s.
Fuel consumption : 16 to 21 mpg.

SM I drove because it is reminiscent of the best vintage sports cars. Returning to it after a considerable lapse of time, I felt at home immediately.

Owing to other commitments, my test was a short one and I was not able to range so far afield as in the original car. The makers claim that the maximum speed is now 141.6 mph and I do not for one moment dispute this, but I was not able to attain it on the timed stretch of road at my disposal. However, I approached this velocity closely with the car still gradually picking up speed on the relatively short straight, so I think we may accept the claim.

The point is, however, that 130 mph is a very easy cruising speed, nowhere near the red part of the rev-counter dial. The makers claim a 0-60 mph acceleration of 8.0 s, but although I did manage to equal this after a lot of practice, I often managed only 8.4 s, due to wheelspin at the getaway. I think that 8.2 s would therefore be a fair figure. Wheelspin is only a problem at standing starts and is never experienced thereafter during normal road driving.

The gearchange is excellent and fourth gear,

with its 115 mph maximum, makes the car very lively when getting clear of fast traffic. The engine is relatively quiet when cruising in fifth gear but never really silent; it is frankly a high-efficiency unit getting on with its job and is distinctly audible when pressed, with a rather metallic note. In this respect, it does not compare with the big 4.7-litre V8 of the Maserati Bora, but it wins hands down on fuel consumption. There are cars which are faster than the Citroën by a small amount, and most of them are in the 10 mpg bracket. The SM, with its smaller engine, may double this while putting up an impressive average.

The cornering power is very high indeed and the car can be flung through quite sharp bends in spite of its substantial size and weight. The natural self-centring of the steering at speed is complemented by power-centring at the lower rates; indeed, the steering straightens itself when the car is at a standstill. This makes town driving easy and restful, but at high speeds it is perhaps the stability in gusty side winds that is most appreciated. The brakes stop the car as if it had been grabbed by a giant hand.

Of the suspension, one can merely say that

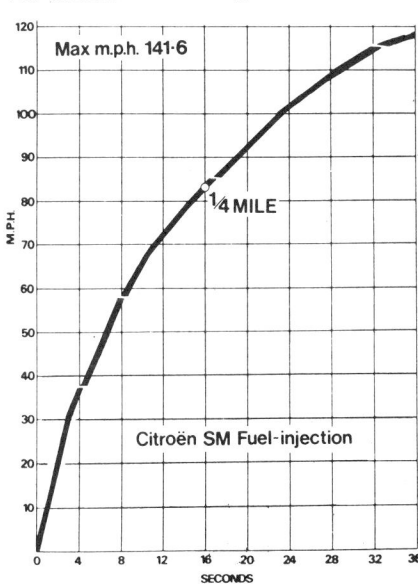

AUTO TEST

CITROEN SM

Ultimate in advanced engineering?

AT-A-GLANCE: Flagship of the Citroen range now with electronic injection. More flexible, more economical and almost as quick on acceleration. More top speed. Unique power steering works well. Excellent self levelling suspension. Fade free power brakes. Not much luggage room.

CITROEN are a company of individualists and any model they design is literally riddled with technical novelties. Even the cheapest and most basic Citroen saloons break totally with convention in such all-important areas as their suspension, and when the new medium-class GS saloon was added to the range it was even more advanced in many ways than the long-established D range. To satisfy the extremist designers, we suspect, as much as to provide France with a prestige high-speed touring car, a very exciting Grand Tourer was introduced in the spring of 1970. Known as the SM (S for special, M for Maserati who supply the engine), it has been on sale in France now for almost three years and to judge by the number seen travelling at very high speed on the *autoroutes,* the model is a huge success.

To improve it slightly, a change was made in the summer of last year from Weber carburettors to Bosch electronic fuel injection and top gear was raised from 0.81 to 0.76. The induction change resulted in a peak power boost from 170 to 178 bhp (DIN) to 5,500 rpm, but no increase in torque. The real reason for adopting Bosch injection is most likely to comply with the new emission controls stipulated in the Economic Commission for Europe's Regulation 15. This will apply in the UK to all cars manufactured after 20 September this year, and it is already in force in France.

In almost all other respects the SM is exactly the same as when we tested it in the summer of 1971. Plans for a right-hand version are still unsettled, the small volume sold here hardly justifying the tooling investment required. It is such an interesting car that we make no apologies for testing it again after only two years.

To recap briefly on the specification, the SM is the fastest front-drive car made anywhere in the world, its Maserati power unit being of unusual 90-deg. vee-6 configuration with four chain-driven overhead camshafts.

Transmission is through a five-speed ZF transaxle, the engine being behind the front-wheel centre-line and the gearbox ahead of it. Suspension incorporates anti-dive geometry and uses the unique Citroen hydropneumatic struts, interconnected front to rear and incorporating self-levelling sensors to maintain a constant ride height regardless of load. Power from the same high-pressure hydraulic system is used to boost brake pedal effort and to energize the servos for the very advanced steering mechanism.

Now that injection is fitted with full automatic temperature compensation, the cold starting procedure is much simpler than before. All that is now needed is a turn on the key and immediately the engine comes to life and

Above: As with all Citroens, the SM has remarkable styling. The spats over the rear wheels can be removed. Top right: All six driving lamps and the number plate are behind the three-piece glass cover

idles evenly. As before it seems to need no warming-up period, a smooth and snatch-free power delivery being available at once after a cold start. The only slight quirk we noticed was a tendency for the exhaust to be a bit smokey (more with oil fumes than over-rich mixture) first thing in the morning.

Because of its unusual cylinder layout, derived literally from cutting down Maserati's own 90-deg. vee-8 into a vee-6, the SM engine is not as smooth as something more conventional like an in-line six or a vee-8. At low speeds the unequal firing impulses can be felt, although they are in no way unpleasant, and on this latest engine there seemed to be more thrash and clatter from the valve gear, probably because the induction itself is better silenced.

Throttle response is always very quick and there was none of the annoying surging at steady speeds which plagues some injection installations on other cars. A long and very progressive pedal action helps provide very

delicate control, which is just as well because at low speed the suspension over-reacts to engine torque, the front rearing up very noticeably. A harsh and insensitive driver could easily upset his passengers if he provoked this motion too often. The trouble stems from one of the inherent features of inter-connection, which in order to be soft in bump must be very soft in pitch. Anti-squat geometry at the rear would improve matters enormously.

Towards the top end of its range the engine becomes extremely smooth and between its torque peak of 4,000 and the rev limit of 6,500 rpm it has distinctly turbine-like qualities. Very occasionally we experienced a brief part-throttle misfire, the cause of which was never established.

As seems to be the way with cars in production, the SM has put on a bit of weight in the past two years and it now turns the scales at just over 30cwt., an increase of nearly 100lb. unladen. This coupled with a test car which had covered rather less miles than before and what we suspect to be an inferior torque at the bottom end made the standing-start acceleration figures slower the whole way through the range. From rest to 100 mph took 25.9 sec. compared with 24.3 sec. with the old carburettor SM and the 0 to 60 mph time is now 9.3 instead of 9 sec. dead. These differences are of academic interest only, the car feeling just as quick on the road and still managing to put up some very respectable times for a large car with an engine well under 3-litres capacity.

The change in fifth gear ratio already mentioned puts the mph per 1,000 rpm up from 22.6 to 23.2, which is not enough to affect top gear flexibility (the SM would pull happily from 20 mph in fifth), but it makes high-speed cruising a little bit easier and gives a useful small boost to the top speed. As before we were able to run over the power peak to 6,000 mph which now means 139 instead of only 135 mph. At high speed the SM is incredibly stable and seems to be totally unaffected by side winds. The novel steering plays its part in this, one of the sensors being connected to the output shaft of the gearbox and hence making one of the steering functions speed sensitive.

Basically the steering provides servo centring as well as servo assistance to wheel movements. At low speed the centring forces are high (enough to turn the wheels back to the straight-ahead position automatically at the kerb), but they can always be countermanded by the driver, whose efforts are boosted in the usual way once the servo valves have reacted to positive steering wheel movement. As speed increases the centring reduces and a very carefully engineered balance in the hydraulic system gives a lot of artificial feel to a mechanism which has been designed "dead" to eliminate road shocks and the strong front-drive effects that are inherent. The overall result is a very pleasant high-geared system that always responds immediately.

Having only two turns between locks, the steering is so high geared that a driver new to the SM finds it difficult to adjust his movements at first and it really takes a few hundred miles before one feels at home behind the wheel. Reducing the amount of wheel twirling so drastically has no other adverse effects, however, and its big plus factor is the apparent way the whole scale of the car is reduced proportionately. With its overall length of just over 16ft and a width of over 6ft, the SM is a very large car by any standards and especially for a close-coupled 2 + 2. Apart from the close confines of heavy traffic or a car park, it does not feel such a large car to drive and the way it can be hurled through bends at very high speed is uncanny.

Like on other Citroens, roll angles are quite large on the SM when cornered fast and, considering all the possibilities available with hydraulic suspension, it seems a pity that more anti-roll (if not absolute no-roll) has not been incorporated at the same time as all the other clever things.

One would expect the Citroen suspension to be very impressive on ride, and there are few disappointments. Big bumps and broken surfaces are soaked up with similar ease and the overall insulation from any kind of surface-induced shock is of a very high order. It takes only a short drive to realize that the SM will storm across any kind of irregularity with total contempt, which explains why it is always the Citroens which are least affected by *chausèe dèformèe* in France. At all times the suspension works very quietly too, the hydraulic pump for all the services actually making more noise than movements of the wheels.

With a high-pressure hydraulic circuit to provide servo assistance, Citroen have chosen a zero-travel pedal action for the brakes of

the SM. A mushroom pad (to put some slight movement and progression into the action) replaces a conventional swinging arm pedal and the way it always feels "hard" even to a heavy dab is most reassuring. Very little effort is required for a maximum-g stop and on this car the judder and harshness we experienced from high speed before were not nearly so marked. Once the linings have fully warmed up there is effectively no fade, but the reponse from the higher speed of the fade test showed up some appreciable speed sensitivity in the system. To record

0.5g from 30 mph required about 25lb. effort with cold linings, whereas this rose to 35lb. from 70 mph with the linings hot. On the road the brakes always feel consistent and never gave us cause to doubt them for even a moment.

Clutch effort is rather on the high side at 40lb., but the travel of 5in. is very reasonable. The ZF gearbox, despite the complications of the shift linkage, works superbly with a clean, positive engagement of each ratio and absolutely unbeatable synchromesh.

The instruments are shielded by a sweeping cowl, and the steering column can be adjusted The button between the accelerator and clutch pedals is the foot brake

Comfort and Equipment

Citroen have shunned conventional two-piece seats in the SM and fitted it instead with a hammock-type design which follows a smooth curve from shoulders to the backs of the knees. It has a firm outer edge with soft squashy rolls inside and gives good support uniformly. We found the cloth trim covering much less slippery than the leather cloth option, but some more lateral support in the padding would improve location on corners still more.

Inclined ramps bring the seat up as it slides forward; the cushion height can be adjusted at front and rear edges. The backrest can be adjusted through a wide angle by a lever on the inboard side. A similar lever outboard releases the backrest and the slides

so that the seat can be doubled up and slid forward for access to the rear. Seats in the back are similar to those in front, but the shape of the roof restricts headroom considerably.. Although there is enough width for three-abreast, at a pinch, the padding is formed as two individual seats with very little upholstery in between.

Releasing a clamp at the base of the steering column surround enables the upper part to be adjusted for reach and tilt, but all our drivers preferred it in its least extended position. It is a bit fiddly to insert the thin key into its slot on the side of the column, but apart from their strange styling all the other controls are well placed and easy to operate.

In front of the driver are two large oval dials for the speedometer and rev counter, flanked by a collection of warning telltales on the right and a fresh-air duct on the left, both in matching oval bezels. Set into the facia rail in the centre of the car, angled towards the driver's sight line, are three supplementary gauges for water temperature, oil pressure and fuel tank contents. Total capacity of the tank is nearly 20 gallons,

Buried under all the ancilliaries is the V6 engine. The key below gives location of the various components

1. Engine oil filler
2. Distributor
3. Intake manifold
4. Intake air duct
5. Air conditioning refrigeration compressor
6. Suspension hydropneumatic unit
7. Brake pressure unit
8. Alternator
9. Headlamp level damper

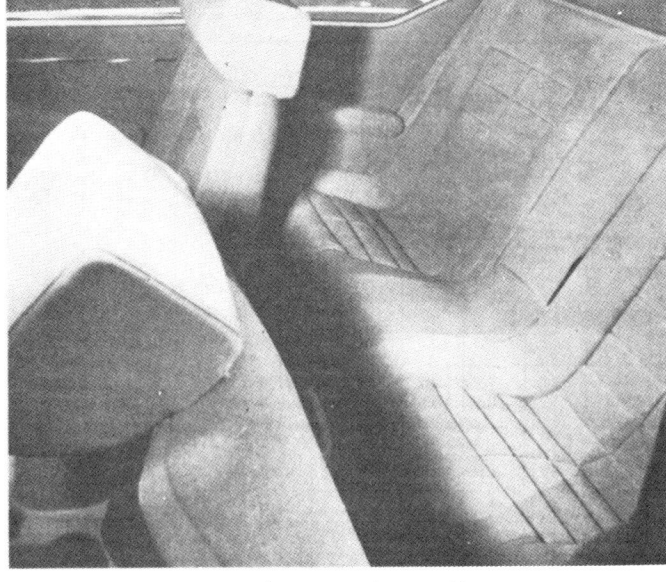

Above: Adjustments on the hammock-type front seats provide for backrest angle, tip, height and leg-room. The head restraints can also be adjusted for height and angle. Above right: The rear seats are shaped to take two passengers, and have armrests built into the ends

which gives a useful range of over 300 miles. A warning light starts to flash when the level is down to the last three or four gallons.

Three stalks and a row of push-buttons take care of all accessory switching, two-speed wipers with intermittent delay being standard, backed up by a powerful electric screen washer. Indicators are non-self-cancelling, which is a peculiar idiosyncrasy of Citroen and not really an inconvenience once used to the system.

Lamps are all operated by a single control, its multi-action taking care of switching and dipping. Curved glass covers streamline a battery of six quartz-hologen lamps, all being levelled automatically to compensate for attitude changes in the suspension and a special long-range pair being additionally connected to the steering. Although the long summer evenings prevented us from sampling the system this time, we remember how effective it is from our previous experience of the SM and our recent re-acquaintance on the Avon Tour of Britain.

Side windows in the doors have electric lifts, which are very slow in operation. The rear quarterlights can be cracked open about an inch to improve ventilation, but the process involves a slow-action thumbscrew.

In addition to a normal and very effective air-blending heater, with thermostatic control, the test car was fitted with refrigeration and we found this invaluable in hot weather. The controls are combined into a simple and easy-to-understand cluster just ahead of the gear-lever. Temperature regulation for heated or cooled air is by means of a single slide, marked in blue and red, and there is a variable-speed booster fan for all outlets including a large area "Texas duct" in the central console. Refrigerated air is emitted by all ducts as required, but with the heater in operation the adjustable vents are fed with ambient air only. Heating-wire in the large back window keeps it clear from misting up and the slipstream soon clears standing water from its outside surface.

Living with the SM

It is to the importer's credit that an estimated price of £5,500 for the SM two years ago has materialized today into only £5,478 with special car tax and VAT. Special seat belts, licence, delivery and number plates bring this up to £5,537 on the road. With air conditioning, tinted glass and a radio, the cost goes up to nearly £6,000, but even at this price the car seems far from expensive. During

a long term of ownership, though the running costs are liable to be even more than usual for this class of car, such routine items as the oil filter element (£3.42) and contact breaker (£6.96) being extraordinarily highly priced. Major replacements like a new exhaust system would cost £116.62 and a clutch renewal would work out at £93.96. Changing the brake pads on all four wheels costs £21.71 and the price for one of those curved glass lamp covers is about £20. The warranty period is six months, regardless of the mileage covered.

With the SM you get three different keys, the largest operating the steering-ignition lock and two smaller ones being for the doors and the fuel filler respectively. The door key also works the boot lock and the glove locker lid.

For such a large car the boot is something of a sham. Lifting up the rear window in its frame reveals a large cavity some 43in. deep and up to 48in. wide, but is mostly filled by the huge spare wheel. The remaining space is awkwardly shaped and it is difficult to insert even a single bulky suitcase. This lack of luggage space is undoubtedly the SM's biggest shortcoming.

Left: For such a car, the boot space is on the small side. The small lever by the spare is for lowering the rear wheels when the car is jacked up

Low and high: The variations in available suspension heights on the SM

Below: The inner pair of headlamps mover with the steering. The centre and outer pairs are fixed, and the lines are part of the optional system

CITROEN SM (2,670 c.c.)

ACCELERATION

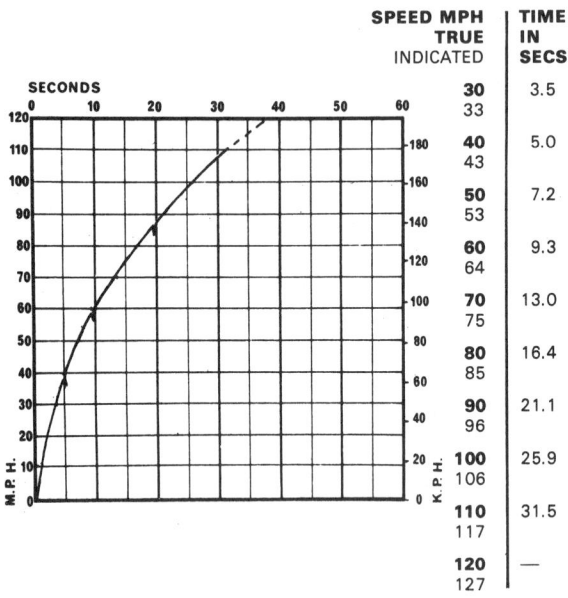

SPEED MPH TRUE INDICATED	TIME IN SECS
30 / 33	3.5
40 / 43	5.0
50 / 53	7.2
60 / 64	9.3
70 / 75	13.0
80 / 85	16.4
90 / 96	21.1
100 / 106	25.9
110 / 117	31.5
120 / 127	—

GEAR RATIOS AND TIME IN SEC

mph	Top (3.33)	4th (4.24)	3rd (5.78)	2nd (8.49)
10-30	—	—	6.9	4.3
20-40	13.0	9.1	6.0	4.0
30-50	12.7	8.6	5.7	3.9
40-60	12.3	8.1	5.8	—
50-70	12.1	8.8	5.9	—
60-80	13.3	9.1	7.5	—
70-90	14.8	9.6	—	—
80-100	15.5	10.4	—	—

Standing ¼-mile
17.1 sec 81 mph
Standing Kilometre
31.0 sec 109 mph
Test distance
981 miles
Mileage recorder
4 per cent over-reading

PERFORMANCE

MAXIMUM SPEEDS

Gear	mph	kph	rpm
Top (mean)	139	224	6,000
(best)	140	225	6,030
4th	118	190	6,500
3rd	87	135	6,500
2nd	59	95	6,500
1st	39	63	6,500

BRAKES

FADE
(from 70 mph in neutral)
Pedal load for 0.5g stops in lb

1	35	6	35
2	35	7	35
3	35	8	35
4	35	9	35
5	35	10	35

RESPONSE
(from 30 mph in neutral)

Load	g	Distance
20lb	0.38	79ft
30lb	0.64	47ft
40lb	1.02	29.6ft
Handbrake	0.27	112ft
Max. Gradient	1 in 4	

CLUTCH
Pedal 40lb and 5in.

COMPARISONS

MAXIMUM SPEED MPH
Citroen SM	(£5,480)	**139**
Porsche 911E	(£5,649)	139
Alfa Romeo Montreal	(£4,999)	137
Fiat 130 Coupe (A)	(£5,531)	116
Triumph Stag	(£2,533)	116

0–60 MPH, SEC
Porsche 911E	6.4
Alfa Romeo Montreal	7.6
Citroen SM	**9.3**
Triumph Stag	9.3
Fiat 130 Coupe	10.6

STANDING ¼-MILE, SEC
Porsche 911E	14.4
Alfa Romeo Montreal	15.4
Citroen SM	**17.1**
Triumph Stag	17.1
Fiat 130 Coupe	17.7

OVERALL MPG
Triumph Stag	20.7
Fiat 130 Coupe	20.6
Citroen SM	**17.9**
Porsche 911E	15.6
Alfa Romeo Montreal	14.9

GEARING
(with 195/70-15in. tyres)

Top	23.2 mph per 1,000 rpm
4th	18.2 mph per 1,000 rpm
3rd	13.3 mph per 1,000 rpm
2nd	9.1 mph per 1,000 rpm
1st	6.0 mph per 1,000 rpm

CONSUMPTION

FUEL
High pressure injection system incompatible with our measuring equipment

Typical mpg . . 20 (14.1 litres/100km)
Calculated (DIN) mpg 25.2 (11.2 litres/100km)
Overall mpg . . 17.9 (15.8 litres/100km)
Grade of fuel Premium, 4-star (min. 98 RM)

OIL
Consumption (SAE 20/50) 500

TEST CONDITIONS:
Weather: Fine Wind: 5-8 mph.
Temperature: 26 deg. C. (79 deg. F).
Barometer: 29.9in. hg. Humidity: 48 per cent.
Surfaces: Dry concrete and asphalt.

WEIGHT:
Kerb weight 30.3 cwt (3,395lb-1,543kg)
(with oil, water and half full fuel tank).
Distribution, per cent F, 62; R, 38
Laden as tested: 33.6 cwt (3,762lb-1,710kg)

TURNING CIRCLES:
Between kerbs L, 35ft 6in.; R, 35ft 10in.
Between walls L, 38ft 4in.; R, 38ft 8in.
Steering wheel turns, lock to lock 2.
Figures taken at 2,500 miles by our own staff at the Motor Industry Research Association proving ground at Nuneaton and on the Continent.

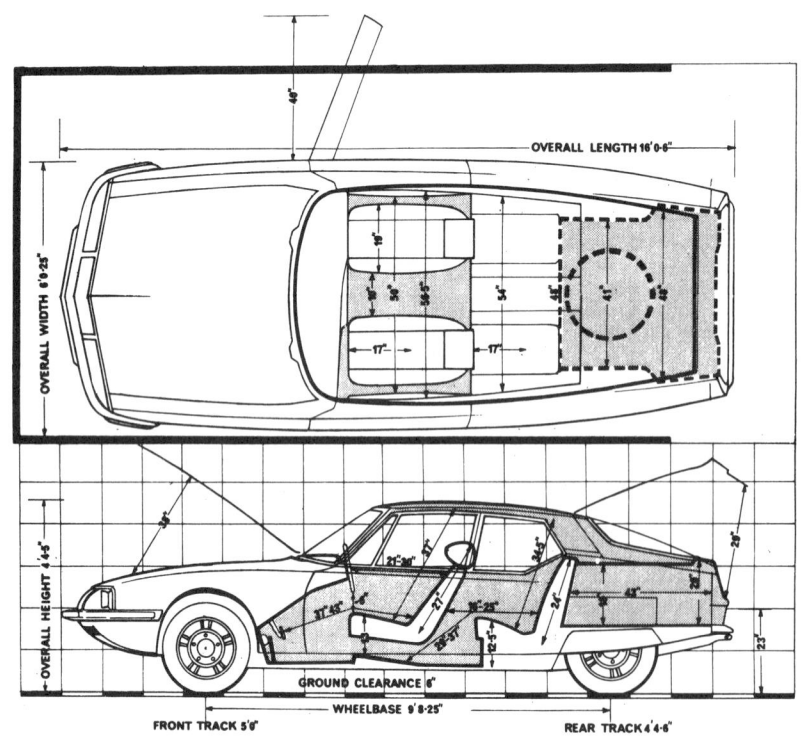

STANDARD GARAGE 16ft x 8ft 6in.

SPECIFICATION

FRONT ENGINE, FRONT-WHEEL DRIVE

ENGINE
Cylinders	6, in 90-degree
Main bearings	4
Cooling system	Water; pump, thermostat and twin electric fans
Bore	87mm (3.42in.)
Stroke	75mm (2.95in.)
Displacement	2,670 c.c. (163 cu. in.)
Valve gear	Twin chain-driven overhead camshafts per cylinder bank
Compression ratio	9-to-1. Min. octane rating: 98RM
Induction	Bosch electronic fuel injection
Fuel pump	Electric
Oil filter	Full-flow, renewable element
Max. power	178 bhp (DIN) at 5,500 rpm
Max. torque	164 lb.ft (DIN) at 4,000 rpm

TRANSMISSION
Clutch	Diaphragm spring, 8.7in. dia.
Gearbox	5-speed all-synchromesh ZF
Gear ratios	Top 0.76
	Fourth 0.97
	Third 1.32
	Second 1.94
	First 2.93
	Reverse 3.16
Final drive	Hypoid bevel, 4.375-to-1

CHASSIS and BODY
Construction	Integral steel hull with bolt-on front wings, aluminium bonnet

SUSPENSION
Front	Independent; trailing arms, hydro-pneumatic struts interconnected and self-levelling
Rear	Independent; trailing arms, hydro-pneumatic struts interconnected and self-levelling

STEERING
Type	Rack and pinion with speed sensitive and self-centring power assistance
Wheel dia.	15 x 13.7 in.

BRAKES
Make and type	Disc front and rear
Servo	Pressurized hydraulics
Dimensions	F 11.8 in. dia.
	R 10.1 in. dia.

WHEELS
Type	Pressed steel, 5-stud fixing, 6 in. wide rim
Tyres— make	Michelin
— type	XWX radial ply tubed
— size	195/70VR-15 in.

EQUIPMENT
Battery	12 Volt 70 Ah.
Alternator	65 amp
Headlamps	Six lamp system 330/220/110 watt (total)
Reversing lamp	Standard
Electric fuses	12
Screen wipers	2-speed with variable delay
Screen washer	Standard electric
Interior heater	Fresh-air blending, refrigeration extra
Heated backlight	Standard
Safety belts	Extra
Interior trim	Nylon jersey seats, cloth headlining
Floor covering	Carpet
Jack	Fixed pillar
Jacking points	2, one each side
Windscreen	Laminated
Underbody protection	Bitumastic treatment after painting

MAINTENANCE
Fuel tank	19.7 Imp. gallons (90 litres)
Cooling system	24 pints (inc. heater)
Engine sump	15.4 pints (7 litres) SAE 20/50. Change oil every 3,000 miles. Change filter every 6,000 miles.
Gearbox and final drive	4.4 pints. SAE EP80. Change every 12,000 miles.
Grease	6 points every 3,000 miles.
Valve clearance	Inlet 0.014 in. (cold) Exhaust 0.020 in. (cold)
Contact breaker	88 deg. dwell
Ignition timing	6 deg. BTDC (static) 22 deg. BTDC (stroboscopic at 2,000 rpm)
Spark plug	Type: Bosch W200T30. Gap 0.025 in.
Tyre pressures	F 32; R 29 psi (normal driving)
Max. payload	838 lb (381 kg)

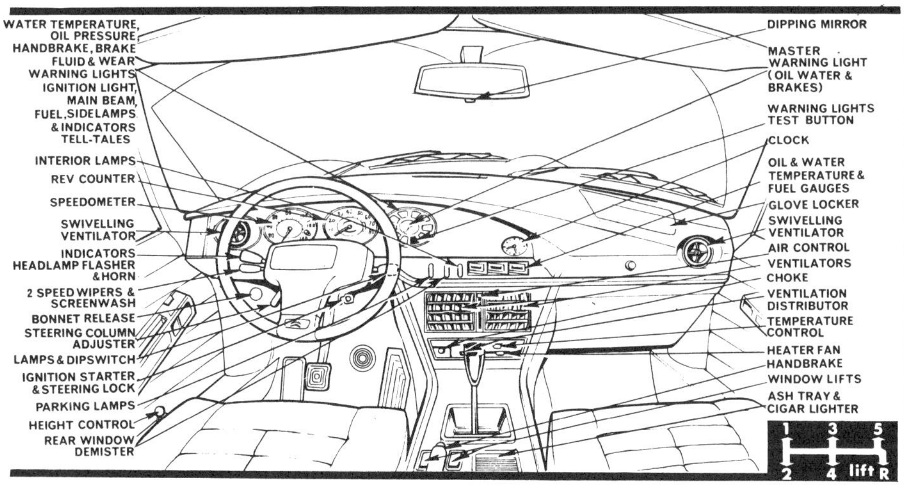

One of the advantages of having a car with pressurized hydraulic suspension is that the chores of jacking can be eliminated to a large extent. In the Citroen tool kit only a pillar is provided for this purpose, the technique being to set the ride-height selector for maximum lift, insert the pillar and retract the wheels. At the rear on the SM it is also necessary to lock the rear height adjuster with a special pin provided.

Although the headlamps are connected to the steering and the suspension, resetting beams is quite a straightforward job which involves no more than the adjustment of four thumbscrews. Changing bulbs is also quite simple, except on the inner steered pair of long-range lamps, when the glass number plate cover must be taken out first. A total of 12 fuses protect the electric circuits and they are colour coded to simplify identification.

In the event of a serious hydraulic leak, the system can, in an emergency, be topped up with "straight" SAE 10 or SAE 20 engine oil. As soon as possible afterwards the system should be drained and refilled with proper green LHM fluid.

Although the view under the bonnet looks fearfully complicated, essential items for routine checking are easy to find. The dipstick is in a tube near the back of the engine and the radiator header tank with its filler close to a wing crown on one side. The hydraulic reservoir has a translucent sight glass on its outside with maximum and minimum levels marked on it.

Conclusions

Apart from its extravagant overall dimensions, which appear to be an essential part of the streamlined styling, the SM is a most rewarding car to live with, even if it does take a lot of learning in the first place. For anyone with technical inclinations, the complicated systems are a marvel, and in our limited experience so far, they seem to function most reliably. To put the model to a much longer test we are adding an SM to our long-term fleet and will report again when a substantial mileage has been covered. As it stands, at well under £6,000, the SM offers a lot of advanced features and behaves on the road most impressively. Apart from the snag of left-hand drive, which may well soon be overcome, it is a most excellent machine in all respects. □

Interior diagram labels:
WATER TEMPERATURE, OIL PRESSURE, HANDBRAKE, BRAKE FLUID & WEAR WARNING LIGHTS, IGNITION LIGHT, MAIN BEAM, FUEL, SIDELAMPS & INDICATORS TELL-TALES, INTERIOR LAMPS, REV COUNTER, SPEEDOMETER, SWIVELLING VENTILATOR, INDICATORS, HEADLAMP FLASHER & HORN, 2 SPEED WIPERS & SCREENWASH, BONNET RELEASE, STEERING COLUMN ADJUSTER, LAMPS & DIPSWITCH, IGNITION STARTER & STEERING LOCK, PARKING LAMPS, HEIGHT CONTROL, REAR WINDOW DEMISTER, DIPPING MIRROR, MASTER WARNING LIGHT (OIL WATER & BRAKES), WARNING LIGHTS TEST BUTTON, CLOCK, OIL & WATER TEMPERATURE & FUEL GAUGES, GLOVE LOCKER, SWIVELLING VENTILATOR, AIR CONTROL, VENTILATORS, CHOKE, VENTILATION DISTRIBUTOR, TEMPERATURE CONTROL, HEATER FAN, HANDBRAKE, WINDOW LIFTS, ASH TRAY & CIGAR LIGHTER

MANUFACTURER:
SA André Citroen, 133 Quai André Citroen, Paris 5e, France.

UK CONCESSIONAIRES:
Citroen Cars Ltd., Trading Estate, Slough, Bucks.

PRICES
Basic	£4,597.00
Special Car Tax	£383.08
VAT	£498.01
Total (in GB)	**£5,478.09**
Seat Belts	£19.06
Licence	£25.00
Delivery charge (London)	£8.50
Number plates	£3.99
Total on the Road (exc. insurance)	**£5,534.64**
Insurance	Group 7

EXTRAS (inc. VAT)
Tinted windows	£55.70
*Refrigeration	£227.10
*Loudspeaker and electric aerial	£40.78
Radio to choice (approx)	£50.00

*Fitted to test car

TOTAL AS TESTED ON THE ROAD	**£5,802.52**

Service Interval
	3,000 miles	6,000 miles
Time Allowed (hours and mins.)	1.00	8.30
Cost @ £3.30 per hour	£3.30	£27.39
Oil Change	£2.77	£2.77
Oil Filter	—	£3.42
Breather Filter	—	—
Air Filter	—	£6.60
Contact breaker points	—	£6.96
Sparking plugs	—	£4.62
Total Cost:	£6.07	£51.75

Routine Replacements:
	Time (hours & mins)	Cost (labour)	Spares	TOTAL:
Brake Pads — Front (set) Brake Pads — Rear (set) }	1.00	£3.30	£18.41	£21.71
Exhaust System	2.00	£6.60	£110.02	£116.62
Clutch	13.00	£42.90	£51.06	£93.96
Struts — Front (pair)	.30	£1.65	£42.56	£44.21
Struts — Rear (pair)	.30	£1.65	£38.37	£40.02
Replace Drive Shaft	.45	£2.48	£82.55	£85.03
Replace Generator	.45	£2.48	£30.69	£33.17
Replace Starter	2.00	£6.60	£44.00	£50.60

ROAD TEST

Citroen SM

FOR: smooth ride; very comfortable in the front; slick five-speed gearchange; tenacious road-holding; superb lights; efficient heating and ventilation; relaxed high-speed cruising; modern interior decor

AGAINST: tricky to drive smoothly; poor visibility; engine rather noisy and thirsty; cramped in the back; left-hand drive only

The Citroen SM has changed little during the three years it's been in production. The most significant modification being the replacement of the original twin-choke Weber carburetters with Bosch electronic fuel injection. As our original test was on an early example and over a lowish mileage, this change in carburation provides a good excuse for us to reappraise the car.

The SM was the first produce of the Citroen/Maserati marriage, and it still tops the French company's range. To recap, it has a V6 Maserati engine driving the front wheels through an excellent Citroen-designed five-speed gearbox. The suspension is basically the soft-riding self-levelling road - hugging hydropneumatic system used for the DS, with the addition of anti-dive and stiffer roll bars. The brakes are power operated discs with automatic compensation for weight transfer, and the steering is a fully powered high-geared rack and pinion system with artificial feel that varies with speed and lock. All very complicated, but does it work?

The SM has a top speed comparable to that of the Jensen Interceptor yet an engine of less than half the capacity, partly because of relatively low drag, partly because Maserati have squeezed a very healthy output from their lovely all-alloy four-cam V6.

However, progress by other manufacturers has forced us to temper our original wild enthusiasm for some aspects of the car's design. For instance, we find the brakes too sensitive, and the unique super-responsive power steering takes a lot of getting used to. The car is also rather noisy: pleasing though the sound of the engine may be, it is tiresome at anything near full throttle. Road noise is also disappointingly high. By way of a

contradiction it is at high cruising speed that the car really comes into its own. Ideal gearing and very low wind noise make light work of continuous 120 mph cruising. So much so in fact, that one has to keep a wary eye on the speedometer. The five-speed gearbox is also a joy to use.

We thoroughly enjoyed our reacquaintance with this unusual motorcar; anyone who can conquer its idiosyncrasies will find it an appealing machine. Others who can't may find the concentration required to drive it well on our crowded roads inappropriate to a price tag of over £6000. It's size doesn't help, either: the SM is an exceptionally large car by European standards—just over 16 ft long and 6 ft wide—and it

bulges out of the driver's sight in all directions. Yet its accommodation is poor as there is little rear-seat legroom and the boot is of quite modest size.

PERFORMANCE

★★ ★★ A couple of churns were always sufficient to start the engine, even after a night out in the frost. Cold start enrichment is automatic and the engine pulls strongly straightaway.

The lovely-looking Maserati power plant (not that you can see much of it) is sited well back under the rearmost part of the enormous sloping bonnet. It is an all-alloy 90 deg V6 with four chain-driven overhead camshafts. French fiscal laws demand high taxes for vehicles over 2800 cc, so the capacity has been restricted to 2670 cc. Even so, the output is excellent; with the new Bosch fuel injection system it produces 178 bhp at 5500 rpm, 8 bhp more than before. Maximum torque of 171 lb ft is developed rather high in the range at 4000 rpm but, as our top gear acceleration figures suggest, the curve is a flat one and the engine will pull strongly from at little as 2000 rpm.

As with all big Citroens, our standing start accelerations were rather traumatic. Too many revs and you provoke vicious and damaging tramp, too few and you fail to induce wheelspin and thus lose time. We achieved our best 0-60 mph times with rather fierce initial clutch slip followed by a little wheelspin: even then we were a little outside Citroen's claim of 8.0 sec. The injected car is 1.3 secs faster to 60 than the carburetter version though, and 2.9 secs quicker to 100 mph.

Acceleration times in fourth and third gear are unaffected by the change in induction; top gear times, however, have increased

The interior is sumptuous with its brushed nylon covered seats and quality carpets. Tilting the backrests forward automatically releases the catch on the base, making for easy entry to the back. Once you are in the rear, head and leg room is limited. We squeezed 9 cu ft of luggage into the cluttered boot

due to a substantial rise in the internal gearing. Citroen claim a top speed of nearly 142 mph: unfortunately we were unable to check this accurately though we feel it is slightly optimistic, considering the small power increase and the 135.2 mph attained with the earlier cars.

In the main the engine is very smooth, though there is a slight harshness between 4500 and 5000 rpm. Also on occasions the engine staggers and stutters momentarily as though the injection system has been caught out and the fuel isn't getting through.

ECONOMY

★★☆ Our test car was inordinately thirsty, giving an overall consumption of just 14.8 mpg on 4-star petrol. At best it rose to almost 19 mpg and at worst it fell below 13 mpg. This compares poorly with the carburetted model which managed 17.2 mpg. We have no way of measuring the steady speed consumption of the Bosch electronic injection at present so we cannot compute a touring consumption. The range, however, would be around 360 miles from the 20-gallon tank.

Oil consumption for the 1300-mile test was negligible.

TRANSMISSION

★★★ / ★★★ Mounted ahead of the Maserati engine is a Citroen-manufactured five-speed gearbox. And very good it is too. The longish lever rocks through a wide gate with the first four gears in the conventional H pattern and fifth up to the right. Reverse occupies the sixth slot and is selected by first lifting the lever upwards.

Fourth gear synchromesh on our test car was weak and resented fast changes, but the other gears could be selected as fast as your hand could move with surprisingly little baulking, making the gearchange a very satisfying one. A spring bias ensures an easy second to third action, though fourth to fifth requires a more careful movement.

Originally the five ratios were closely stacked, providing a continuous surge of acceleration through the range. Now, though the lower four remain unaltered, top has been raised significantly in the interests of relaxed and unstrained cruising.

The clutch engages very smoothly, but is a mite heavy and long in travel for continuous town driving. It also slipped

rather too readily on the 1 in 3 start.

One unfortunate trait of the transmission is the snatch that sometimes occurs at low speed, making it difficult to exploit the engine's excellent low speed tractability.

HANDLING

★★ / ★★ Initially the steering feels very strange indeed and most drivers didn't like it at first. At low speed it seems impossibly direct with just two turns from lock to lock; it also has a strong self-centring action, even at a standstill. As the speed rises, the amount of artificial feel, or resistance at the wheel rim increases and the directness becomes less noticeable. Transferring from a low-geared car with heavy unassisted steering can be really alarming, as the tendency is to apply too much lock too quickly, making the car swerve and snake.

Only when fully accustomed to this exceptional response (and most drivers would probably need several hundred miles to acclimatise), can you really appreciate the car's exceptional handling. You aim rather than steer, as little knowledge of the increas-

ing understeer is transmitted via the small steering wheel and the limit of dry road adhesion is high. Even with deliberate provocation we never succeeded in making the tail break away. In the wet, you have to be careful not to apply too much power out of the corners, when the inside wheel will spin and tend to make the car snake. The understeer also builds up much more rapidly on wet surfaces of course, but the tendency is for the driver to lift off long before he comes to any harm.

BRAKES

★★★ You need powerful brakes to stop 1½ tons of motor car. The SM has them. There are separate circuits for the front and rear discs which are power operated by a small rubber-covered button in place of the conventional pedal.

A mere 40 lb pressure is all you need to give a 0.97g stop from 30 mph. Just 25 lb is sufficient for 0.60g. In consequence very controlled footwork is needed, especially in the wet when it is all too easy to lock the wheels. This lightness makes the brakes too sensitive in town and you have to be very careful and gentle to avoid jerking. At higher speeds, the brakes feel much better and the anti-dive geometry of the suspension does make the car a little more comfortable to drive than the ordinary DS, though there's still a lot of attitude change according to whether the car is braking or accelerating.

Our 20-stop fade test caused an initial rise in pressure of as much as 50 per cent, to the accompaniment of a very strong smell of cooked linings and juddering from the front. However, after the ninth stop the brakes virtually recovered though the smell re-occurred later on. The water splash had no effect whatsoever.

Sadly, the SM's handbrake failed to meet even the minimum legal retardation from 30 mph (as did that of the last car), managing a meagre 0.18g. Admittedly it is unlikely to be required in an emergency thanks to the divided circuits, but it wouldn't even hold the car on a 1 in 6 slope, let alone the 1 in 3 that many cars manage.

ACCOMMODATION

★
  ★

There is ample legroom in the front when using the car as a two seater: for four occupants there has to be a certain amount of sharing. Even with the front seats well forward, there is little leg or head room behind. The rear backrest is also too upright for comfort on long journeys. A central armrest can be folded down to provide the necessary lateral support.

Access to the rear is good. A lever on the side of the front seats releases the tilting and the catch on the seat runners, allowing the whole seat to slide forward. To return to the same setting you just push the seat back, whereupon it locks automatically.

Oddments can be stowed within the four armrests, which have neat flip-up lids; in the tray on the console; and on the large parcel shelf at the rear. The spare wheel steals a lot of boot space but we managed to pack in 9.0 cu ft of our test luggage.

RIDE COMFORT

★★★
★★

The SM's ride is noticeably firmer than that of the DS though we didn't feel any less comfortable because of it. It doesn't wallow or crash on to the bump stops on hump-back bridges as does its sister car, though there is a certain harshness at low speeds when crevices jar the body far more than they would an XJ6. Brisk crosscountry travel, when you're constantly transferring from throttle to brake, emphasises the pronounced change in pitch attitude to which the car is prone. Some people found it quite disconcerting. Travelling fast on main roads, however, the car develops that uncanny magic carpet ride that is unique to these hydropneumatic Citroens ; we know of no better-riding car in such circumstances.

MOTOR ROAD TEST No. 60/73 ● CITROEN SM

PERFORMANCE

CONDITIONS
Weather	Overcast ; Wind 0-18 mph
Temperature	53-60°F
Barometer	29.95
Surface	Dry tarmac

MAXIMUM SPEEDS
	mph	kph
Banked circuit	See text	
Terminal speeds :		
at ¼ mile	87	140
kilometre	109	175
Speed in gears (at 6500 rpm) :		
1st	39	63
2nd	59	95
3rd	86	138
4th	117	188

ACCELERATION FROM REST
mph	sec	kph	sec
0-30	3.4	0-40	2.7
0-40	4.7	0-60	4.3
0-50	6.4	0-80	6.3
0-60	8.3	0-100	9.2
0-70	11.3	0-120	12.7
0-80	14.4	0-140	16.8
0-90	18.2	0-160	22.8
0-100	23.2		
0-110	30.0		
Stand'g ¼	16.5	Stand'g km	30.2

ACCELERATION IN TOP
mph	sec	kph	sec
20-40	12.2	40-60	7.8
30-50	12.9	60-80	7.7
40-60	12.2	80-100	7.9
50-70	12.2	100-120	8.0

60-80	13.5	120-140	8.6
70-90	14.7		

ACCELERATION IN 4th
mph	sec	kph	sec
20-40	8.5	40-60	4.3
30-50	8.0	60-80	5.9
40-60	7.9	80-100	5.1
50-70	8.0	100-120	4.9
60-80	8.6	120-140	5.9
70-90	9.4	140-160	7.4
80-100	9.8		
90-110	12.1		

FUEL CONSUMPTION
Overall	14.9 mpg
	18.9 lt/100 km
Fuel grade	4 octane (RM)
	98 star rating
Tank capacity	20.0 galls
	90.9 litres
Max range	See text
Test distance	1345 miles
	2164 km

*Consumption midway between 30 mph and maximum less 5 per cent for acceleration.

BRAKES
Pedal pressure deceleration and stopping distance from 30 mph (48 kph) :
lb	kg	g	ft	m
25	11	0.60	50	15
40	18	0.97	31	9
Handbrake		0.18	167	51

FADE
20½g stops at 1 min intervals from speed midway between 40 mph (64 kph) and maximum (89 mph, 143 kph)
	lb	kg
Pedal force at start	21	9
Pedal force at 10th stop	25	11
Pedal force at 20th stop	24	11

STEERING
Turning circle between kerbs
	ft	m
left	32.4	9.8
right	32.4	9.8
Lock to lock	2.0 turns	
50 ft diam circle	0.7 turns	

CLUTCH
	in	cm
Free pedal movement	1.0	2.5
Additional to disengage	3.5	8.9
Maximum pedal load	42 lb	19.1 kg

SPEEDOMETER (mph)
Speedo	30	40	50	60	70	80	90	100
True	28	37	47	56	75	74.5	84	93

Distance recorder : 1.9 per cent fast.

WEIGHT
	cwt.	kg
Unladen weight*	29.5	1498.7
Weight as tested	33.2	1686.6

* With fuel for approx 50 miles.

Performance tests carried out by Motor's staff at the Motor Industry Research Association proving ground, Lindley.

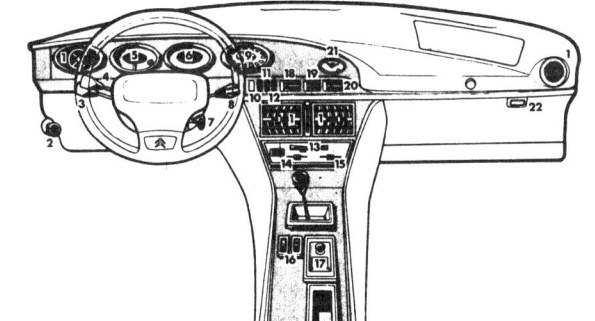

1 face vents	13	temperature control
2 bonnet release	14	distribution
3 wash/wipe	15	fan boost
4 indicators/ horns/ headlamp flash	16	electric windows
5 speedometer	17	cigar lighter
6 rev-counter	18	water temperature gauge
7 ignition switch	19	fuel gauge
8 light switch	20	oil temperature gauge
9 warning lights	21	clock
10 parking lights	22	map reading lamp
11 rear demister		
12 interior light		

COMPARISONS

	Capacity cc	Price £	Max mph	0-60 sec	30-50* sec	Overall mpg	Touring mpg	Length ft in	Width ft in	Weight cwt	Boot cu ft
Citroen SM EFI	2670	6154	see text	8.3	12.9	14.9	—	16 0.5	6 0.5	29.5	9.0
Alfa Romeo Montreal	2593	4999	135.2	8.1	8.8	13.8	—	13 10	5 5.75	25.1	3.2
BMW 3.0CSL	3003	7399	132.5	7.2	7.3	17.2	—	15 3.25	5 11	25.4	6.2
Mercedes-Benz 350 SL	3499	6995	127.8	8.1	3.8	15.4	19.5	14 4.75	5 10.25	30.4	6.6
Fiat 130 Coupe	3235	5531	115.6	10.6	3.9	18.8	—	15 10	6 0	31.7	12.3
Jensen Interceptor	6276	6981	138.5	7.3	3.4	11.3	15.0	15 .8	5 10	33.0	8.5
Daimler Double-Six	5343	4812	135.7	7.4	2.6	11.5	13.5	15 9.75	5 9.25	34.8	11.8

*in fifth for Citroen, Alfa ; kickdown for automatic Mercedes, Jensen, Daimler, Fiat
Touring fuel consumption not recorded for cars with fuel injection

STAR GRADE KEY ★★★ excellent ★★ good ★ average ★ poor ▪ bad

MOTOR ROAD TEST No. 60/73 ● CITROEN SM

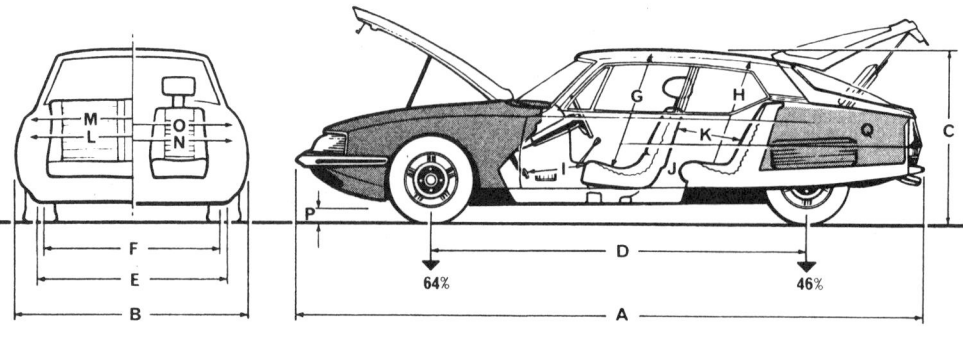

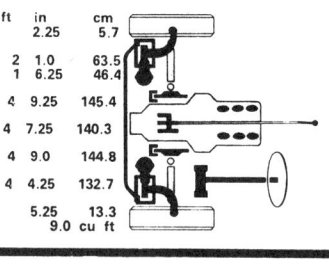

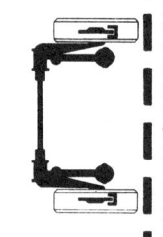

		ft	in	cm			ft	in	cm
A	overall length	16	0.5	488.9		min		2.25	5.7
B	overall width	6	0.5	184.2	K	front to back			
C	unladen height	4	3.25	130.2		seat max	2	1.0	63.5
D	wheelbase	9	8.25	295.3		min	1	6.25	46.4
E	front track	5	0.5	153.7	L	front elbow			
F	rear track	4	5.0	134.6		width	4	9.25	145.4
G	com seat to				M	front shoulder			
	roof front	3	3.5	100.3		width	4	7.25	140.3
H	com seat to				N	rear elbow			
	roof rear	3	0.5	92.7		width	4	9.0	144.8
I	pedal to seat				O	rear shoulder			
	max	1	8.5	52.1		width	4	4.25	132.7
	min	1	2.75	37.5	P	min ground			
J	kneeroom					clearance		5.25	13.3
	max		8.5	21.6	Q	boot capacity			9.0 cu ft

GENERAL SPECIFICATION

ENGINE
Cylinders — 90° V6
Capacity — 2670 cc (163 cu in.)
Bore/stroke — 87/75 mm
(3.42/2.95 in.)
Cooling — Water
Block — Light alloy
Head — Light alloy
Valves — Twin dohc
Valve timing — Not disclosed
Compression — 9.0 : 1
Carburetter — Bosch electronic fuel injection
Bearings — 4 main
Fuel pump — Electric
Max power — 178 bhp (DIN) at 6250 rpm
Max torque — 171 lb ft (DIN) at 4000 rpm

TRANSMISSION
Type — 5-speed manual
Clutch — 9 in. sdp diaphragm spring
Internal ratios and mph/1000 rpm
Top — 0.75 : 1/23.4
4th — 0.97 : 1/18.1

3rd — 1.32 : 1/13.2
2nd — 1.94 : 1/9.0
1st — 2.92 : 1/6.0
Rev — 3.15 : 1
Final drive — Spiral bevel 4.375 : 1

BODY/CHASSIS
Construction — All steel monoshell with bolt-on panels.
Protection — Electrophoretic primer and paint.

SUSPENSION
Front — Ind by transverse arms, anti-roll bar and hydro-pneumatic springing with self-levelling.
Rear — Ind by trailing arms, anti-roll bar, and hydro-pneumatic springing with self-levelling.

STEERING
Type — Unique rack and pinion with variable assistance.
Assistance — Yes

Toe-in — 3-5 mm
Camber — 0 to ¼ in. negative
Castor — 1° 38'-1° 47'

BRAKES
Type — Power operated discs all round.
Circuit — Split back and front
Rear valve — Automatic weight transfer compensation.
Adjustment — Self-adjusting

WHEELS
Type — Steel disc type
Tyres — Michelin 205 x 70 XVX.
Pressures — F 32 ; R 29

ELECTRICAL
Battery — 12 volt, 70 Ah
Polarity — Negative earth
Generator — Alternator
Fuses — 12
Headlights — 6 QI, two of which are directional, all self-levelling.

STANDARD EQUIPMENT

Adjustable steering .... Yes
Anti-lock brakes .... No
Armrests .... Yes
Ashtrays .... Yes
Breakaway mirror .... Yes
Cigar lighter .... Yes
Childproof locks .... No
Clock .... Yes
Coat hooks .... No
Dual circuit brakes .... Yes
Electric windows .... Yes
Energy absorb steering col .... Yes
Fresh air ventilation .... Yes
Grab handles .... No
Head restraints .... Yes

Heated rear window .... Yes
Laminated screen .... No
Lights
  Boot .... Yes
  Courtesy .... Yes
  Engine bay .... Yes
  Hazard warning .... No
  Map reading .... Yes
  Parking .... Yes
  Reversing .... Yes
  Spot/fog .... Yes
Locker .... No
Outside mirror .... Yes
Parcel shelf .... Yes

Petrol filler lock .... Yes
Radio .... No
Rev counter .... Yes
Seat belts
  Front .... No
  Rear .... No
Seat recline .... Yes
Seat height adjuster .... Yes
Sliding roof .... No
Tinted glass .... No
Combination wash/wipe .... Yes
Wipe delay .... No
Vanity mirror .... Yes

IN SERVICE

GUARANTEE
Duration .... 6 months

MAINTENANCE
Schedule .... Every 3000 miles
Free service .... At 600 miles

DO-IT-YOURSELF
Sump ...... 12.5 pints, SAE 20W/50

Gearbox/Rear axle ... 3.9 pints, SAE EP80
Steering gear ....
Coolant .... 23 pints
Chassis lubrication...10 grease points
Contact breaker gap ... 0.4±0.05 mm
Spark plug type **Golden Lodge HL/ Champion N10Y**
Spark plug gap .... 0.6 mm
Tappets (cold) **0.30/0.35 mm inlet 0.50/0.55 mm exhaust**

REPLACEMENT COSTS
Brake pads/linings (front) — £16.81
Clutch unit — £50.12
Complete exhaust system... — £124.77
Engine (part exchange) ... — £1537.44
Front wing — £84.10
Gearbox (part exchange) — £247.67
Oil filter — £3.41
Starter motor .... — £91.31
Windscreen — £71.20

Make : Citroen.
Model : SM
Makers : S. A. Ándre Citroen, 133 Quai Andre Citroen, Paris, 15e, France.
Concessionaires : Citroen Cars Ltd, Trading Estate, Slough, Bucks.
Tel: Slough 23811.
Price : £5164.00 plus £430.33 car tax and £559.3 VAT equals £6153.76. Plus tinted windows, £77.46, plus air conditioning, £267.13 gives total as test of £6498.35.

AT THE WHEEL

★★★
★★★

The seats are narrow and unusual in that the backrest tilts from the lumbar region rather than from the base of the spine. Fore and aft adjustment is sufficient rather than generous and the cushion has three alternative tilt positions at either end. Though very comfortable, the seats lack lateral support. The steering column is adjustable too, and with the clamp released both rake and reach can be set to taste.

At first the pedals feel odd and awkward, as they're all quite different. The clutch is of the pendant type, the brake is a small button on the floor and the throttle a big organ pedal, set well above the brake. Surprisingly you can heel-and-toe with practice, even though the throttle requires as much, maybe more, pressure than the brake.

The minor controls are excellent. The foremost of the two left-hand stalks operates the (non-return) indicators, the horn and headlamp flasher. The one behind controls the two-speed wipers and electric washers. On the right a single stalk looks after the complicated lighting system.

The only control that is badly placed is the handbrake, which is set too far back—particularly in our test car as it didn't have any effect until the lever was in the upright position and at the limit of its travel. The static Toric belts are easy to put on (though difficult to adjust for length) but they have to be kept tight otherwise they slide off your shoulder. What a pity the car doesn't have Toric's marvellous inertia reel belts.

VISIBILITY

★
★

Visibility is not one of the car's strong points. Initially, most people will choose a high seating position to help them aim this six-feet wide giant, otherwise you can't see the far side of the bonnet let alone the tip of the drooping nose. Rear three-quarter vision is poor because of the up-swept tail, and dirt soon collects on the heavily canted rear screen. The headrests and reflection from the chrome strips at the base of the facia don't make matters any easier.

Two door mirrors assist the dipping interior one, which is just as well as the rear view is constantly changing due to the considerable pitch movements. The enormous anti-lift wipers do their job well but leave a large unswept area in the bottom left-hand corner of the screen.

The lights are fantastic ; with the powerful swivelling beams in action no car comes with better lights, though the big glass windows that encapsulate them need regular cleaning. Again, the attitude of the car, particularly the tail droop under acceleration, badly effects the aim of the lights. The suspension's self-levelling

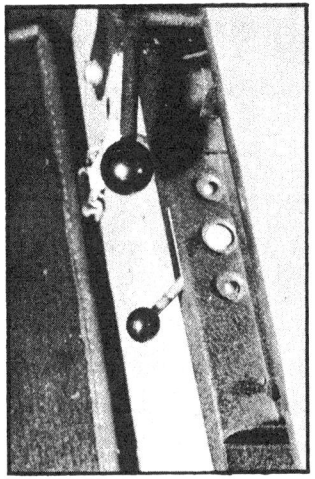

Left : the heating and ventilating is easy to control. Demisting is slow however. Above : this lever allows full adjustment of the steering column. Right : the front seat cushions are adjustable for tilt at the back and front. The large lever controls fore and aft movement

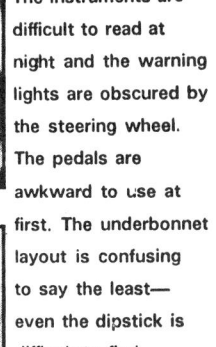

The instruments are difficult to read at night and the warning lights are obscured by the steering wheel. The pedals are awkward to use at first. The underbonnet layout is confusing to say the least— even the dipstick is difficult to find

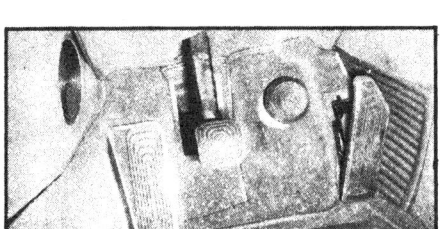

system doesn't compensate quickly enough to prevent this snag.

INSTRUMENTS

★★★ Citroen have perhaps been too concerned with symmetry rather than easy reading; the warning light cluster, for instance, is hidden behind the rim of the steering wheel and the oval speedometer is graduated in 5 mph steps and is not easy to read at night. We doubt if anybody would have time to make use of the stopping distances that are calibrated alongside the speeds. A useful gimmick however, is the button with which you can test all the major warning light bulbs.

The auxiliary instruments, including oil and water temperature gauges and the fuel gauge, are set into the lip of the facia and angled towards the driver. All instruments are illuminated with subtle green lighting at night. On our test car the water temperature needle would sometimes move into the red zone before the fans were heard to cut in.

HEATING

★★ Heating is easily controlled. One horizontal slide regulates temperature, one distribution and a third the volume, including a four-speed fan. Not only is it immediately

obvious how to work the heater, but it all works very well, providing fine control over a powerful set-up. Our only quibble is that it would not demist the screen as quickly as we'd like.

VENTILATION

★★★ Our test car was fitted with the optional air conditioning so getting cold air was no problem. The fan can be used to force ample air out of the multi-position centre vents and thus assist the effective ram system of the eyeball vents at each end of the facia.

NOISE

★★★ It seems reasonable to expect peace and quiet in a car of this quality and price. In this respect the SM has a Jekyll and Hyde character. Wind noise is very low with no more than a hiss building up around the exterior mirrors and the seal at the front of the doors. Road roar, is disappointingly high, though, and there is also a fair amount of bump thump. The worse offender, however, is the engine, which makes a nasty rattly noise when idling, a loud induction roar on full throttle and a high-pitched whine when nearing peak revs. Only when cruising in fifth is engine noise unobtrusive. Other infrequent rattlings would appear to come

from the hydraulic pump, though it is not as obtrusive in the SM as it is in the DS.

EQUIPMENT

★★★★ The SM has most of the amenities you would expect of a car of this type and price, plus one or two rather unusual ones. Electric windows, reclining seats, power steering and headrests are standard. There is a central ashtray with built-in cigar lighter and two more ashtrays at each end of the back seat. There are two fold-out sun-visors with a vanity mirror for the passenger. A clock, heated rear screen and reversing and parking lights are also included.

More unusual are the swivelling, self-levelling lights and, of course, the variable height suspension. Extras included on our test car were the air-conditioning unit and tinted windows. A radio is not fitted as standard.

FINISH

★★★★ The standard of finish is high and to us very pleasing and modern in design. The brushed nylon seats and combed stainless steel facia emphasise this ultra modern decor which is refreshingly different to that of most luxury cars. Carpets line the footwells and outer sills as well as the floor

itself. A coarser-grained one is used to cover the interior of the boot and the spare wheel.

Outside, rubber inserts in the wrap-around bumpers help prevent those odd dents and scratches. The paintwork didn't look very durable in places though, some of the (unstressed and replaceable) panels being thinly covered at the edges.

SERVICE

With its new fuel injection system the SM's engine is practically invisible. The long inlet tracts swoop over it, completely obscuring the sparking plugs. Even the dipstick is hard to find, hidden away at the back of the engine under the long bonnet. Certainly the mass of pipes, hoses, pumps and reservoirs that together fill almost every square inch of the engine compartment, will be more than enough to dissuade the average owner from getting his hands dirty. Even the battery looks as if it is cocooned for life.

However, when you've worked out where they are, you can at least get at the oil filter, the hydraulic reservoir and the radiator header tank.

The spare wheel is located in the boot together with the accessories required for jacking the car up. There is no twiddling of handles with the Citroen; the hydropneumatic system does all the work.

Elegant complexity

The Citroën SM can claim to be the world's most advanced car. Is all the complication worth the cost? After a long-term test which has encompassed two different SMs and journeys ranging from long Continental trips to 50 mph-limited commuting, we believe that it is.

This story really begins last summer when *Autocar* entered a Citroën SM in the BRSCC's first Tour of Britain. Howden Ganley and I drove it. Our result was nothing to get excited about; the car had proved less competitive than we had hoped and more difficult to handle than we had anticipated. I remember asking Howden what he thought we had learnt from the exercise. His answer was succinct: "Well," he said, "Now we know why people don't race Citroëns". With hindsight, it was a pretty rotten thing to do to a fine car, which, like all Citroëns had been designed with a "clean sheet" approach to meet certain specified conditions. Those included the need for quiet, high speed cruising, a superbly comfortable ride over all sorts of surfaces, and a. very sophisticated power steering system. But they did not include racing.

In our original road test of the SM (*Autocar* 10 June 1971) we described it as "technically the world's most advanced car". One of our intentions had been to find out how reliable its many complex systems would be under the stresses and strains of competition as well as in normal use. On the Tour they had given no trouble and a few weeks later, denuded of its roll cage and with the dents knocked out, the car came back for us to gain further experience with it under more typical road conditions.

It was running well, though both engine and gearbox were noisier than they had been originally. From the long-term test point of view the snag was that very little was known of this car's history; it had been prepared as a Group 1 rally car by the Citroën Competitions Department in Paris and had seen action as a practice car for the Moroccan Rally (which an SM

won in 1971). Furthermore, it was not the latest model as it had the triple-Weber carburetted engine which had been superseded by the Bosch electronic fuel injection version. Citroën Cars Ltd. very generously agreed to the long-term loan of a never-raced-nor-rallied Injection SM in its place. It had done 4,000 miles as a press demonstrator; we aimed to add a minimum of another 10,000.

Actually it could not have come at a worse time. It was the beginning of December and the height of the fuel shortage around London. None of us were using cars for long journeys if we could avoid it and those who would normally have been so keen to drive the SM were squabbling over our Renault 5 and Fiat 127. Experience suggested that we would be unlikely to get more than 15 mpg around town, though even at that rate its big tank gave it a useful 300-mile range—providing you could find somebody to fill it up. But then there was the 50 mph limit which succeeded in its intention of boring us away from the motorways, and at which speed the SM would not run cleanly in fifth gear. In any case it seemed anti-social to be using a car so obviously designed for the enjoyment of motoring in those petrol-starved times. The miles went on slowly.

From a driveability point-of-view I am not convinced of the advantages of fuel injection. The SM *Injection Electronique* (EFI) had excellent throttle response when accelerating and none of the "hunting" at low speed and idle that is associated with some electronic systems, but does not have the reassuring shut-off when the throttle is lifted like an old-fashioned carburettor engine. It had an occasional light-throttle hesitation. Furthermore, it turned the SM's already frighteningly complicated underbonnet scene into a mechanic's nightmare with its system of air ducts, filters, intakes and banana-shaped inlet manifolds. Having spent a frustrating hour removing five of the six sparking plugs on the carburettor car (the sixth was totally inaccessible) I was glad that the fuel injection version did not share its tendency to foul its plugs in traffic. In fact, cold starting and subsequent drive-away were always excellent. The rich mixture control is automatic.

Our road test of the injection SM (*Autocar* 23 August 1973) had suggested that apart from maximum speed (4 mph up) as a result of higher gearing, performance was slightly down compared to the earlier model. Figures taken with our long-term car at 11,000 miles, published here, show an improvement over the original injection test car in step-off, though as a whole they are still a little slower than the first SM that we tested. Such observations are really only of theoretical interest because the SM is not a car that is bought for ultimate performance alone. Performance is in any case remarkably good for a car that weighs over 30 cwt and is powered by an engine of only 2.7 litres.

Altogether the SM is an odd amalgam of characteristics. Its startling, super-streamlined body couldn't be anything but a Citroën and its aerodynamic efficiency, shown by its maximum speed and lack of wind noise, are what one would expect from the flagship of this very imaginative firm. The Maserati V6 engine on the other hand, emits a splendid racing growl under hard acceleration and has quite a harsh feel to it when working hard. Similarly, the manual five-speed gearbox has a precise "gated" change that would not be out of place in an Italian sports car, and belies the transmission's distant location from the cockpit. Somehow, with such a futuristic appearance a conventional power unit and transmission seems out of place; it deserves a gas turbine and fully automatic transmission at the very least.

These things and others, therefore, give the Citroën SM a truly unique character. It is not everyone's cup of tea. Certainly it takes some getting used to, which is why we encouraged anyone driving it for the first time to do a longish journey which would give him time to adapt to its peculiarities and also use the car under the conditions for which it was primarily intended. Not everyone returned convinced. For me it was a taste quickly acquired, like eating an avocado pear for the first time: you are unsure at first, come to appreciate its subtle qualities and then can't have enough of them.

The thing that needs acclimatization (and can catch you out when you come back to the SM

from another car) is the very high geared steering. It is like driving a go-kart; at first one tends to over-steer and over-correct, and progress is twitchy. When mastered, it is one of the best features of this remarkable machine. Mechanically it is one of the most complex of the car's systems and its method of operation is unique. It is perhaps worthwhile to take a little space to examine what Citroën's engineers set out to do and how successful they have been in meeting the object.

The SM is heavy, and has a substantial front weight bias; it has front-wheel drive; and big tyres (205/70 VR 15 Michelin XWX on the injection version—the same as we used on our "racer"). Power steering was clearly essential. It needed to be light for low speed manouevring since the SM is a big car with an unusually long wheelbase. They wanted to have the degree of positive control that only a racing car with very high geared steering could attain. Two turns from lock-to-lock was judged to be ideal, but with the light control envisaged for parking, would make the steering far too sensitive at high speeds. Their solution was to build an artificial "feel" that increased with the speed of the car and they used ideas from aircraft control systems to achieve it. So, as the speed increases, the resistance at the steering wheel is increased, giving it the feel of an unassisted set-up with the advantage of very high gearing. An adjunct to this is that the steering has servo self-centring. At low speed or when stationary this means that the front wheels automatically return to the straight-ahead position, though any hand movement by the driver causes a positive reaction in the hydraulic valve system which then assists his movement like a more conventional power-steering arrangement. Furthermore since all the "feel" is artificially created, the steering wheel is very largely insulated from kick-back over bad surfaces and some of the less favourable characteristics of front-wheel-drive.

The mechanics of this system have been dealt with in detail in these columns (*Autocar* 21 January 1971). It works exceedingly well and plays a very large part in the confident and accurate way that this large car can be rushed through twisting roads like a sports car. Many of the less attractive characteristics of the front wheel drive layout are disguised by it under normal conditions, including the understeer and its tendency to pick up and spin the inside front wheel. Progress that seems very dramatic from the outside feels very secure from within, and as a result one often finds that one has entered a corner much faster than expected. It contributes to the car's excellent "hands off" straight line stability. The self-centring makes the car

steering to keep the car on a straight course.

I mentioned manoeuvring a while back. From the steering point of view this is easy, but the very wide front and long sloping nose means that like the DS Citroëns it is hard to judge its not inconsiderable size (16 ft long and 6 foot wide) when turning in confined spaces. My colleagues are fond of telling stories about the many people who have misjudged the gates of the office car park with DSs. I made the mistake of boasting that I didn't understand the problem; I had never

from rock steady cruising at very high speed on motorways (120 mph is quiet and comfortable; roads, laws and traffic permitting), to snow-covered mountains in Andorra. Fast main roads with long sweeping curves are the SM's forte; for much of France there can be few cars quicker. On slower, sharper corners its biggest disadvantage becomes apparent— the amount of roll. The car really isn't happy being driven through a series of *lacets* with verve. No sooner has the suspension caught up with the car's attitude for one corner than it is unsettled again

and just the dull drone of the engine in its high fifth gear; the impression from within is in some ways more like a small aeroplane than a car. There is the feeling of insulation from the outside world, yet with a solid aura of security and the confidence of complete control. I was not surprised to hear from Citroën that a large percentage of the 400-plus British customers for SMs use them for long journeys, particularly on the Continent. One such customer is Mike Hailwood, who has had his SM for three years, yet previously changed his cars on whim every

surprisingly easy to park at the kerbside, for once a gap has been entered, straightening up is simply a matter of letting go of the wheel between each backward or forward manoeuvre.

There are a few disadvantages too. Even when used to it, in town it does need a fairly delicate approach, which not everyone is able to muster. It is a quirk of the system that it is still a little *too* sensitive around the immediate straight-ahead position. Correct adjustment to the steering wheel's straight-ahead position is critical (and quite easily done by moving the rack; a single bolt job). We found that out on the Tour of Britain when the steering was deranged by an argument with the Armco at Oulton Park. A bottom wishbone mounting was slightly bent and I remember driving down the M6 applying perhaps one-eighth of a turn of lock to keep the car straight; a job that became increasingly harder on the wrists as the car went faster. More serious though was my discovery that the very steeply cambered roads that are found in some parts of France had the same effect (with the steering in good order) and that driving fast along them became physically tiring as one struggled against the

had any trouble with them. The very next morning I confidently swung the SM through the gateway only to hear a sickening clang. In fact, all I had done was to break off the thick rubber facing on the bumper that wraps round the nose, but it illustrated just how close I had been judging things without realizing it. The SM is longer—and wider—than it seems.

In another make of car the suspension and ride would be remarkable. Suffice to say that the SM uses the well-tried Citroën interconnected hydropneumatic struts which make it self-levelling and has ride comfort second to none. It has a three position ride-height adjuster to give it adequate ground clearance for any sort of bad road. As with the DS and GS, bumps and bad surfaces are ironed out with ease, and only hump-back bridges and the like catch the suspension out. For reasons that are not entirely clear to me, its performance over cobbles is less impressive, a sort of uncomfortable patter being set up from the rear wheels. Road noise is high, being particularly sensitive to bump-thump from cat's eyes.

I took the car to the Spanish Grand Prix at Madrid, which involved all aspects of motoring

for the next. The result is a lot of bucking around to accompany the inevitable tyre scrub and a very uncomfortable time for your passengers, who are not helped by the lack of sideways location in the seats. In general, it is better to adopt the rear-wheel drive technique of "straightening out" corners as much as possible to keep the roll to a minimum.

Hard acceleration produces a noticeably nose-up attitude but under heavy braking the anti-dive geometry reduces the opposite reaction. I find the DS-type no-travel brake button very reassuring for a fast car and the all-disc set up proved very consistent in normal use except on one occasion when unexpected front wheel lock on a slippery country road caused me some anxious moments. Out of curiosity I tried to reproduce this in tests at MIRA and found that after four or five repeated heavy stops the rear wheels did have a tendency to jack up and slew sideways as the fronts locked. Under normal circumstances, however, the brakes are without fault.

One could not fail to be impressed by the SM's performance on our trip to Madrid. By the effortless way that it ate up the miles, with virtually no wind noise

few months. "It's nice and comfortable on main roads—I just like it", he says, confessing that he doesn't look after it very well and that it had been reliable "except when there was no anti-freeze in it last winter—that messed it up a bit".

Strangely enough, the water system gave me some cause for alarm on the return from Spain. Slightly higher than normal water temperature and the need for three or four pints of topping up water a day suggested either a leak (which wasn't visible) or head gasket trouble. When safely back home it was found to be the latter —a problem not unknown previously and which had resulted in a new design of gasket. Otherwise, the 3,200 mile round trip was marred only by a bad engine-induced vibration, irritatingly transmitted through the chassis at a steady 4,500 rpm, which represents just over 100 mph in fifth gear and 80 mph in fourth. Apart from discouraging cruising at these otherwise convenient speeds, this was no doubt one reason why several minor bolted-on components like door and boot locks and one headlamp mounting came adrift during the trip.

Vibration also tended to cause the adjustable steering column to

slip to its lowest position. In and out and up and down column adjustment is only one of the factors which go towards producing a perfect driving position for everyone. The seats can be adjusted for height front and rear, and thus for rake as well, while the backrests are, unusually, hinged half way up instead of from the base. This looks as if it ought to be uncomfortable but in fact provides the fine adjustment to get the driving position just right. The thick, soft head restraints are also fully adjustable. Stuart Bladon has an irrational fear of headrests and the like and ejected them before even sitting in the car when he took it to the Geneva Show. A pity, for had he tried the SM's, he would have found them most comfortable; both for supporting the driver's neck and as a pillow for the front seat passenger.

The test car differed from our Tour SM in having leather, rather than nylon cloth-covered seats. These add a hefty £258 to the price, but their smoothness only accentuates the lack of sideways location, and the far from ideal placing of the unusual socket-clasped Toric seat belts did little to help.

Though a driver and one passenger could travel all day in the SM without getting uncomfortable—and arrive fresh at their destination—carrying four people for any distance is less satisfactory. The rear seats are well upholstered and nicely shaped but headroom and, more particularly, leg room are a problem, though rear passengers' feet can be tucked under the front seats. In recognition of this, the front passenger's seat has less adjustment than the driver's. Even someone of average height feels more comfortable with the passenger seat near its rearmost point. One is forced to concede that in terms of packaging, the SM does not come out very well. Like many American cars of similar (and bigger) dimensions it is really only a 2+2. Neither is the luggage space over-generous. The big spare wheel occupies a great deal of boot space. We managed to ac-

Top, left: The EFI test car was trimmed in expensive leather. Seats are comfortable and infinitely adjustable, but they lack side support. Facia is simple and features multi-purpose warning light system (inset). The big red light in the centre is additional warning of hydraulic failure, loss of oil pressure, or overheating. The button is to check that these warning lamps are working

Left: If it breaks down, call a plumber . . . Underbonnet view is daunting, with V6 engine buried beneath injection system and inlet manifolds

Citroën SM *Long Term Report*

commodate all our luggage plus typewriters and a lot of camera gear in it for the Spanish trip, but only by using a number of soft bags instead of suitcases. The boot leaked. Inside stowage space for oddments is provided by some useful side bins (in the doors and at the rear) and a disappointingly small facia locker.

Though it looks very futuristic at first glance, the facia is actually quite straightforward. It is possible to adjust the steering column to the point where the working range of the speedometer and rev counter are not visible. The third matching oval dial has no less than 14 warning lights, for everything from indicators to hydraulic failure and a test switch so that you check that the bulbs are working in the more important ones. The three smaller gauges at the centre are for water and oil temperature and fuel, the latter being very vague (the same system flashes the low fuel warning light on bends with nearly half a tank left). The heating and ventilating controls are nice to use and easy to understand; air distribution is good though the heater isn't all that powerful. Our car had the optional air conditioning—pleasant, but £291 extra. On the centre console, trimmed like the facia with a bronze satin-finish aluminium, is the switch for the electric windows which are maddeningly slow in operation, the handbrake, and the radio slot. I was disappointed to hear that casette players should not be mounted

How it started. The Group 1 carburettor SM on a stage of the 1973 Avon Motor Tour of Britain

vertically; we fitted a Radiomobile 330 radio which was reported on in the issue of 13 July 1974.

Lighting, wipers and indicators are dealt with by finger-tip stalks. The bank of six quartz-halogen lights is yet another SM novelty and they too are self-levelling as well as the inner pair moving with the steering. The spread of light that they produce is fantastic, though unfortunately they prove very difficult to adjust satisfactorily. One of the toughened glass headlamp covers was smashed by *gravillons* on my return through France. The wipers—which have two speeds, intermittent (variable by rheostat) and not fast enough —are, however, really not up to the performance of the car.

No one would expect a car of this price, let alone of this complexity, to make concessions to the home mechanic. Servicing and repairs are a specialised business for which mechanics are specially trained. 25 of Citroën's 180 British sales outlets are officially "SM dealers". During our tenure the sight tube on the big green canister which contains all the hydraulic fluid never dropped below "maximum". Access to oil and water fillers, washer bottle, even the distributor and alternator is not bad. Checking and topping up the battery is more awkward and if it needs to be removed it has to be taken out through a hatch in the right hand wheel arch. Aside from those items mentioned we had no troubles or failures with

the car. Front brake pads needed to be renewed at 6,000 miles and again at 14,000; at which point it also needed a new pair of front tyres. These running costs are included in the accompanying table. To put the overall fuel consumption figure into perspective, the average for the Spanish trip was 20 mpg. General use, including commuting, varied between 15 and 19 mpg with an all-time low for 150 miles around London of 10.5! Overall, the car proved more economical than the carburettor SM.

Only the privileged few can afford a car that costs nearly £7,000. But even leaving price aside, the SM is not for everyone. Opinions among our testers range from great enthusiasm to "no thanks". It is a true Grand Touring car and needs to be used as such. Around town and in little country lanes it is rather unwieldy —and this country made worse by being left-hand-drive. Citroën acknowledge that they lost a lot of potential customers when plans for a right-hand-drive version were dropped.

As enthusiasts we have tended to dwell on its technical marvels but let us not forget that as an attention-getter the SM is supreme. Even in France it turns heads and in the little villages of La Mancha in Central Spain the inhabitants treated it with the suspicion and wonder of something from Outer Space. It is a strange mixture, the SM. Mechanically ornate; simple in line; beautiful yet functional. A girl friend of mine described it as "the sexiest car in the world". I know what she means. □

PERFORMANCE CHECK
Maximum speeds

Gear	mph R/T	mph Staff	kph R/T	kph Staff	rpm R/T	rpm Staff
Top (mean)	139	137	224	220	6,000	5,900
(best)	140	139	225	224	6,030	6,000
4th	118	118	190	190	6,500	6,500
3rd	87	87	135	135	6,500	6,500
2nd	59	59	95	95	6,500	6,500
1st	39	39	63	63	6,500	6,500

Standing	R/T: 17.1 sec	81 mph
¼-mile	Staff: 17.1 sec	81 mph
Standing	R/T: 31.0 sec	109 mph
kilometre	Staff: 31.0 sec	109 mph

Acceleration

R/T:	3.5	5.0	7.2	9.3	13.0	16.4	21.1	25.9	31.5
Staff:	3.2	4.7	7.1	9.3	12.9	16.1	21.3	26.2	33.2

Time in seconds 0										
True speed mph		30	40	50	60	70	80	90	100	110
Indicated speed R/T:		33	43	53	64	75	85	96	106	117
Indicated speed Staff:		30	40	51	62	72	82	92	102	112

Speed range, Gear Ratios and Time in Seconds

mph	Top R/T	Top Staff	4th R/T	4th Staff	3rd R/T	3rd Staff	2nd R/T	2nd Staff
10-30	—	—	—	—	6.9	5.8	4.3	3.9
20-40	13.0	11.5	9.1	8.2	6.0	5.7	4.0	3.5
30-50	12.7	12.0	8.6	8.3	5.7	5.5	3.9	3.5
40-60	12.3	11.8	8.1	8.6	5.8	5.5	—	—
50-70	12.1	11.2	8.8	9.0	5.9	5.7	—	—
60-80	13.3	12.8	9.1	9.8	7.5	6.3	—	—
70-90	14.8	14.4	9.6	10.2	—	—	—	—
80-100	15.5	14.9	10.4	13.3	—	—	—	—

Fuel Consumption

Overall mpg	R/T:	17.9 mpg (15.8 litres/100km)
	Staff:	18.1 mpg (15.6 litres/100km)

NOTE: *"R/T" denotes performance figures for Citroën SM EFI tested in AUTOCAR of 23 August 1973*

COST OF OWNERSHIP

Running Costs	Life in Miles	Cost per 10,000 miles £	Cost per 10,000 miles p
One gallon of 5-star fuel average cost today 55p	18.1	303.86	
One pint of top-up oil, average cost today 29p	550	5.27	
Front disc brake pads (set of 2)	6,000	25.41	
Rear disc brake pads (set of 2)	12,000	8.99	
Michelin XWX 205/70VR-15 tyres (front pair)	15,000	68.80	
Michelin XWX 205/70VR-15 tyres (rear pair)	35,000	29.48	
†Service (main interval and actual cost incurred)	6,000	118.00	
Total		**559.81**	

Running cost per mile	**5.6p**

Approx. standing charges per year	128.10
*Insurance	25.00
Tax	

Depreciation	**712.91**
Price when new	6,107
Trade in cash value (approx.)	4,700
Typical advertised price (current)	5,300
Depreciation (over 12 months)	807

Total cost per mile (based on cash value)	**21.2p**

Insurance cost is for 34 years old driver, with 65 per cent no claims bonus and with car garaged in Byfleet, Surrey. Subject to compulsory excess of £250. Named drivers only.
†*Estimated with the help of Eurocars Ltd., as typical; repair of blown head gasket at 14,000 miles not included (see text)*

Tilting at windmills

A Spanish diversion and some thoughts on the Citroën SM

By Ray Hutton

"*LOOK over there where more than 30 monstrous giants appear. I intend to do battle with them and take all their lives.*"

"*What giants?*" asked Sancho Panza.

"*Those you see there,*" replied his master, "*with their long arms.*"

"*Take care, your Worship,*" said Sancho, "*those things over there are not giants but windmills and what seem to be their arms are sails, which are whirled round in the wind and make the millstone turn.*"

"*It is quite clear,*" replied Don Quixote, "*that you are not experienced in this matter of adventures. They are giants, and if you are afraid go away and say your prayers, whilst I advance and engage them in fierce and unequal battle.*"

We too spotted the giants, a neat row along a ridge of hills overlooking the village of Mota del Cuervo. On a flat open plain like that which forms most of the region of La Mancha, the odd hill and ridge provides a windy, exposed viewpoint. The bigger hills have castles; the smaller ones the distinctive white, conical-roofed windmills that provide the mistaken enemy in one of the most famous tales of Don Quixote, the legendary Knight of the Sad Countenance.

In a way, we too were in search of adventure. The car was a Citroën SM that we were fortunate to run for an extended period last year. Cars like that can be frustrating in Britain. Not just because of the speed limits (it is becoming increasingly difficult to escape those anywhere) but because the daily routine is not the right role for such a blatantly hedonistic car. Thoroughbred machinery, like Don Quixote's faithful Rocinante, needs to stretch its legs from time to time. On this occasion it had been a stimulating 1,500 mile journey to Madrid. Business completed, two days off gave an opportunity to go exploring in La Mancha – a

land made familiar by Cervantes' writing and the many stories, films and musicals resulting from it, but well off the usual tourist track.

Incongruous as the storybook Knight and his Squire may have seemed, they would scarcely have been met with more curiosity and wonder than the metallic blue SM. One can imagine that the layout of the little villages of La Mancha was little different in the sixteenth century. The SM, with hissing hydraulics as it raised its haunches to climb the rougher unmade streets and alleys, might as well have been a spaceship. Everyone stopped and stared while in those rural havens of modern technology, the service stations, interested groups gathered round to marvel at how *complicado* it was under the bonnet.

The people of La Mancha are mostly poor, proud and reserved. Their villages are, in the main, unremarkable, even drab. But there are some glorious exceptions like the galleried town square at Tembleque, the dreamy castle at Belmonte and, of course, the windmills. They stand in orderly rows, close to but above the villages. Of the six at Mota del Cuervo, only one is in full working order, the others have been restored with original materials; elsewhere many have sails missing.

La Mancha, the heart of Spain, is bordered to the west by Toledo and Ciudad Real and to the east by Cuenca and Albacete. We started at Toledo, a couple of hours' drive from Madrid, and stayed overnight in the comfortable *parador* of Conde de Orgaz overlooking the town. La Mancha is not well served with tourist hotels. There is another *parador* at Cuenca; these state-owned inns set out to reflect the character of the region and are both unusual and reasonably priced.

The walled city of Toledo itself is interesting, though care is needed in negotiating its narrow streets. We found ourselves travelling down a winding one-way street and were confronted

with a sign suggesting that its maximum width ahead was 2·5 metres. The SM is a quarter of an inch over 6ft wide so it was going to be a tight fit. But this street led into a square from which the only exit (also one-way) was signposted 2 metres! With a little help from pedestrians and at the expense of some front door-mats we got through. Moral: park the car near the city gates and walk.

As a sporting car, the SM is also too big for Spanish secondary roads. Those of La Mancha are typically narrow and poorly surfaced and with no-overtaking signs (plus double yellow lines) at anything that remotely resembles a corner. Progress was quicker during *siesta* time (2–4 p.m.) when the trucks were off the road.

The SM's performance over poor surfaces is excellent inasmuch as it remains flat when other cars would be bucking around, and it has a solid, secure feel even when travelling fast over indifferent roads. But regular undulations like cobbles set up a noisy patter at the rear wheels and some combinations of speed and surface generate a most uncomfortable vibration that seemed to be transmitted direct to the base of the spine.

The same vibration – which was present to a lesser extent at around 100 mph on smooth motorway – was responsible for the detachment of various parts of the car. The boot lock fell to bits, while the steering column adjuster gradually worked its way down to its lowest position. Worst of all, one of the triple headlamp units came off its mountings which made the impressive spread of light even farther-reaching, while the "steering" headlamps became capable of independent direction.

Electrical things are probably the SM's worst feature. It badly needs a continuous slow-speed facility for the windscreen wipers. The window winders are infuriatingly slow. The hydraulics, as one expects from Citroën's flagship, work

beautifully. The speed-sensitive power steering is so high geared that it needs careful acclimatization, but once that is achieved its advantages become apparent. Its servo self-centring is useful when parking. The Citroën "one-shot" brake button takes some getting used to as well, and although not all my colleagues agree, I find the high-pressure system very reassuring for a fast car. The five-speed gearbox is possibly Citroën's best, while the Maserati V6 engine has a splendid growl which forgives some harshness which is otherwise out of place in an altogether "smooth" car.

What happens to the SM now? Our long term test car is, sadly, no longer with us (report: *Autocar* 7 September 1974).

La Mancha, the land of Cervantes' Don Quixote. We followed the trail of the imaginary Knight with the thoroughly modern Citroën SM, seen here amongst the windmills at Mota del Cuervo and the 15th century castle at Belmonte

---

There have been rumours that the model is to be discontinued for some time, and Maserati's recent demise seals it. Production, latterly transferred to Guy Ligier's factory (described elsewhere in this issue), will cease in September. Also abandoned are production plans for the splendid Maserati Quattroporte II which was built round SM running gear. This was in some ways a more logical application for the complicated systems of the SM, which is oversize for the two-plus-two accommodation it provides. But both are cars of a dying breed – the transcontinental express, capable of safe and superbly comfortable 100 mph-plus cruising on main roads, designed for the pure enjoyment of motoring.

Four hundred years on, Don Quixote, always in search of the impossible, would have mourned their loss. □

84

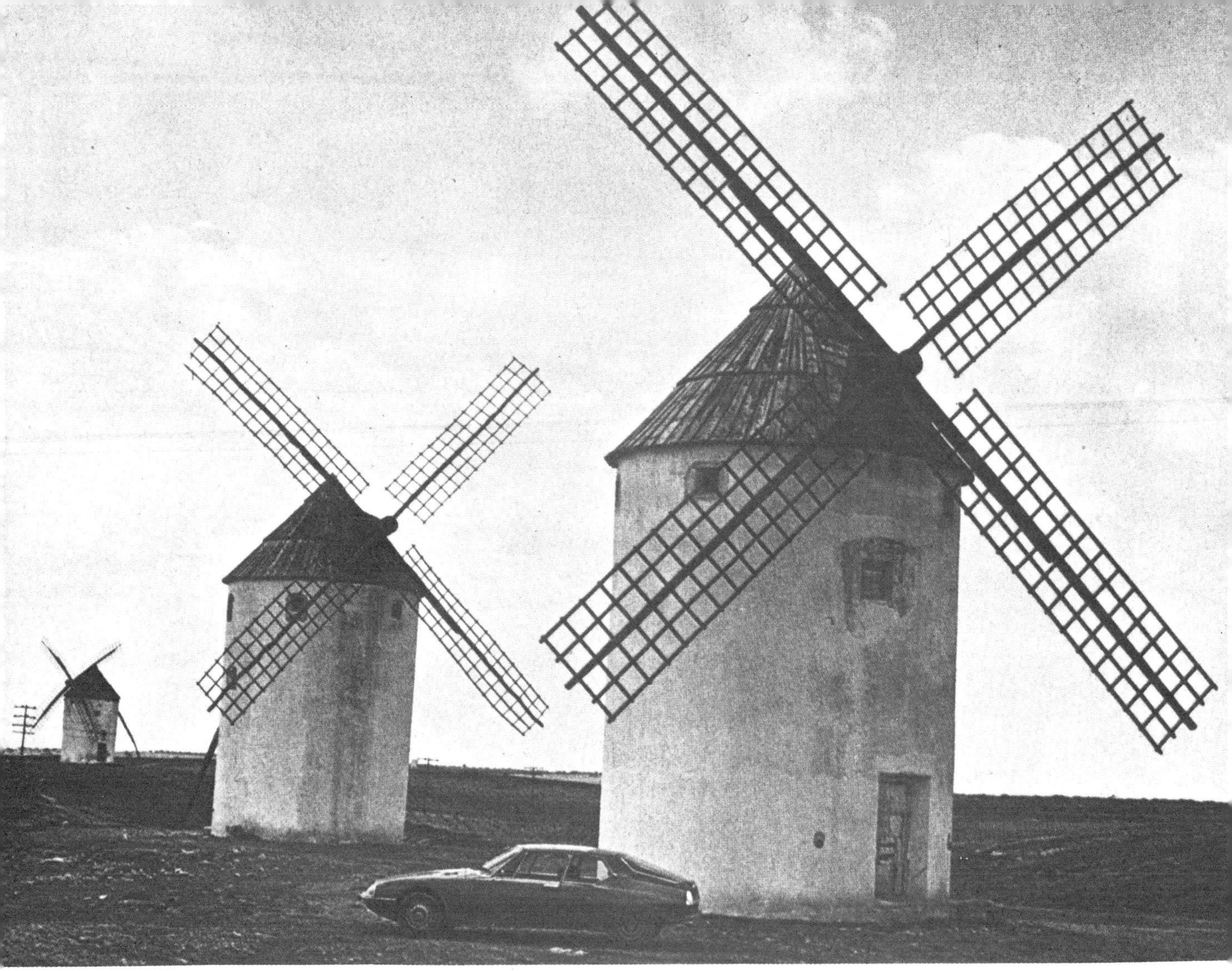

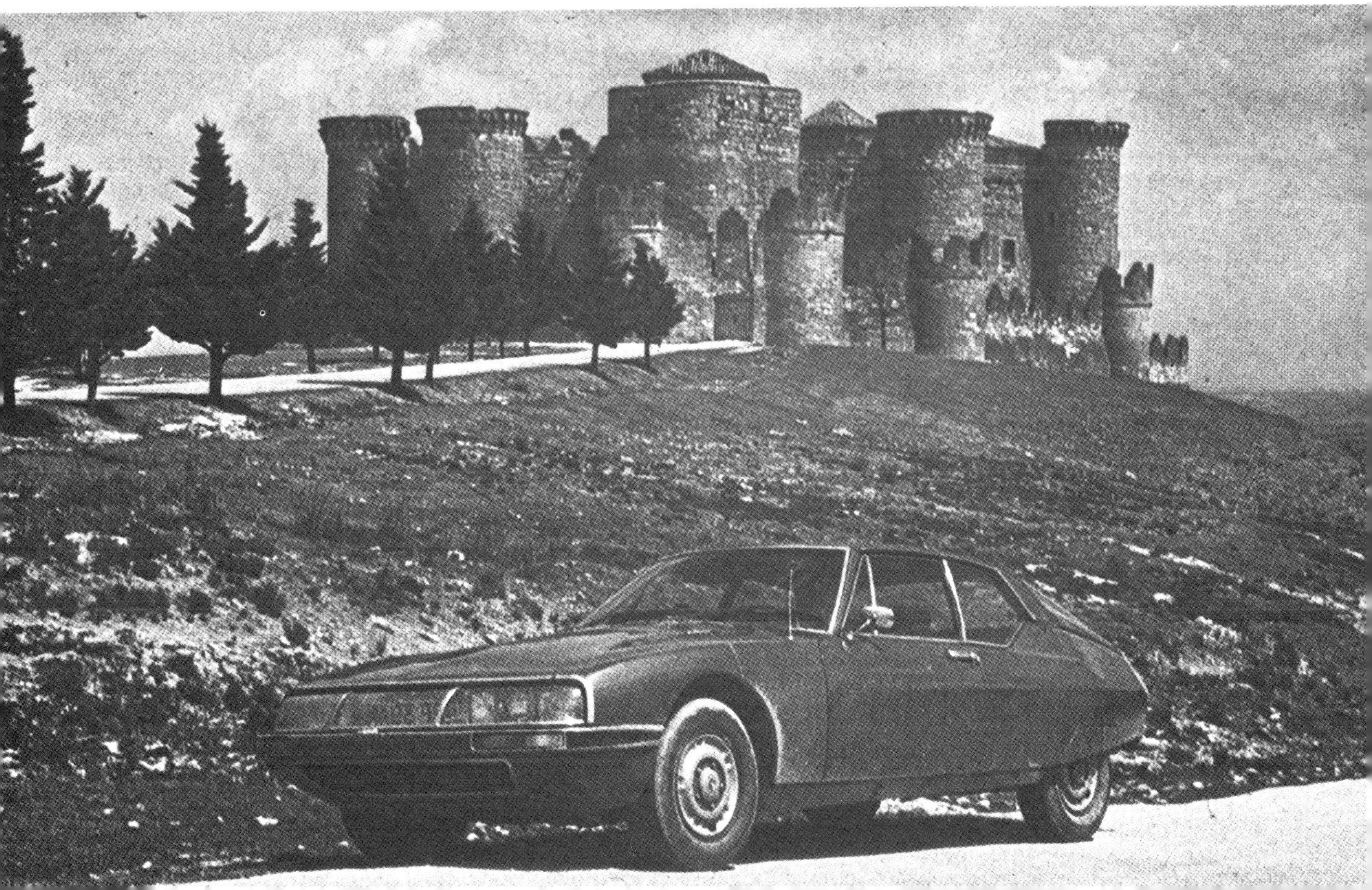

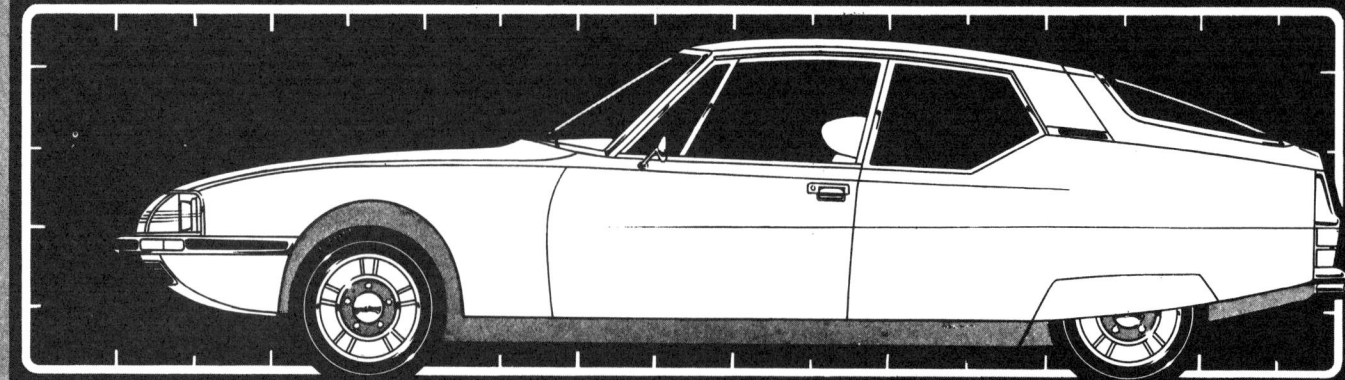

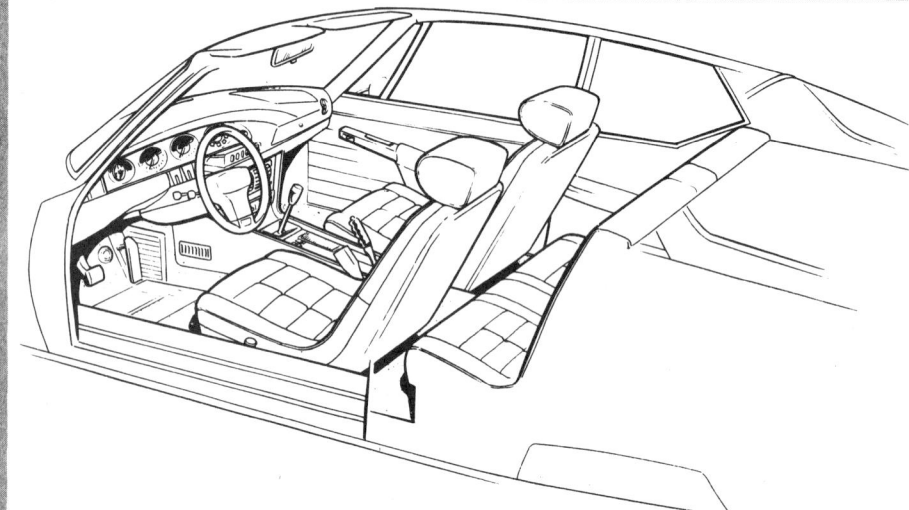

PRICES
(Including car tax and VAT): £6,815·14
Extras
1	Leather upholstery	£258·59
2	Tinted windows	£83·41
3	Air conditioning	£291·96
4	3 Speakers/power aerial	£46·47

As tested with 2,3,4 £7,236·98

ENGINE
Capacity: 2670 cc (163 cu.in)
Configuration: V-6 with dohc per bank
Bore × stroke: 87 × 75 mm
           (3·42 × 2·95 in)
Compression ratio: 9·0:1
           (98-octane RM)
Carburetters: Bosch electronic fuel in-
jection
Power: 178 bhp (DIN) at 6250 rpm
Torque: 171 lb.ft (DIN) at 4000 rpm

TRANSMISSION
Gear ratios:	Top	0·75
	4th	0·97
	3rd	1·32
	2nd	1·94
	1st	2·92
Final drive:		4·375

Mph per 1,000 rpm: Top 23·4
                      4th 18·1

RUNNING GEAR
Suspension: Front, independent
leading arms with hydropneumatic
springing and anti-roll bar; rear,
independent with trailing arms,
hydropneumatic springing
and anti-roll bar
Dampers: Incorporated with
hydropneumatic suspension
Brakes: Power operated discs front
and rear
Tyres: Michelin 205/70 VR 15 XWX
on 6J × 15 steel wheels

CAPACITIES
Fuel tank	20 Imp gallons
Oil	12½ pints
Water	23 pints

DIMENSIONS
Wheelbase: 9 ft 8¼ in
Track: 5 ft 0½ in F, 4 ft 5 in R
Overall length: 16 ft 0½ in
Height: 4 ft 3¼ in
Width: 6 ft 0½ in
Weight: (kerb with fuel for 50 miles)
29·5 cwt
Weight distribution: 64/36 F/R

PERFORMANCE

In gears
MPH	Top	4th
20–40	12·2 sec	8.5 sec
30–50	12·9	8·0
40–60	12·2	7·9
50–70	12·2	8·0
60–80	13·5	8·6
70–90	14·7	9·4
80–100	—	9·8
90–110	—	12·1

Standing starts
0–30	3·4 sec
40	4·7
50	6·4
60	8·3
70	11·3
80	14·4
90	18·2
100	23·2
110	30·0
SS. ¼-mile	16·5
SS. km	30·2

Maximum speeds
Top	App. 140 mph
Fourth	117
Third	86
Second	59
First	39

Brakes (from 30 mph in neutral)
Pedal load (lb)	Retardation	Stopping distance
25	0·60 g	50
40	0·97	31
Handbrake	0·18	167

FUEL CONSUMPTION*
(at steady speeds in top)
30 mph	30½ mpg
40	30½
50	30
60	28½
70	26½
80	23½
90	21½
100	18½

Overall fuel consumption over 740
miles 16·5 mpg (17·1 litres/100 km)
Overall oil consumption negligible

STEERING
Turning between kerbs: 32·4 ft
Turns lock to lock: 2·0

* Consumptions from carburetted SM
with 0·81 top gear and 195/70 × 15
tyres
Figures taken by the staff of Motor
at the MIRA test track

Road Test
Citroen SM

Haute Couture from the House of Citroen, the SM provides the French version of grace and pace at a price

CITROEN have long produced some remarkable cars, cars that start life as trend-setters but still stay fashionable throughout a long model life—this is as true for the DS series as for the 2CV. With the SM they went several steps forward from the DS range, incorporating the best ideas from that—suspension, brakes and swivelling main-beam auxiliaries all appropriately uprated for a high performance sports car—in new graceful aerodynamic lines. For the power unit, they went to the then recently acquired Maserati concern for a four-cam V-6 with light alloy

block and head, now equipped with Bosch fuel injection to produce 178 bhp at 6250 rpm from the relatively small capacity of 2670 cc; to this was mated a new 5-speed box designed by Citroen mounted ahead of the engine for the inevitable and highly effective front-wheel drive. And then there is the steering.

Motoring journalists have long decried the American-inspired obsession with overlight power-steering coupled to low gearing, an obsession explained by Rolls-Royce under the heading of the "Sneeze Factor". Perhaps Citroen owners don't get colds, because the SM steering design has apparently taken such criticisms more than seriously; requiring only two turns from $32\frac{1}{2}$ft lock to lock it is also extremely responsive as the natural product of Michelin 205/70 x 15 XWX tyres and substantially roll-free suspension. Artificial feel is built in with a variable self-centering which decreases as speed rises when the pneumatic trail effect—tyre self-aligning torque—increases. Thus the overall level of effort required seems to stay more or less constant at all speeds. At rest the power-centering is so strong that the wheels return to the straight-ahead position, a fact of which Citroen remind you in the handbook as it can affect un-parking. The steering generally, though, is part and parcel

of a superb and different motor car; it is astonishingly direct and a pleasure to use once you are used to it. Such response doesn't take kindly to one-handed steering, the small movements required need two hands and smooth progression; you have to watch it too when turning into narrow gateways as the combination of a wide car and long wheelbase—9ft 8¼in—can easily put the rear wheels over the pavement if lock is applied too quickly.

We have laboured this point at some length for two reasons: firstly, it is an unique system still and secondly, if you get as far as a test-drive, unfamiliarity could deter you from appreciating the car as a whole. With most cars even 10 miles can be enough, with the SM you need a good 50 on all roads.

Unfortunately all the SMs are left-hand-drive. Despite the car's 6ft width, this is rarely a disadvantage unless you are caught in heavy traffic which requires frequent overtaking; you sit well towards the outside of the car and can easily see along the inside of vehicles you can't see through. The performance is lively enough to make such manoeuvres quick and safe; despite the unladen 30 cwt and the maximum 171 lb ft of torque occurring at 4000 rpm, the engine pulls usefully throughout the rev range so you don't need to stir the convenient gear lever too often. Fifth gear

gives 23½ mph per 1000 rpm for a very leisurely overdrive gearing on an engine that takes 6500 rpm very happily; fourth at 18·1 mph per 1000 rpm is the town gear and ideal for cruising along country roads without the need to change down for most corners, as the roadholding is so good and doesn't upset passenger equilibrium if indulged in. Fourth gear 20 mph speed increments are all well under 10 seconds from 20 to 100 mph.

From rest the SM can reach 60 mph in 8·3s, where the carburetted SM took very nearly 10s, and 100 mph comes up in 23s. so it is a quick car despite its mere 2·7-litres. For most normal driving you will probably stick to around 4000 rpm; beyond this engine noise increases considerably—there are many ancillary pumps all whirring round as well—but much of this must be intake noise as the noise level drops when you settle down to a steady speed over 4000 rpm. The noise is not unpleasant but aesthetically comes midway between that of a hard-working mass-production frenzy and the refined combination of the mechanical chorus and exhaust burr of a thoroughbred multi-cylinder.

Any practical cruising speed is supremely comfortable in the SM up to its maximum around 140 mph; a wind-cheating shape with good sealing keeps wind noise to a comfortable minimum and the engine becomes less audible at steady speeds. With the Bosch fuel injection system we were unable to measure steady speed fuel consumptions but those from the carburetted car should be very similar as the power required to drive the same shape has to remain the same although the gearing is now some 4 per cent higher. With 28½ mpg at 60 mph and 18½ mpg at 100 mph, the car can be fairly economical; we recorded 16½ mpg over some mixed hard motoring but on long 70 mph runs it should be possible to get 20 mpg which, with a 20-gallon tank, gives a good grand touring range.

Starting from cold was no problem but you have to wait for the hydraulic pressure to raise the car to running height as it is easy to stall the car with the extra load of the hydraulic pump. An occasional fault with the injection system is a hiccough during mid-range acceleration in a high gear.

Citroen's self-levelling hydraulic suspension is well known and that on the SM follows the established pattern with firmer settings and some anti-dive built into the trailing link front suspension. The ride is extremely restful over any surface apart from hump-back bridges when the "landing" can jerk the car onto the bump stops quite easily; generally it is far more comfortable than all but the very best saloons, swallowing all sorts of irregularities in an effortlessly level fashion. Around town you can sense bump-thump as the big fat tyres hit ridges, but this is not transmitted to the occupants. The front seats are extremely comfortable and have a wide range of adjustment, with three settings for height at front and rear plus fore-and-aft and reclining positions, the back-rest "breaking" above the angle to vary lumbar support as well. Additionally the steering wheel moves in an out and up and down taking the steering column nacelle and stalks with it, so that any size driver should get comfortable. The scuttle is quite high and average size (5ft 8in) drivers lose the right front end unless you move forward for manoeuvring, but on the open road this seems to be no disadvantage.

Three column stalks control indicators, wash/wipe and the powerful quartz iodine headlights; on main beam the inner of the three pairs of lights come on and these are attached via wire to the steering so that they swivel with applied lock. For road use this is a really outstanding system giving an array of light when cornering that gives an almost daylight field of view. This may be of less advantage to rally drivers but if you argue that the car body and fixed lights are pointing the way you ultimately want to go and the front wheels, and thus swivelling lights, point where you are currently going it should work as effectively in such conditions.

With such high gearing the slight ovality of the small steering wheel is quite acceptable and blends in well with the oval instruments and warning light cluster. This latter includes a check button to show that all the important warning lights are functioning, including one for brake pad wear. The brakes work on the normal Citroen system with independent circuits and full power braking. You soon get used to the initial sinking feeling when you try to apply a brake that doesn't seem to be there, but it is still difficult to get smooth heel and toe operation of brake and accelerator unless you are braking heavily; only 40 lb pressure is required for a maximum stop so anything less demands a light foot, which isn't ideal for pivotting on.

For access to the rear seats, a release catch "breaks" the seat back and allows the seat to be slid forward; there isn't much instep room for those in the back unless the front occupants compromise well forwards, and headroom is limited for tall adults but those that fit are very comfortable. All the armrests have flip-up lockers incorporated.

Our test car was fitted with the optional air-conditioning which was extremely effective and uses the same controls as does the conventional system—slides for up/down, temperature and fan speed. There are outlets in the centre console, facia eyeballs and in the footwells, so that the atmosphere can be adjusted very quickly while the fan is not too noisy even on its fastest setting.

A large spare wheel absorbs a considerable amount of space in the boot which is thus rather oddly shaped, but you can get an adequate number of large suitcases inside. Wheelchanging follows the usual DS-range pattern using the ride-height control and jack stand; apart from the high and low wheel-changing positions there are three ride-height positions.

Wheelchanging is about all you would dare do on the SM since the array of equipment under the bonnet dwarfs the engine and looks thoroughly daunting to any but a fully qualified Citroen mechanic; it requires servicing every 3000 miles.

The SM is a complex car, so the question must be—is the complexity justified? It is, and will remain so until others can make their cars as fast, safe and comfortable for less complexity and less money. Jaguar and Mercedes are the obvious rivals in safe, comfortable high performance—the Citroen is not only very different but does some things better. For a man to whom Citroen driving came naturally the choice might be difficult and ultimately be largely decided on the basis of internal space, torque, styling and left-hand-drive, if one considers the car on its merits rather than value. It is expensive but superbly designed and built. ●

It must surely say something for the state of the motor industry in 1970 that two volume car manufacturers should think it fit, let alone viable, to launch highly expensive, limited production models purely as promotional exercises. Petrol prices were low, the performance race was still in full swing, and aerodynamics had not yet erased aesthetics from the stylists' handbook.

Such unique circumstances saw the Alfa Romeo Montreal and the Citroën SM appear, after lengthy development — they were totally dissimilar in approach yet almost identical in concept.

The Alfa Romeo conception effectively took place in 1967 at the EXPO 67 Montreal World Fair. That occasion was staged to celebrate Canada's centenary and nations were invited to submit examples of their finest achievements in art, culture, science and industry. Alfa Romeo was the only motor manufacturer to be asked to display 'an expression of man's ultimate aspirations in the automotive field'.

With the help of Nuccio Bertone, Alfa produced the car which later became known as the Montreal, the two show cars being based on the then current 1600 Giulia coupé. The cars, one red and one white, were exceptionally beautiful and caused something of a minor sensation when they were unveiled.

The public acclaim forced Alfa Romeo to see the Montreal through to fruition. Whether or not the car was originally designed as a future production model remains in some doubt, but, by the nature of Alfa's EXPO 67 brief, the project had to have 'feasible mass production possibilities in the not too distant future'.

Clearly such dramatic styling deserved a far more powerful engine than Alfa's 1600cc twin-cam unit so, rather bravely, the famous Tipo 33 V8 was borrowed from Alfa's racing division and neatly accommodated within the Montreal's sculpture.

Racing engine

This engine was at the heart of Alfa's return to motor racing in 1967 with the mid-engined 2-litre Group 6 T33. The car, while not sweeping the board, certainly proved highly competitive, frequently beating Ferrari and being vanquished only by Porsche in the 1971 Sports Car Championship. Enlarged to a 3-litre, the engine had no success in a number of Formula 1 cars, having been adopted by March, McLaren and Cooper.

For a road car the Type 33 unit was torrid material indeed. It was a 90 degree V8 with four overhead camshafts, Spica fuel injection, dry sump lubrication (which helped in keeping a low frontal aspect), and hemispherical combustion chambers. A racing engine in a production road car — fantastic!

An exciting engine was also an important factor in the development of the Citroën SM. The idea of a self-indulgent sporting car defining everything innovative about Citroën had first been discussed in Paris in the early sixties. An appropriate power unit could not readily be found and the SM did not reach production until 1970.

Citroën were leagues ahead of other manufacturers in many aspects of design. Only the DS series demonstrated the extent of their expertise and these,

BACK TO BACK

Très chic

Near identical in concept, but opposites in execution, the Citroen SM and Alfa Romeo Montreal had lots of glamour. Richard Sutton compares them

apart from a few convertibles, were all saloon cars. Not one sports model was available. Every other manufacturer in the DS price bracket had a sports car to keep the track suit over the spreading corporate figure. All, that is, except Rover, who, realising the problem, were hard at work with their sensational P6BS mid-engined project.

The SM became inevitable on the day in 1968 when Citroën bought out a company with a fine racing heritage — Maserati S.P.A. of Bologna. With Maserati in the kitchen, Citroën not only acquired a substantial amount of cake, with fresh ingredients like Alfieri, Bertocchi and Cozza, but also all the icing a saloon car manufacturer's marketing department could ever want. In classical style, Alfieri designed, manufactured and ran the new SM engine within three weeks.

To comply with French fiscal horsepower regulations, the engine — a 2.7-litre V6 — was remarkably unorthodox. Being a V6 it should have had an included vee-angle of either 60 or 120 degrees — this

V6 had a 90 degree angle and an unusual camshaft drive positioned half way along the crank.

The reason for these two anomalies was that Alfieri had based the engine on a 3-litre V8 he had designed some years previously with the correct 90 degree piston angle and four overhead camshafts. For ease of manufacture, using in-house tooling, the V8's fundamental specifications were retained for the new V6 unit. To overcome any problems induced by the 90 degree layout, Alfieri adopted a stronger crankshaft which allowed a very short stroke of only 65mm, thus enabling the necessary crankpin overlap to be attained.

In addition to engine development there are many other similarities between the Montreal and SM concepts. Their purchase prices by the end of 1972, when supplies and sales were settling in an ordered fashion, were both just over £5000, or five times as much as a new Cortina and about the same as the Fiat 130 coupé and Ferrari Dino 246. Both cars had race bred engines of similar capacity, power, construction and fuel consumption. *Motor* recorded that both cars reached 50mph in 6.1secs and topped 138mph. Having said that, the SM was really not as quick as the Alfa through the gears and reached its high top speed by nature of the car's remarkable aerodynamics. A claimed drag coefficient of 0.24 is about as far away from Audi's modern flush-glass marvels as an E-Type was from a Safari Land-Rover with roof rack and horse box.

Show car becomes reality

Development of the two cars also took similar lines. The Alfa, bar its engine and details of bodywork and trim, was virtually identical to the 1967 EXPO cars when it reached the production line. This meant that chassis and floor-pan, suspension, steering and drivetrain came directly, with minimal modification, from the standard production Giulia cars. Independent front suspension by coil springs and wishbones, recirculating ball steering, four wheel disc brakes, and a live rear axle with coil springs, radius arms and 'A' bracket, were all attached to a pressed steel floor pan.

The Citroën was similarly derived from the long established DS saloons. The manufacturer's 'statutory' front wheel drive, hydropneumatic self-levelling suspension with struts and wishbones to the front and struts and trailing arms to the rear, power assisted rack and pinion steering, disc brakes all round, were also all attached to a pressed steel chassis unit.

The purchase price of each car was the same, the performance and fuel consumption virtually identical. They were both 2+2s, both beautifully styled and both derived from volume production cars. Rarity and exclusivity was shared and they both entered the market and were withdrawn in the years 1970 and 1976.

Despite the strong similarities, the cars differed widely. Perhaps their national characteristics were the most evident, one being classically French, the other typically Italian.

The Citroën's graceful, curvaceous bodywork has no sheerline angles, no sudden drops or corners. To me it's a paragon of automotive art — *chic alors* — and

Instruments within the Alfa Romeo Montreal's massive cowls are not among the most legible

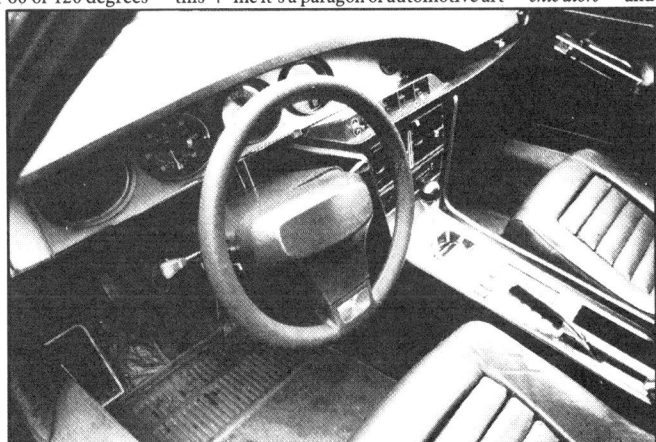

Citroën SMs always came with left-hand drive with an interior looking like up-market GS

Alfa Montreal has undeniably sensational lines, but suffers from a fussiness irritating to some, liked by others

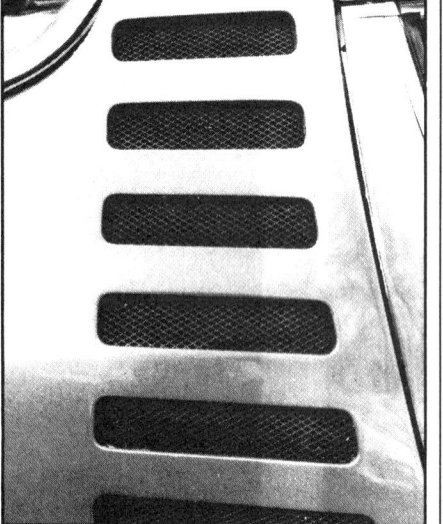

Stylised air intakes on rear pillar serve no function

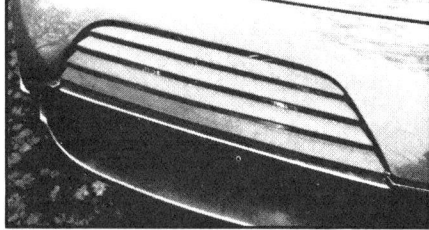

Gimmicky powered slats revolve to expose the headlights

Montreal's sophisticated 2.6-litre dohc V8 delivers 200bhp

The Citroën SM has graceful, curvaceous bodywork with no angles: paragon of automotive art, or just plain ugly?

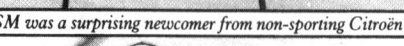

SM was a surprising newcomer from non-sporting Citroën

Even the cockpit air intake has Citroën's chevron badge

Inner lights of triple set-up swivel with the steering

SM's under-bonnet is awesome: 2.7-litre V6 is hidden!

one of the finest looking cars of all time. To many it's mis-shapen, even ugly.

The Alfa's appeal is undoubtedly more widespread but ultimately just as controversial. Its styling is straight from an Italian Art College blackboard — almost the work of amateurs with all the right ideas but with an inability to co-ordinate and style features sympathetically. The result is a car which, thanks to the oversight of Nuccio Bertone, is undeniably sensational but suffers from a fussiness which is irritating to some, relished by others. By rights it should never have been allowed.

Inside, the cars are equally luxurious and eccentric. In keeping with their styling, the Citroën is space age, the Alfa pedantically detailed, and both are thoroughly over-the-top.

And then there are the gimmicks. A look at the headlight arrangements on both cars says it all. The SM has six lamps enclosed behind a glass band extending right across the front of the car, covering even the licence plate. The space behind this cover is kept dry and free of condensation by a constant flow of warm air, which ensures that the innermost lamps can be seen turning directionally with the steering. The Montreal has the upper half of its twin headlamps partially obscured by venetian blind-like screens which, when the headlamps are switched on (assuming the engine is running), rotate across the front of the lamps to disappear beneath. This intriguing nonsense must rate as one of the most amusing pieces of power-assisted paraphernalia ever fitted to a production car.

Elizabeth Rose, who co-owns the Montreal with Robert Gordon-Blacker, is a helicopter pilot and Irish Setter judge and breeder. She actually bought the car after splitting up with an old boyfriend. He had one and she had become inextricably attached to it, covering 15,000 miles in the car in the last two years. Robert is an accomplished musician and solicitor and has used the car regularly for his job. They, and Kevin Johnston of Alfissimo, have maintained the car to a very high standard.

Stunning blonde

Brian Wilkinson, who is also a pilot, has only had the SM featured here for a few months, but has used one on a day-to-day basis since 1973. "I decided I had to have one after seeing an immaculate metallic car in the South of France. A stunning blonde French girl stood beside it, arguing." Brian has since owned 10 SMs, in carburetted and later fuel injected guises. He presently also owns a Ferrari Mondial, and rates them both as "very much drivers' cars".

Getting into the Citroën it immediately felt well made. The doors closed with a hefty thud, and there were no rattles or insubstantiality here. Your feet sit low in the car, a deep box sectioned sill to your left, wide centre console to the right. The leather seating (a very expensive option this, amounting to almost a fifth of the original purchase price when new) is supremely comfortable but gives little side support.

The small steering wheel, adjustable for rake and reach, sits far out in front. The left arm settles comfortable on the door's continental style armrest and the wheel is held between thumb and middle fingers. The chrome plated gear lever leads down to a similarly endowed gate — real juke box decor. The dashboard is similar in style to the GS Citroëns but more dramatic. All instruments are visible either in the three circular dials ahead or on the rectangular gauges in the centre console.

The SM starts immediately and rises on its hydraulics. Snick it into first gear, ease up the clutch, palm the wheel to the right and the SM eases sideways. Let go of the wheel and the steering moves straight ahead automatically. Acceleration through the gears is quick rather than staggering, the turbine-like engine happy to rev to 6500rpm. The gearbox is equally impressive. Changing is easy, albeit through a noisy gate. There is a distinct gap between second and third, but the change from fourth to fifth is perfect for swift overtaking. Only when accelerating is the car noisy, the engine note being almost harsh — but then it does sound like a sports racing car.

Like any hydropneumatic Citroën, the SM demands a gentle hand. The self-centring steering, on/off brake pedal and remarkably forgiving suspension system all contribute to an initial feel of undriveability. A dramatic change in driving style is demanded and, once adopted, the SM presents a highly rewarding combination of ease and excitement. Be gentle, be respectful, be cool.

It doesn't take long before the SM can be driven confidently. The steering soon becomes very precise, at least under normal driving conditions. It does become a little irritating on the motorway though, where keeping to the straight and narrow is nearly impossible — a sneeze and you've changed lanes. While the car is supremely accurate to steer into fast corners, coming out is rather different . . . practice, undoubtedly, would make perfect.

The same principle applies to the brakes, which are very reassuring but the pedal gives the impression that nothing is going to happen, and then it all does, and very quickly.

SM's handling 'superb'

Under the relatively limiting conditions in which I was able to drive the SM it was impossible to make any ultimate test of its roadholding and handling characteristics but there can be no doubt that the car is extremely capable. Both *Autocar* and *Motor* contemporary road test reports describe the SM's roadholding as nothing short of 'superb' and *Autocar* even went so far as to draw parallels with the Lotus Elan's handling — that's high praise indeed, and all at a gentle touch. Maximum response from minimal effort, that's the SM way.

V8 Alfa Romeos are from a very different *genus*. Gone is the passivity and elegance of the French *bourgeois* and in comes the brash, brawn and brio of the Italian footballer. Just getting into the Montreal tells you this car is Italian. Flash first, longevity last. Even the driving position is from a rate car. Arms outstretched, gearshift at neck height, feet just touching the pedals and a bonnet view which looks like the Mont Blanc foothills — breathtaking.

Directly in front of the driver sit two Lamborghini Miura sized instrument cowls. They house the clocks and warning lights in a bizarre pie chart fashion and are very difficult to read. Velour upholstered front seats are very comfortable (there was no leather option), while the rear seats are considerably more useless than the Citroën's and the bootspace . . . what bootspace? Visibility in every direction but forwards is miserable and most of the switches are confusing to the point of being dangerous.

A few churns and the V8 fires as soon as the injection system is primed. Wow! It sounds just like a Camaro! Into the dog leg first gear, lever the firm clutch up and we're off. First is quite a high gear but the engine is incredibly flexible and perfectly suited to its gearbox. Changes are easy and quick through a faultless synchromesh (although reverse can be difficult to find). The Montreal can be left in fourth almost indefinitely and the car is quite happy travelling around at 1500rpm.

The ride is commendably soft for a sports car, although roll is a penalty, and noise levels are uncannily low at any speed. It's a very refined car.

While regretting the lack of unused acceleration potential in the engine, it's consoling to remember that the Montreal's basic drivetrain and suspension systems would severely restrict the use of any more available power. With its live rear axle, the car already has difficulty in keeping its wheels firmly on the ground, especially under the wet conditions prevailing when I tried the car. Outright acceleration has been intelligently sacrificed for the inherent benefits of great flexibility and refinement.

It does not hold the road as well as the SM, nor does it corner as undramatically, but with rear wheel drive, and a tendency towards progressive understeer with plenty of power to counter it, the Montreal, at least in the dry, is greatly controllable and very enjoyable.

Back at base, with the two cars together, idling with their bonnets up, their contrasting characters are again perfectly demonstrated.

The Alfa growls quietly, oozing aggression and muscle, with the added bonus of looking right. The Citroën's V6, in contrast, is constantly interrupted by snorts, gurgles, hisses, clicks and rumbles as the multitude of compressors, pipes, pumps and relays set about the tasks they were put on earth to do.

Running either of the cars when they were new was a Swiss Bank Account affair. Having said that, Robert feels his Montreal has consistently been cheaper to run than any of the BMWs he's owned, and Brian is happy that the SM is competitive with moderns as long as nothing major goes wrong. Fortunately, both cars *are* reliable. Criticism of the Citroën's hydraulic system was probably caused by its daunting complexity rather than any real reliability problem.

Haphazard supply

So what sank the flagships? Between 1970 and 1976 when production ceased, only 3925 Montreals had been made, 200 in right-hand drive form. The car suffered from neglected development. During the five years it was made, the model remained unchanged when detail improvements would have made it significantly better. Supply was haphazard and marketing half-hearted. When the fuel crisis took its toll, the Montreal was discontinued.

The SM also died because of the fuel crisis, and, perhaps more significantly, due to the sale of Maserati to the de Tomaso group by Citroën. Nearly 12,000 SMs were made, but, like the Montreal, production dropped in the later years, a mere 294 being made in 1974 and fewer than half that number in 1975.

Which car you would choose would probably depend on your ultimate aspirations or even prevailing lifestyle. May I suggest that if you are keen on chasing intelligent, unmarried Countesses around Parisian boutiques the SM would be perfect. If, on the other hand, you are a dog lover with a keen eye for charming lady helicopter pilots, the Montreal would be as surefire as Bolognese sauce.

SPECIFICATION	CITROËN SM	ALFA ROMEO MONTREAL
Engine	V6	V8
Bore stroke	87mm × 75mm	80mm × 64.5mm
Capacity	2670cc	2593cc
Valves	dohc per bank	dohc per bank
Compression ratio	9.0:1	9.0:1
Power	178bhp @ 5500rpm	200bhp @ 6500rpm
Transmission	Five-speed manual (three-speed auto' option)	Five-speed manual
Brakes	Discs	Discs
Suspension front	Ind by twin transverse arms, trailing mountings, lever operated hydropneumatic spring dampers interconnected with rear	Ind with transverse wishbones, coil springs and anti-roll bar
Suspension rear	Ind by trailing arms, lever operated hydropneumatic spring dampers interconnected with front	Live axle with coil springs, twin trailing arms and 'A' bracket
Steering	VariPower with artificial feel system	Re-circulating ball
Body	Combined steel chassis and body, aluminium bonnet	Unitary all-steel construction

DIMENSIONS		
Length	16ft ½in	13ft 10ins
Width	6ft ¼ins	5ft 5¾ins
Height	4ft 4ins	4ft ¾in
Wheelbase	9ft 8ins	7ft 8½ins
Kerb weight	3197lbs	2830lbs
Tyres	195/70 VR15 on 6J rims	195/70X VR14 on 6½J rims

PERFORMANCE		
Max speed	138mph	138mph
0-60mph	8.3secs	8.3secs
Standing ¼ mile	17.1secs	16.7secs
Average mpg	16-20mpg	14-18mpg

PRODUCTION		
Years built	1970-5	1970-5
Numbers built	12,920	3925
Price new (1972)	£5342	£5549

This is Brian Wilkinson's 10th SM since falling in love with one in the South of France in '73

Elizabeth Rose, a helicopter pilot, loves the Montreal in which she covers 7500 miles a year

CITROËN'S MASERATI

Technical *tour de force* or just too complicated for its own good? Whatever the critics now make of the Citroen SM and its intricate hydraulics, delicate V6 engine and sensitive steering, there can be little doubt that it is one of the most stunning-looking sports saloon cars ever to take to the road; or that, despite its reputation for breaking at the drop of a hat, in the hands of a sympathetic owner it can be as reliable as a modern BX. Enthusiast Richard Horne here looks at the SM's strengths and weaknesses and points out a few expensive pitfalls for the unwary

Lines of later CX clearly visible in SM. Still looks remarkably up to date nearly 20 years on

The Citroën SM was launched at the Geneva Salon in March 1970. The car was a technical *tour de force,* considering it took just under two years to develop it. Citroën had just bought Panhard and the Berliet truck company and Maserati seemed to be a necessary cog in its future plans; the two companies merged in early 1968.

Citroën had always been innovative in its design and the SM was to be its crowning glory, a truly prestigious Gran Turismo car in the fading tradition of the Grand Routier machines of the late 1930s and 1940s. Development work began during the 1960s when the company used some cut-and-shut V6-engined DS coupés in several rallies.

Citroën's sporting car needed a powerful engine to compete with the likes of Jaguar, Mercedes and Porsche, so Maserati's Ing Alfieri was asked to design a brand-new 150bhp engine in a mere six months.

Citroën had to cope with France's punitive tax laws on engines above 2.8 litres, so capacity was reduced to 2670cc. This was only arrived at after much reduction work. Alfieri originally adapted a V8 Maserati Indy unit which had a capacity of 4146cc. He cut off two cylinders, reducing the size to 3102cc, and then reduced the stroke by 10mm to 75mm. This was still too

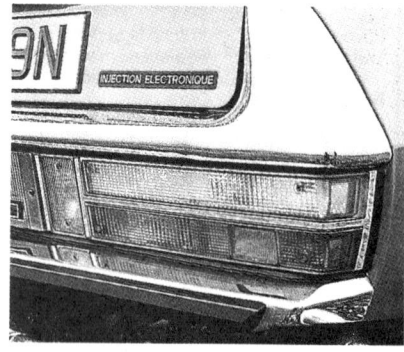

Specialised body components biggest problem in restoration; go for secondhand items

large, pushing the volume above the 15CV *puissance fiscale* rating so, by reducing the bore size to 87mm, he achieved that capacity of 2670cc.

UNEQUAL FIRING

The engine was bound to be rougher than a V8, and not surprisingly considering the usual secondary imbalance and unequal firing impulses. This was caused by the 90 degree angle between the banks. If, like most V6s, the inclined angle had been 60 or 120 degrees, then the problem would not have arisen. The engine showed its racing parentage, however, and thanks to the four-bearing crankshaft's rigidity was very keen to rev right up to its peak-power point at 6250rpm. The engine was made of aluminium alloy for the cylinder heads and block, with 'dry' cast-iron cylinder liners. This material was always used by Maserati, and was and inclined with an approximate 78 degree angle between intake and exhaust, with inverted-bucket tappets adjusted by means of shims. Almost flat-topped pistons formed the bottoms of the hemispherical combustion chambers. The four overhead camshafts were operated by an unorthodox ing length, and allowing identical cylinder-head castings to be used for both banks.

The early engines were fed by three downdraught Weber 42 DCNFZ twin-choke carburettors. The power output was 170bhp with peak torque of 170lb ft developed at 4000rpm. The distribu-

Battery of self-levelling halogen headlights controlled by hydraulics. Should stay level, whatever attitude of car; innermost pair swivel

Photography: Derek Goard

beautifully die-cast. The engine had great rigidity thanks to its five main castings, which were the two cylinder heads, block, lower block and sump. The lower block acted as a spacer between the sump, main block and crankshaft. Thus the sandwiched crank ran in two sets of half-bearings, again contributing to rigidity.

The valves were operated by twin-overhead camshafts per cylinder bank, two-stage duplex chain drive, with the primary chain from the crankshaft driving a central jackshaft.

This unique SM item was of massive hollow construction with three double sprockets and a skew gear which drove the distributor. The secondary chains (manually adjustable) ran between the cylinder centres. The advantage of this system was the splitting of the drive, reducing vibration and sav-

tor was unusual in having two sets of contact breakers. These operated in conjunction with two coils and it was thus quite difficult to set the timing. An oil cooler was standard, plus two thermostatically controlled electric fans.

The car had front-wheel drive through a five-speed gearbox and a conventional hydraulically operated diaphragm-spring dry-plate clutch some nine inches in diameter. The combined gearbox and final-drive unit was mounted ahead of the engine and differential in Citroën DS fashion. It was also ahead of the wheel centre line. The main input shaft ran above and over the right-hand side of the differential case, transmitting through the gears to the layshaft below, which drove rearward on the spiral-bevel drive to the differential. The car had a high final-drive ratio of 4.375:1 giving some 22mph per 1000rpm in top gear.

INDEPENDENTLY SPRUNG

The four wheels were independently sprung and the front suspension had equal-length transverse arms. The rear suspension was by trailing arms joined by an anti-roll bar and operated by hydropneumatic struts.

The other major part of the suspension was the hydropneumatic system as used successfully in the DS. This consisted of liquid-nitrogen-filled spheres which acted as the springing units. Each wheel had a sphere with the hydraulic fluid carried in the lower half. The high-pressure pump supplied the fluid to operate the front and rear levelling systems. In traditional Citroën fashion, this arrangement automatically maintained the front and rear of the car at a constant height regardless of payload. Another benefit was the rising-rate property of the gas spring units which automatically stiffened in relation to load.

There was also a four-position lever by the driver's seat for varying the height of the car. This was particularly useful when driving in snow or over rough tracks. It could also be used to change a wheel. By raising the car to the 'high' position, inserting a strut below the vehicle and then setting the suspension lever to the 'low' position one had a pair of wheels off the ground. An additional control inside the boot, operating on the rear levelling valve, would cause the retracted rear wheel to reappear for removal.

The drive shafts had constant-velocity joints at their outer ends with sliding pot-joints at the inboard end. The steering was hydraulically operated and as revolutionary in 1970 as the suspension had been in 1955 at the time of the DS19's launch. It was fully powered from the central hydraulic system and had the sensitivity associated with a racing car. It was a very highly geared rack-and-pinion system with a ratio of 9.4:1, which corresponded to just two turns lock to lock. This gave the car a 34½ ft turning circle. The Vari-Power system was like no other power-steering arrangement. The steering was totally 'artificial', being a true servo mechanism. The main advantage was that the steering wheel was largely insulated from kickback over rough surfaces and un-

favourable front-wheel-drive characteristics. It also gave quick, accurate control over the front wheels which, being heavily laden, helped to give the SM its legendary stability at speed.

Citroën used ideas from aircraft control systems to achieve the artificial feel. Having a hydraulic governor and cam-follower arrangement attached to the front of the gearbox, Citroën produced a system where steering effort increased with speed. This worked by increasing the pressure applied to the cam follower as the car's speed increased. Thus the steering was extremely light at parking and town speeds, but became progressively heavier as speed increased.

The steering also provided full self-centring, urging the driving wheels to point forward and ensuring straight-line stability. At rest the wheels return to the straight-ahead position when one releases the steering wheel. Overall, the high-geared system is very pleasant. Besides the instant response, there was the advantage of delightful precision through corners, achieved by minute, smooth wheel movements. Because of this complete isolation at the steering wheel, tyre blowouts at any speed had little, or no, discernible effect on the steering.

FULLY POWERED

Like the steering, the brakes were also fully powered by the hydraulics, with solid discs all round. The SM's footbrake-brake pad, resembling half a tennis ball, activated a sophisticated valve arrangement supplying separate front and rear circuits from two independent pressure sources. The 11.8-inch diameter front discs were mounted inboard, reducing unsprung weight. The 10-inch rear discs were mounted outboard with proportioning front to rear. The front discs incorporated auxiliary handbrake pads.

The brakes were activated by a strange mushroom-shaped pedal, rather than the normal pendant arrangement. It required just a very light touch to give full braking and the unwary could easily lock the wheels until they became accustomed to the car. There was, however, a system of feedback circuits which applied caliper pressure to the apportioning valves in the system to provide genuine 'feel' at the pedal.

The final hydraulically controlled system was the battery of six self-levelling halogen headlights. Whatever the load or the car's attitude under acceleration or braking, they maintained their station. The inner pair of driving lights also swivelled with the steering, giving advanced warning of what might be around the corner, a typical piece of advanced Citroën engineering first seen on the DS21.

Three different engines were used during the SM's all too brief life. First was the carburettor version of the V6 that we have already talked about. This car weighed around 3200lb and achieved a maximum speed of 137mph and a 0-60mph time of approximately nine seconds. This version was produced until July 1972 and cost £5342 including tax when it was phased out. Fuel consumption averaged around 17.5mpg, with the possibility of 25mpg with gentle driving.

INJECTION ADDED

From July 1972 the SM was offered with Bosch fuel injection. This engine had a power output of 178bhp achieved at the same peak revs. The only other alteration was the fitment of 205/70VR15 Michelin tyres. This slightly increased the overall gearing (by 1.8 per cent) helping achieve a new maximum speed of 142mph with the 0-60 time dropping to about 8.2 seconds. The major reasons for the change to fuel injection were to improve mid-range torque (up to 174lb ft at 4000rpm), enhance traffic manners and improve fuel consumption, and to comply with the impending emission-control regulations.

The car's weight increased to 3300lb, however, and the injection system also made it more difficult to remove the spark plugs. The fuel consumption did not improve much, but slight gains were obtained when cruising at motorway speeds.

Optional extras included leather upholstery, tinted glass, a special radio with three loudspeakers, electric aerial and air conditioning, the last of which did nothing for fuel consumption.

The final development was an automatic model, introduced as a sweetener for the American market. This appeared in July 1973 and had a 2965cc engine with bore and stroke figures of 91.6mm and 75mm.

However, because there were problems matching the fuel injection to the requirements of the automatic gearbox, Citroën reverted to Weber carburettors. Power output rose by just 2bhp, to 180bhp, at a higher 5750rpm. Torque rose to 181lb ft at 4000rpm — achieving the aim of the exercise.

In practice, however, performance was considerably reduced. The car only attained a maximum of 127mph with a 0-60mph time of 10 seconds. The touring fuel consumption fell to 21mpg. Sales of automatic cars were, not surprisingly, always very low.

IN-HOUSE STYLING

The SM's exquisite aerodynamic body was styled in-house by Robert Aupron, with the metalwork built by Chausson. The car had a Cd figure of about 0.34

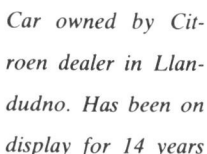

(not bad, even by today's exacting standards) and, unlike many modern cars, was not unduly affected by crosswinds. This was because the self-levelling suspension maintained a constant angle of incidence.

The steel monocoque body shell had detachable front wings with an aluminium bonnet and front undertray. Unlike most cars with 'soft' aluminium panels, the SM used aircraft-quality LT72 aluminium which is cured at 505°C and comes out rock-hard. The car was long, with an overall length of 16½ feet and a front-end width of six feet, with a taper towards the rear. There was an eight-inch difference between front and rear tracks.

Getting into an SM is fairly easy thanks to the wide-opening doors, which have two click-stop stays. They shut with a satisfying clunk. The front seats are comfortable, not the usual soft, sinking Citroën seats, but harder, if slightly less supportive. The seats adjust in all directions with no fewer than six controls. The headrests adjust fore and aft as well as up and down, and it is not too difficult to find a comfortable driving position. The rear seats are rather cramped for adults, however, due to the relatively low roof.

The steering wheel adjusts for reach as well as rake, taking the various column stalks with it. The dashboard is as revolutionary as the exterior, curving up to the driver's side with a polished metal panel housing the oval speedometer, tachometer and multi-purpose warning-light dial. There is a check button to ensure that the lamps are working, with a large 'stop' light in the centre to inform of any major malfunctions. There are three supplementary gauges, angled towards the driver and set in the facia rail. To their left are three minor switches. Windows are power-operated, albeit very slow.

The long, chromed gear lever is beautifully positioned in its metal gate. The gear ratios are well-matched, with unbeatable synchromesh, correlating well with the engine's torque character-

istics. The enthusiastic driver will very probably be encouraged to change gear just for the pleasure it brings.

REAL GEM

The engine is a real gem, too, emitting an eager, hard-edged racing growl, which sounds better the higher the revs rise. Throttle response is almost instantaneous from about 3500rpm. The ultra-high fifth gear is ideal for cruising, with 106mph equating to 5000rpm.

The high-powered self-centring steering, brakes and suspension take a little while to become accustomed to. The car understeers as one would expect from its front-wheel drive. Roll is noticeable when travelling quickly but roadholding is good at all times, even in the wet.

The ride is outstanding, soaking up rough roads and any sudden undulations far better than other sporting saloon cars. This characteristic is similar to the DS, but the SM is rather more firm. It does not float on long undulations, but follows the overall road contours. It offers a real 'magic carpet' ride and causes one to wonder why other cars still have coil- and leaf-springs.

The SM was axed before it really had a chance. Now, though, it is beginning to be appreciated for its undoubted qualities and even average SMs sell for around £5000, although a prospective buyer should set aside at least another £1000-£1500 for immediate repairs. Good examples of the marque with an average mileage of 40,000 sell for around £7500. They might still need a few hundred pounds spent on them to bring them up to scratch.

Just like any other car, the SM rusts, and panels are fairly expensive to replace. Needless to say, new body/chassis units are no longer available, but specialists do exist: Middleton Motors at Potters Bar can repair crunched cars, for example.

The main rust areas are the boot floor, the rear wing spats, the front wings and the bottoms of the doors. Front wings cost £250 and spats £50. The aluminium panels are prone to corrosion, with an underpan costing £120 and a bonnet a fairly steep £500. Other items are just as expensive, but there are economies to be found if you go to the specialists rather than to Citroën themselves.

The standard cloth trim, if damaged,

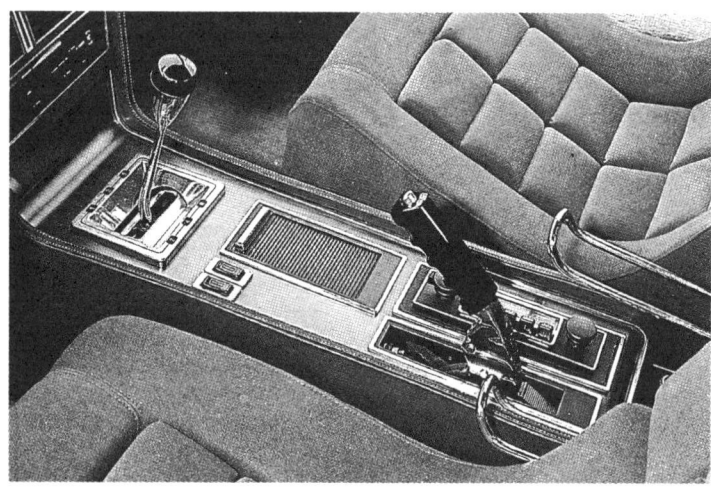

Interior shows much stylised detail, much use of chrome. Seats better than they look

is impossible to repair, and requires complete re-covering. ICI do not make the original cloth anymore. This left the factory with a silicone treatment protecting the upholstery from the ingress of dirt. If you clean the cloth, reproof it or it will be filthy again in minutes.

The leather can be repaired but it is fairly expensive. Look out for leather that's dry, shrunk, cracked or badly scratched. The stitching may have perished, but people like Connolly will be able to help. The front seats on earlier cars broke. After 1974 the seats had a massive reinforcing plate built into the sides, stopping the backrests breaking. A lot of owners let the seats become very shabby, requiring a major stripdown to repair them. It is best to buy a car with leather trim which will wear well if maintained occasionally with hide food.

Instruments are easily available, but a new battery is difficult to fit, being located, rather inaccessibly, below the offside front wing. The air conditioning used to run constantly if the interior fan was on, so the answer is to fit a cut-out switch, which costs around £20.

HYDRAULICS

The hydraulic piping is inexpensive to replace, and copper piping should be used if possible. There may be problems in that Citroën had their own types of union. The hydraulic pump can wear out, but new seal kits are readily available for about £25.

Always use mineral fluid and change it every 20,000 miles. No other fluid should be used, as this will eat away every seal. The suspension-sphere and brake accumulator pressures gradually drop due to the diffusion of the nitrogen gas. This can be cured by repressurising, which costs around £50 for all five spheres.

The anti-roll bar should be greased twice a year, as it can rust through – and even break at the ball joints. Reconditioning the bar is expensive and new ones are unobtainable. If the

car rolls a lot through corners then the bump stops may have melted because of a leaking suspension gaiter. These are inexpensive to change. Look for wear on track-rod ends, steering swivels and steering joints.

It is advisable to have the engine checked thoroughly, regardless of the previous owner's assurances. A tune-up will cost up to £100. The biggest weak point may well be the previous mechanic who worked on the car.

The SM had a tendency to eat valves and put pistons through the block. This was due to the timing chain losing tension because of the breaking up of the chain tensioner. There should be no timing-chain noise. The rear chain costs £300 to replace, the top ones £150-£200. A sensible modification to guard against such problems is to fit the approved Renolds chain tensioner kit, costing £75, plus £300 for fitting. Fitting *can* be done by the DIY mechanic and, surprisingly, requires no special tools. This modification should last for many thousands of miles.

SEEM EXPENSIVE

Engines normally require attention at about 100,000 miles. Engine components also seem expensive: camshafts cost £250, crankshafts £800, intermediate shafts £350, and crankcases over £1000. A complete gasket set costs £200. Have the car serviced by specialists every 5000 miles and you should have no problems. The prices are not really high considering it's such an advanced car. Fitting a good electronic ignition system can alleviate the dual contact-breaker/distributor problem. The Weber carburettors should give no problems. If they do, then a complete stripdown and clean with an air-line will restore them. The fuel-injected cars are susceptible to catching fire, mostly because penny-pinching owners won't replace fuel pipes, which are inexpensive, or change the injectors. The injection 'brain' is very reliable but if it fails then

have a new Bosch unit fitted. This costs £180 instead of the £650 that Citroën charge! A new stainless-steel exhaust system costs £420 from Andrew Brodie, compared with about £370 for a mild-steel one from Citroën.

The gearbox is very robust and problems are rare except for weak synchromesh. A modified version of the unit is still used by Lotus in their Esprit Turbo, so spares should be no problem to find. The front discs may be worn; new ones cost £300 to have fitted. A clutch should last 40,000 miles, but some specialists are experimenting by fitting a CX plate which is 1mm thicker.

Tyres have to be the specified Michelin XWX type. It is possible to fit 215-section tyres at the front further to improve top-end performance.

SOUND INVESTMENT

A total of 12,920 SMs were produced, all left-hand drive, and 327 were sold in this country. Two automatic models made their way here and Middleton Motors converted three to right-hand drive. Two of those cars now survive.

An SM is a sound investment if you are prepared to spend money on it. If there was one car from the 1970s that should have been updated and kept in production, then the SM is it. Given a 3-litre injected engine, Kevlar or aluminium bodywork and anti-lock brakes, it could have been an outstanding marketing success instead of the rather half-baked automotive curiosity that many now consider it to be.

Yes, the SM has its problems, and yes, it can be very expensive to put right, but that is not really the car's fault. In many ways it was more complex and sophisticated than a light aircraft, and anyone trying to maintain a Cessna Citation as if it was an Austin 7 will soon come unstuck. Treat the Citroën SM as you would any high-grade piece of machinery and you'll be agreeably surprised at just how good it can be to drive and own.

FEBRUARY MEANS
FORMIDABLE

Brian Palmer assesses the remarkable Citroën SM portrayed in this year's stunning Classic Cars *Calendar portfolio*

Brightening up those dark days of winter in our 1989 *Classic Cars* calendar the Citroën SM provided a suitably exotic counterpoint to the chill and gloom outside. It made one yearn for Spring, lengthening days, warmth and sunshine. Indeed it had us keen to drive that very car – for this intriguing Seventies sub-supercar hybrid had so far escaped our clutches. I then imagined myself heading off down some arrow straight, Poplar-lined French arterial road in search of adventure.

Well I missed out on the typical French roads, so rapidly urbanised Hertfordshire had to suffice, but thanks to owner Andrew Brodie of Hypertronics, a north London firm specialising in the Citroën marque, I managed to drive that very same calendar car and fulfil a long standing ambition.

Of course the name Citroën and the term *avant garde* are so naturally associated with each other as to appear totally inseparable. And, quite simply, some of the world's most innovative and truly great cars are those that have proudly borne the famous double chevron motif. In popularising front-wheel drive, the pre-war *Traction Avant* Citroën literally led the world by its nose. In the Fifties the DS shocked the motoring world by adding hydro-pneumatic suspension, with self-levelling facility, powered steering, brakes and clutch and a sleek aerodynamic shape to its catalogue of achievement.

The big Citroën offered a glimpse of what motoring could be like in the future – indeed so ahead of its time was it that the model ran for a staggering twenty years, boldly flaunting convention with its Gallic idiosyncrasies. It is doubtful that its successor the CX, excellent car though it may be, will be remembered quite as affectionately.

Yet the model which gave Citroën by far its most dramatic profile on the world stage was built for a mere five years and actually came about through an unlikely collaboration with another firm. The Citroën SM of 1970 was, by any standards, a remarkable and uncom-promising vehicle. Probably no other mass-producer, before or since, has or could have offered for public sale a more audacious design. I've no doubt, either, that the long-dead master magician André Citroën himself must have had a hand in this extraordinary creation even

The SM was not designed to be a racer but some examples did make it to the race track, like this works car run by Ligier in the '74 Spa 24 Hours. Migault is driving

if through some form of divine intervention. His stamp of genius is present in every fibre. The SM has the look of a real Citroën. Its stance, the long wheelbase, the defiantly individual styling, the brilliant technical *tour de force* beneath, all combine to make the SM quite simply a Citroën for connoisseurs.

And so unmistakably a Citroën – perhaps the quintessential Citroën – is the SM that they could have happily omitted all marque labels. The car was, you might say, its own emblem, and its own advertisement.

I know there are those who profess not to like the looks of the Citroën SM, but to my eyes, the car is a modern styling masterpiece. Not beautiful, I'll grant you, but handsome certainly. It is, as much as anything, a bold statement.

The hunched rear hints at the latent power lurking beneath the bonnet, the smooth flanks and bevelled front were clearly designed to cleave through the air, and the whole character radiating out of the metal is that here is a machine bristling with every auto-technical innovation known at that time. And why not? The SM not only looked out of the 21st Century, but it boasted the best and most sophisticated suspension medium in the world, high pressure powered brakes, clutch and variable ratio power steering. The SM's frontal aspect was unusual to say the least, with six headlamp units lurking

behind a curved glass cover. Further-more, the headlamps were kept level at all times and the inner four contrived to pivot in unison with the front wheels!

It was the engine that was the single element in this manic mechanical melange that set the SM apart from all other Citroëns. To be honest, apart from being wet-linered, previous Citroën power units – fours all – were not exactly going to set the world alight for their ingenuity, power or smoothness.

However, the SM project – though long a gleam in the eye of Citroën's engineers – had only been made possible by an unlikely liaison between the French company and the then ailing Italian supercar manufacturer Maserati. Citroën and Maserati had signed an agreement to co-operate on design and manufacture in January 1968, but this gentlemanly courtship abruptly turned into a shotgun marriage within three months when the French giant grabbed a majority shareholding in Maserati.

Undoubtedly the acquisition gave Citroën considerable publicity, and made the upcoming SM hybrid seem a good deal more exotic on paper. The deal offered the Italian firm the prospect of strong finincial backing from an established mass-producer. The flow wasn't all one way. The Bora and Merak both contained Citroënesque features, the latter sharing the SM's engine. And, in turn, this useful cross-fertilisation also held the prospect of reduced unit costs for Maserati.

Not that this was to prove to be the case – by 1974 Maserati's losses amounted to more than the capital value of the company. Then there was the little matter of a clash of two totally different Latin temperaments. It was, perhaps, from the inception an ill-starred liaison. Nevertheless, early on in the marriage, Citroën all bright eyed and bushy-tailed at their good fortune requested Guilio Alfieri – Maserati's much respected engineer – to come up with something scintillating by way of a new engine for the upcoming SM. What's more it was wanted inside six months.

He is said to have replied, to an amazed Citroën management, that they could have their engine – not in six months, but in three weeks! Alfieri, who was used to making a lire stretch a long, long way for Maserati, had already run experimental V6 engines by the simple expedient of lopping two cylinders from the company's stock V8. The resultant unit was nominally a little over 3-litres in capacity but had its stroke reduced and a specially made crankshaft machined from solid billet to bring it down to 2.7-litres to fit-in with French taxation laws. The Merak, and later SMs, went back up to 3-litres.

The new engine was also highly unusual in having a very wide, 90 degree angle between the cylinder banks – indeed wider than strictly desirable for smoothness and balance – but this allowed the existing rudimentary tooling to be retained. The cylinder dimensions at 87 x 65mm were handsomely oversquare, each block of six boasted twin-overhead camshafts, maximum power generated being 170bhp at 5500rpm.

Unusually the drive to the camshafts was split; primary chain drive went from the crank nose to a jackshaft running the entire length of the engine vee, while the secondary drive ran to sprockets part way along the camshafts. Even so, the SM's engine has proved a reliable unit in service. And, it must be said, a lusty performer.

Despite hauling a bulky and commodious coupé/saloon body of 28½cwt around, top speed, of the later fuel-injected model, was close on 140mph with 0-60 coming up in an impressive 9.3 secs. certainly fast enough to put the Citroën firmly in the supercar bracket nearly twenty years ago. Comparing the amazing Citroën with its contemporaries makes for interesting analysis. Top speed, for instance, was achieved on half the power needed by a Jensen Interceptor, say, which is an indicator of just how advanced were those early Seventies' Citroën aerodynamics.

A further indicator of this, is the car's impressively steady fuel consumption readings. At 30, 40 and 50mph the SM returns 30mpg and drops gradually thereafter. Only above 95mph does it drop below the magic 20mpg level.

Above, the SM had considerable beauty of line, retaining many classic elements of Citroën styling yet projecting a supercar image

Far left, the engine itself is a fairly compact unit, but all the ancillary equipment gives the impression of massive complexity. Centre left, optional carbon fibre wheels. Left, the maker's mark taken from Andre Citroën's patented gear pattern

FEBRUARY MEANS FORMIDABLE

Overall consumption averages 17mpg, a great deal more frugal than most supercars of the period, and over 20mpg was attainable when touring.

The 0-60mph acceleration figure, though good, could still be matched by something like a Cortina Lotus on a power to weight basis simply because aerodynamics have an insignificant effect up to this point. The Citroën's real advantage came later, as the 26 second 0-100mph figure shows. To illustrate their not inconsiderable effect, the far smaller and lighter Lotus Elan Plus Two, given the same 170bhp, would have been a mere 3mph faster overall.

The Maserati engine and aero-dynamics were but two assets in the SM's extensive armoury. The famous hydropneumatic suspension from the DS21 was developed further to maintain ride comfort, while allowing for more sporty handling, together with self-levelling. The rear suspension pivoted on familiar trailing arms; at the front are found a pair of transverse arms, just single links not wishbones, turned through a right angle to give a longitudinal axis.

Slightly different lengths, upper and lower, prevented the wheel from inclining with the body and were thus kept flatter on the road. Massive 195/70 HR 15 Michelin XVR tyres, as used on current Ferraris, helped too.

Andrew Brodie's car is also fitted with the optional extra carbon-fibre road wheels as fitted to the Moroccan Rally winner's car and available from 1971-on. Weighing less than half that of the conventional wheel, they are truly amazingly light. Try lifting one and it's feather-light

Then there's Citroën's unique power steering. For a kick-off the Citroën used rack and pinion steering, adopted first

"You feel you wouldn't want to sneeze mid-way round a mountain hairpin"

on the Traction Avant cars of the Thirties, which incurs little or no lost motion at the steering wheel whilst providing the maximum of information to the driver. The Citroën engineers then, perversely you might think, designed out all traces of true 'feel' inherent in the system. They then added variable ratio power-assistance, providing maximum help at zero speed for parking, and building up as lock increases – together with a self-centring system so strong that the wheel always returns to the straight ahead position if let go. Further the gearing was extremely high so that those unfamiliar with the car tend to depart in a series of hilarious zig-zags.

Another Citroën foible concerns the brakes, again powered and operated through separate circuits, and activated from the cockpit by a rubber button on the floor instead of the usual pedal.

So much for the background – though that's important with such an unusual and rarely seen machine – but what's the beast *like* to drive? One has heard so many stories about this car, some of them verging on the horror variety, that it seems almost impossible to retrieve fact from fantasy.

To do the Citroën SM justice you need rather longer behind the wheel to become fully accustomed to it than a conventional car. But for all that, the SM holds no terrors, nor does it require special driving skills. It does, however, require a deft touch and a degree of finesse to extract the best from it and, indeed, full enjoyment. If your driving style is of the brute force and bloody

ignorance variety, then the SM's definitely not for you. Take the steering, for instance.

Grasp the wheel like a panic-stricken learner driver and you'll veer-off down the road like you've had one over the eight. Learn to caress the wheel, and there's no problem. You also have to modify your steering input, especially around the tight street corners, other-wise you'll be clipping the kerb with the rear wheels of this 16ft long vehicle.

At speed, the steering feels just like a manual system even though the sensation is entirely artificial. To underline that, the Citroën will make no deviation whatever in the event of a tyre blow-out at speed. Even so, a certain degree of concentration is required at speed due to the very small steering inputs needed – you feel you wouldn't want to sneeze mid-way round a mountain hairpin!

Similarly, with the brakes, stamp your size eleven un-caringly on the brake button and likely as not your loved-ones will all disappear through the windscreen. So you learn to stroke the thing gently with your foot.

The gearchange is a bit odd too. Well, you'd expect it to be wouldn't you? Sprouting out of the floor in the usual place, it may be, but this five-speeder appears to operate not in a gate but in a horizontal slot. It does both. Though it works well enough, I'm always dis-appointed by Citroën manual gearboxes.

Somehow, something so base, so crude and irretrievably linked-in with the dawn of motoring, seems totally at odds with the French firm's lifelong dedication to sophistication and modernity. An automatic gearbox has to be the answer – they *were* made incidentally – or at least something after the style of the French Cotal electric 'box of pre-war days.

The engine displays a somewhat Jekyll and Hyde-like character, being relatively unobtrusive at lowish speeds but emitting a delightful snarl as the revs soar above 3000rpm. The big Citroën also has enormous levels of grip once you overcome the initial mental hurdle of throwing such a big vehicle headlong into bends. You simply power it round, letting the front wheels drag you through.

Yet for all that dynamic competence, I feel that the SM is not in reality a sport car, or even a supercar, but a distinguished modern day member of very class of car the French invented before the war – the *Grande Routier*.

Is not the SM, for all its technical wizardry and forward thinking, a car very much in the mould of a big Bugatti or Delahaye of pre-war days?

The SM is big, bold, highly – even dramatically – styled, comfortable, competent and fast. The SM is a car for a marathon rather than a sprint. A car for travelling somewhere exotic and far away in good time, by virtue of high cruising speeds, and arriving as refreshed as on a trip to the corner shop. A car for travelling South; away from all worries and all other cars.

The interior is well equipped and comfortable with large well-shaped seats. Note the unusual gearchange gate and the distinctive steering wheel